✑ *Strained Sisterhood* ✑

GENDER AND CLASS
IN THE BOSTON FEMALE
ANTI-SLAVERY SOCIETY

Debra Gold Hansen

The University of Massachusetts Press

Amherst

Copyright © 1993 by
The University of Massachusetts Press
All rights reserved
Printed in the United States of America
LC 92-40310
ISBN 0-87023-848-5
Designed by Dorothy Thompson Griffin
Set in Electra
Printed and bound by Thomson-Shore, Inc.

Library of Congress Cataloging-in-Publication Data
Hansen, Debra Gold, 1953–
      Strained sisterhood : gender and class in the Boston female anti-
slavery society / Debra Gold Hansen.
      p.   cm.
      Includes bibliographical references and index.
      ISBN 0–87023–848–5 (alk. paper).
      1. Boston Female Anti-slavery Society.   2. Women abolitionists—
Massachusetts—Boston—History—19th century.   3. Sex role—
Massachusetts—Boston—History—19th century.   4. Slavery—United
States—Anti-slavery movements.   I. Title.
E449.H25   1993
305.42′09744′61—dc20   92–40310
                                                                        CIP

British Library Cataloguing in Publication data are available.

For Art

Contents

Acknowledgments

I accumulated many debts during the years that I worked on this book, and at last I have the opportunity to acknowledge them. My deepest intellectual debt goes to my history professors and mentors at the University of California, Irvine (UCI), and California State University, Fullerton (CSUF). As a doctoral student at UCI, I was the beneficiary of a challenging curriculum that introduced me to exciting new scholarship in social, gender, family, and ethnic history and the use of social theory in interpreting the past. My graduate adviser there, Mary P. Ryan, helped establish the historiographical and theoretical foundations for this study, and my association with her on this and other projects taught me well how a first-rate historian works. Michael P. Johnson, my dissertation adviser, was instrumental in the conceptualization and completion of this book, and for his timely encouragement, sage advice, and many kindnesses, I will always be grateful. I also am indebted to my other professors at UCI, particularly Spencer Olin, for their stimulating classes and embodiment of productive, committed historians. Although UCI was pivotal in my scholarly development, I continue to appreciate the academic training I received at CSUF, and especially the direction and advice of history professors David Pivar, Nancy Fitch, Lawrence de Graaf, and Ronald Rietveld. My current teaching area is not in history, but the CSUF history department has continued to embrace me as a colleague, which I value very much.

California's system of higher education has sustained me financially as well as intellectually. The University of California provided research funds in the form of a Regents Fellowship, a Patent Fund Award, and a Humanities Research Grant, while the California State University System promoted my research through a CSUF Departmental Association Council grant and a Summer Fellowship. In these times of fiscal austerity I increasingly appreciate the resources made available to me.

Now that I am a professor of library and information science, I must salute the great work done by anonymous librarians and archivists in creating, organizing, and making accessible the fabulous historical materials pertaining to antislavery, women, local history, and genealogy in New England. In particular, I would like to thank the professional and support staffs of the following libraries for their assistance in locating and making available the material in their collections: American Antiquarian Society, Andover-Newton Theological Seminary, Boston Public Library, Church of Jesus Christ of Latter-day Saints Genealogy Library (Salt Lake City), Columbia University, Cornell University, Essex Institute, Jaffrey (N.H.) Public Library, Massachusetts Historical Society, New England Historic and Genealogical Library, Schlesinger Library of Radcliffe College, and Smith College. I also acknowledge the hard work of Nancy Caudill and Ruth Palmer, interlibrary loan librarians at California State University, Fullerton, and Claremont Colleges, respectively, who patiently and resourcefully searched for the obscure materials I had to have for my research.

At various stages in the writing of this book scholarly reviewers have provided careful readings of and judicious comments concerning the manuscript. Although these readers remain anonymous, I am ever indebted to their incisive criticism and astute recommendations for revision. I can thank directly Jean Fagan Yellin and Anne Boylan for generously sharing with me their knowledge and data pertaining to women abolitionists. I also would like to thank the individuals at the University of Massachusetts Press for their professional efforts, particularly Barbara Palmer, whose exacting editorial pencil spared me from needless errors of spelling and fact, and Director Bruce Wilcox for his encouragement and promotion of this project. If, despite the diligence of these individuals, errors remain, they are entirely my own.

Few creative endeavors are sustained without the commitment and cooperation of immediate colleagues. I owe special thanks to my good friends and associates at the Honnold Library of the Claremont Colleges, the California State University, Fullerton, Oral History Program, and San Jose State University's School of Library and Information Science—Fullerton Campus. These individuals provided unwavering encouragement and support, even when it meant sacrificing themselves so that I would be free to pursue my "muse." In addition, I would like to thank my students, particularly the men and women enrolled in my "Women in Librarianship" classes. Our challenging and often intense discussions of women's theory and the feminization of a particular profession helped keep my reading and thinking on this topic fresh and taught me never to make assumptions concerning gender roles and women's issues.

Finally, my heartfelt thanks go to my friends and family who vicariously wrote this book with me and who were equally jubilant to see its completion. Sharon Beattie, Linda Gunter, Jacque Sundstrand, Martha Smith, Elizabeth Stein, and Janet Green are constant reminders of the power of female friendships, while Anna Hansen, Ron and Annette Larson, and Jack and Duff Griffith contributed in ways that never can be repaid. Many thanks, too, go to my parents, Jim and Jean Gold, who provided me with the intellectual tools as well as the emotional and financial resources to pursue a scholarly career. On numerous occasions they selflessly assumed responsibility for my house and pets so that I could pursue the Boston Female Anti-Slavery Society in distant archives. Finally, I'd like to thank Arthur A. Hansen—my mentor and life companion—for this book is as much his as it is mine. As I reviewed my notes and drafts for a final time, Art's unmistakable handwriting on these many pages reminded me of the countless contributions that he has made to my development as a historian and a scholar. I dedicate this book to him with love.

Strained Sisterhood

Introduction

IN THE LATE AFTERNOON OF 21 OCTOBER 1835, HARRIET MARTINEAU WAS traveling through Boston en route to Providence, Rhode Island. Seeing the streets thronged with people, the English author inquired of the other passengers as to the cause of the excitement. Such a crowd, surmised the others in the coach, must have been attracted by the arrival of the foreign mail at the post office located in the Old State House in the center of the city. When Martineau reached Providence, she learned the real cause of the commotion on State Street. A women's abolition society, holding its annual meeting in downtown antislavery offices, had incited a riot.

The mob action culminated events that over the past year had pitted Boston abolitionists against popular local opinion. During the summer and fall of 1835, angry crowds, fearing that the activists were undermining accepted race relations and threatening the harmony of the states, regularly disrupted antislavery meetings. Full-blown riots had occurred in the nearby towns of Lowell, Lynn, and Abington, where British abolitionist George Thompson preached, while in Boston local officials and merchants held an emotional meeting in Faneuil Hall, denouncing the "professed agitator" for hurling "firebrands, arrows, and death."[1] For their part, abolitionists refused to curtail their activities, insisting they were defending their own rights and freedoms as much as those of blacks.

The stage was set for violence when the Boston Female Anti-Slavery Society announced that George Thompson would address the group at its annual meeting on 21 October. That morning placards appeared urging Bostonians to "Snake Thompson Out!" and, as the meeting time neared, the streets around the antislavery office on Cornhill filled with angry, brick-toting men. During the ensuing fracas, the crowd tore the entry door to the offices from its hinges and splintered the wooden "Anti-Slavery Rooms" sign. Inside, the fifty members of the Boston Female Anti-Slavery Society who had managed to thread their way through the crowd sat reading Scripture and talking quietly among themselves.

Presently Mayor Theodore Lyman arrived, hoping to use his authority to disperse the crowd. When the mayor found he had little influence over the men in the street, he tried to disband the women, a request to which abolitionist Maria Weston Chapman boldly replied: "If this is the last bulwark of freedom, we may as well die here as anywhere."[2] Eventually, Lyman did persuade the women to leave. As they made their way into the street, lawyer Samuel Sewell, whose wife Louisa was a society member, rushed to their protection, shielding the black and white women as they walked arm-in-arm through the shouting crowd. Afterward, the mob, not finding Thompson on the premises, turned their wrath upon William Lloyd Garrison (whose wife Helen was also in the Boston Female Anti-Slavery Society), dragging the infamous radical through the downtown streets until the police rescued him and deposited him in the Leverett Street jail.

Hearing of these events, Harriet Martineau, known for her abolition work in England, was dismayed at Boston's illiberality, not only for turning a blind eye toward slavery but also for its shameless suspension of free speech and quick resort to street violence. When Boston Female Anti-Slavery Society officers requested that Martineau attend the reconvened annual meeting scheduled for 19 November, she accepted, even though her Boston host, the Reverend Henry Ware, Jr., predicted, "You will be mobbed. You will certainly be mobbed."[3] His fears notwithstanding, on the day of the women's meeting Ware chauffeured Martineau and her lady traveling companion to Louisa and Ellis Gray Loring's home, where the Englishwomen dined before the gathering.

Other guests at the Lorings' table included the Reverend Samuel J. May, Maria Weston Chapman, and one of Chapman's younger sisters. It was Martineau's first meeting with Chapman, with whom she was to become a lifelong intimate:

I still see the exquisite beauty which took me by surprise that day;—the slender, graceful form;—the golden hair which might have covered her to her feet; the brilliant complexion, noble profile, and deep blue eyes;—the aspect, meant to be soft and winning only, but that day, (as ever since) so vivified by courage, and so strengthened by upright conviction, as to appear the very embodiment of heroism.

As the group prepared to leave for the meeting, Chapman confided to Martineau, "You know we are threatened with a mob again today: but I do not myself apprehend it. It must not surprise us; but my hopes are stronger than my fears."[4]

The diners walked together to the mansion of merchant Francis Jackson who had offered the use of his new home after it became apparent that no meeting hall in the city was open to the women. There they found only a half-dozen boys in front of the house amusing themselves by harassing the black women who dared enter the residence. In all, 130 women came to the Boston Female Anti-Slavery Society's reconstituted annual meeting, comfortably accommodated in the adjoining drawing rooms of Jackson's impressive home. Toward the end of the proceedings, some of those present invited Martineau to address the society, which she did, declaring herself in complete sympathy with abolitionist sentiments.

As a result of her public support of the antislavery women, the Boston citizenry condemned and ostracized their English visitor. But despite this popular resentment against her, Martineau claimed she never regretted her decision to participate in the meeting; she had no conscionable choice but to attend. Her one disappointment was the narrow bigotry she found in the so-called Athens of America. "I hope the Boston people," she later commented, "have outgrown the childishness of sulking at opinions." Moreover, Martineau denied that she was a martyr for the abolition cause. In her opinion, the courageous women in the Boston Female Anti-Slavery Society were the true martyrs in this case. "I was going home in less than a year; and should leave peril and slander behind me. But these women were to pass their lives in the city whose wrath they were defying; and their persecutors were fellow-citizens, fellow-worshippers, and familiar acquaintances."[5]

Harriet Martineau's writings about Boston's female abolitionists have helped create the legend surrounding their personalities, conflicts, and accomplishments.[6] With affection and admiration she portrayed these committed women as educated, articulate members of Boston's Unitarian upper class, the wives, sisters, and daughters of prosperous and eminent men like Samuel Sewell, Ellis Gray Loring, Francis Jackson, Henry Chapman, Samuel May, Samuel Cabot, and Robert Shaw. These were strong, accomplished, propertied women who were uncompromising and steadfast in the face of social ostracism and physical danger, and they struggled for nearly thirty years to free the slaves. In the end, their endeavors as social reformers set in motion the first organized women's rights movement in the United States.

Martineau's depiction is correct as far as it goes, but it fails to provide a comprehensive or completely accurate picture of either the society's membership or its history. Martineau encountered the organization at its apex, defiant and unified in the face of oppression, thriving upon common myths of heroism and accomplishment. In fact, over the next year and a half, the society would become one of the most famous and influential women's groups in the country. This harmony of sentiment and action, however, was more apparent than real. In actuality, the Boston Female Anti-Slavery Society was a coalition of diverse women that included not only wealthy, cosmopolitan women but also blacks from Boston's Belknap Street ghetto and self-supporting individuals recently arrived from rural New England and still suspicious of urban life. Moreover, despite the abolitionists' self-applause for the heterogeneous character of their organization, these women worked together harmoniously for fewer than five years. After 1837 the Boston Female Anti-Slavery Society was racked with factionalism, with every meeting paralyzed by contention over religious and moral philosophy, race relations, and women's rights. In April 1840 the society voted itself out of existence.

I discovered the Boston Female Anti-Slavery Society more than fifteen years ago while searching for a suitable topic for my master's thesis.[7] A study of female abolitionists presented an exciting prospect. For one thing, women abolitionists had been sorely neglected by historians of the antislavery movement. Preoccupied with political issues like leadership and power, ideology and rhetoric, elections and war, "movement" historians, by the very nature of the questions they asked, ignored the contributions of women, which were more personal than public, supportive not administrative.[8] Indeed, the persistent interest in the abolitionists' role in the creation of the Republican party and the coming of the Civil War led one historian to suggest that the topic had simply "run dry."[9] The so-called new social histories helped resuscitate abolition scholarship providing fresh insights into the sociological, psychological, and economic underpinnings of the movement and incorporating heretofore neglected groups, such as African Americans and workingmen, into the narrative.[10] Yet, despite these new approaches and topics, antislavery histories still largely exclude women, either by considering only male patterns of participation or by giving women only token reference, usually in a separate chapter devoted to them. Even now there are only a handful of book-length studies of women abolitionists, the most important of which are Alma Lutz's *Crusade for Freedom* (1968); Blanche Glassman Hersh's *Slavery of Sex* (1978); Jean Fagan Yellin's *Women and Sisters* (1989); and Shirley Yee's *Black Women Abolitionists* (1992).[11]

Women's liberation and the flowering of feminist scholarship during the 1970s and 1980s redressed this situation somewhat and brought to light information about women's involvement in antebellum social movements.[12] In searching for feminist political traditions, historians quickly discerned the prominent role played by abolitionists (male and female) in the formation of the nineteenth-century women's rights movement as well as significant parallels between the civil rights and feminist movements of the 1830s and those of the 1960s. Historians like Ellen Du Bois, Keith Melder, and Blanche Glassman Hersh described how the actions taken by women in their antislavery work raised issues, set precedents, and provided role models that led some female activists to confront their own oppression.[13] As Hersh observed in *Slavery of Sex*, nineteenth-century feminism was practically an "inevitable outgrowth of a radical movement which had as its goal the emancipation of all enslaved humanity."[14] Jean Fagan Yellin's study has added a significant postscript to our understanding of these feminist-abolitionists. While she, too, believes that they "inevitably embodied and projected versions of true womanhood that challenged patriarchal versions," she exposes how their new feminine model was eventually depoliticized by the dominant culture and stripped of its liberating potential.[15]

As significant as these studies are, historians' preoccupation with the feminist implications of female abolitionism have made the exception the rule. In the case of the Boston Female Anti-Slavery Society, most of its members were hostile to the introduction of the "woman question" into the abolition movement. At the very time the more radical women were soliciting signatures on petitions, participating in boisterous debates, and lecturing to large audiences on behalf of the slave, most in the society pursued more customary female benevolent projects, such as teaching African-American children, running orphanages, and working in Sunday schools and sewing circles. Moreover, while the minority of Boston's

female abolitionists pushed for equal membership in male abolition societies, the majority preferred working within their own exclusively female
organizations.

Many scholars have made similar observations about the problems
inherent in a political approach to women's history, arguing that the
preoccupation with female activists and other overachievers misrepresents
and undervalues the experiences and life styles of the vast majority of
women.[16] As an alternative, historians like Nancy Cott, Carroll Smith-
Rosenberg, and Carl Degler, to name some of the most influential, have
developed a woman-centered model for historical inquiry that looks not at
the male world of politics and power but at the female world of home and
family. These scholars have shown that within the private boundaries of
their so-called separate sphere women developed a distinctive counterculture with values and priorities that both originated from and validated their
prescribed roles. According to this "female culture" model of women's
history, then, the impulse to form organizations like the Boston Female
Anti-Slavery Society came from popular conceptions of women's character
and duties and not from a consciously feminist rejection of what today
seem to be limiting stereotypes.[17]

Here again, although this interpretation is useful in understanding the
sociocultural factors that motivated women to join the antislavery movement in the 1830s, it does not do justice to the myriad needs and expectations of Boston Female Anti-Slavery Society members. Some joined out of
traditional upper-class noblesse oblige, others out of religious conviction.
Many women became abolitionists because of their burning hatred of
racism and segregation, while some did so because their mothers, sisters,
and other family members were involved in the movement. In the end, this
mixture of motives and goals among Boston Female Anti-Slavery Society
members made it virtually impossible for them to agree on policy matters
or cooperate on specific projects. Indeed, these differences proved so
extensive and irreconcilable that the society, as noted earlier, disbanded in
1840.

Historians are now beginning to confront the diversity of female experience to show that ideas about the female character are socially constructed
and thus constantly evolving in response to complex socioeconomic and
cultural change. As Linda Alcoff has explained, women's identity is "defined not by a particular set of attributes but by a particular position . . .
[within] a network of elements involving others, the objective economic
conditions, cultural and political institutions and ideologies, and so on."[18]

Building upon the work of Mary Ryan, Carroll Smith-Rosenberg, Barbara Epstein, and Nancy Hewitt, historians of women currently are exploring how the changing definitions of gender in the early nineteenth century were related to wider changes in the economy and society, particularly to the development of class consciousness and class values.[19] As Christine Stansell notes, "Class formation was related to, but not synonymous with, the thorough-going transformation of the gender system in the first half of the nineteenth century."[20] These works, as well as more recent studies by Lori Ginzberg and Anne Boylan, are beginning to make clear that women's organizational activities (not to mention their occupational patterns, family relationships, denominational affiliations, and leisure pursuits) can be class, ethnic, and/or generational based, depending upon women's particular position within society at that time.[21]

In *Strained Sisterhood* I will be taking this type of positional or constructionist approach to the study of the Boston Female Anti-Slavery Society and the women who became its active members. Because I envision this as more of a social history of antebellum women than an examination of the female antislavery movement, my narrative will focus not upon the chronological history of the society but upon the different attitudes and activities of its members to see what can be learned about the life styles and ideologies of women at that time. The thesis shaping my analysis is that women abolitionists disagreed among themselves as to what constituted female character and that they constructed their competing models of womanhood in response to the specific socioeconomic conditions of 1830s Boston and their position within the city's social hierarchy. To this end, I will explore how the abolitionists' competing models of womanhood are revealed in their occupational situations, religious beliefs, moral codes, leisure pursuits, use of symbols and rituals, and modes of discourse.[22]

Strained Sisterhood will commence against the backdrop of social change and increasing cultural diversity in the city of Boston and the beginnings of the antislavery movement there. Chapter 1 provides a skeletal history of the women's abolition society. It details the society's origins and major projects as well as the issues and events leading to its dissolution but leaves extensive analysis for future chapters. The next chapter describes the geographic setting: Boston in the 1830s. In the forefront of New England's industrialization and urbanization, Boston itself was undergoing tremendous demographic, environmental, and economic change. These transformations put extreme pressure upon the city's traditional social and political structures, and for the first time distinct neighborhoods, churches, political parties, and cultural and charitable institutions based upon class, race, and ethnicity appeared. Chapter 3 focuses upon women's situation within the changing milieu of antebellum Boston. In this chapter, I discuss women's employment opportunities, religious and charitable concerns, and leisure pursuits and attempt to relate these patterns to the emergence of distinctive socioeconomic groupings in the city.

Having established the physical and social setting of Boston and the hierarchies within its world of women, I return to the Boston Female Anti-Slavery Society. Chapter 4 analyzes the composition of the women's group in terms of the abolitionists' socioeconomic standing, religious affiliations, and family backgrounds. The survey reveals that the white activists were distinctly upper and middle class, a coalition of women drawn from the city's traditional mercantile elite and its emerging bourgeoisie. Typically New England–born and of Anglo-American heritage, these Boston Female Anti-Slavery Society members represented various Protestant denominations ranging from Baptist to Episcopalian. As for the African Americans in the organization, they were members of their community's social and economic elite and belonged to local African Baptist and Zion churches.

Chapter 5 addresses the questions that originally attracted me to the Boston Female Anti-Slavery Society. What were the sources of discontent in the society, and what factors led some members to advocate women's rights and others to retreat into traditional forms of female benevolence? It seems fairly clear that the women connected with Boston's upper class— the wives and daughters of merchants, bankers, lawyers, and high-standing government officials—were the individuals who rebelled against social and cultural restrictions placed upon them. The more traditional faction consisted of women from the city's new middle class who were self-supporting as teachers, social workers, and boardinghouse keepers and/or married to clerks, proprietors, skilled artisans, and clergymen. In the following chapter, I use the society's annual fundraiser, the antislavery fair, to explore the different cultural tastes and the religious, political, and moral concerns of these competing upper- and middle-class factions.

The politicization of the Boston Female Anti-Slavery Society and the emergence of competing factions among the white women had the effect of marginalizing blacks in the society. Though African-American support was coveted by both white groups as a testament to the legitimacy of their antislavery goals, black opinions and preferences were generally unsolicited. As a result, after 1837 African Americans played a minimal role in the development of white antislavery programs and policies, and, not surprisingly, they had little direct impact upon the ideologies that the white factions would espouse. Thus African-American women largely disappear from my analysis at this point in the book, which in itself provides further evidence of Boston's strained sisterhood.

Chapters 7 and 8 bring together scattered conclusions, observations, and surmisals as to the origins and central components of the different conceptions of womanhood that emerged among the whites in the organization. In "Models of Womanhood within the Boston Female Anti-Slavery Society," and the Conclusion, I compare the ideologies put forth by white upper- and middle-class abolitionists regarding women's rights and responsibilities and try to link these ideologies to the context within which they developed. The feminist attitudes of the elite women were an outgrowth of republican ideals, Unitarian and Quaker beliefs, and upper-class assumptions concerning wealth, status, and power, which led them to advocate equal social, political, and moral rights for all human beings. In contrast, women of the urban middle class articulated a philosophy of womanhood based upon a strict division of labor by gender. Predominantly Congregationalist and Baptist, bourgeois women used biblical teachings, patriarchal social organization, and beliefs about the innate differences between the sexes to construct a female sphere that emphasized women's biological and psychological predisposition toward domesticity, nurture, and morality. Middle-class Boston Female Anti-Slavery Society members, like their upper-class counterparts, sought to improve the condition and status of women. However, they felt this object could be achieved not through equal political and social rights but through a revaluation of women's domestic, familial, and religious functions.[23]

In studying the Boston Female Anti-Slavery Society, I found the organization's failure at least as compelling and instructive as its success, for the events leading to and the consequences of its division exposed the limits of women's commitments to social reform, and to each other. While African-American women were marginalized, white women were unable to communicate or cooperate among themselves. Indeed, the debates that took place among whites over the society's dissolution elicited a variety of interpretations of women's roles and responsibilities, with upper-class women advocating economic, political, and spiritual equality and women of the middle class defending domesticity and motherhood. Both models of white womanhood were feminist insofar as each stressed the centrality of women in the emerging social order. Both models, too, suggest the importance that gender and class would assume in industrial society. In short, the history of the Boston Female Anti-Slavery Society suggests to me not the bonds but the very fragile ties of womanhood.

⚜ CHAPTER 1 ⚜

The Boston Female Anti-Slavery Society:
A Brief History

ON AN OCTOBER AFTERNOON IN 1833, TWELVE WOMEN ORGANIZED THE Boston Female Anti-Slavery Society. Despite its far-reaching objective, the group had modest beginnings and was quite typical of early-nineteenth-century female benevolent societies. The members selected Charlotte Phelps, wife of a Congregational minister, as their first president, though it was her husband, the Reverend Amos A. Phelps, who guided them through the proprieties of associational conduct and intercourse.[1] Even with Phelps's direction, it took the women more than six months to construct a constitution, and they did not have the document printed in local reform newspapers until five months after that. In it, the society promised to "aid and assist" the antislavery movement "as far as lies within our power," primarily by disseminating antislavery propaganda and improving the "moral and intellectual character" of the community's free blacks.[2]

Meeting as a body only four times a year, the Boston Female Anti-Slavery Society initially was more a symbolic than a truly functioning organization. As an auxiliary to the Massachusetts Anti-Slavery Society, the women initiated few projects of their own, preferring to contribute their efforts to male-run organizations and enterprises. They sat in the audiences of Massachusetts Anti-Slavery Society meetings, listened to sermons preached by local abolitionist ministers, and attended monthly

13

"concerts for the slave" to sing protest songs and pray. In retrospect, the society itself admitted that at the outset their activities warranted little attention, that their "first year of association was marked by no event of peculiar interest."[3]

Some more enterprising members found additional ways to assist African Americans during this period. For example, Lydia Maria Child and Louisa Loring organized an abolition fair in December 1834, though, as was expected, they automatically deposited the sale's $300 earnings into the Massachusetts Anti-Slavery Society treasury. Sisters Martha and Lucy Ball opened a school for "young ladies of color" and employed several other society members including Maria Ray and Julia Williams (herself black) as teachers. Others courageously confronted the pervasive racism in the city. On one occasion, Lydia Maria Child rebuked Samuel Gridley Howe, then director of Boston's Perkins Institute for the Education of the Blind, for barring the admission of a black child so as not to offend current inmates or public opinion. "If the children of the poor and despised are to be excluded to please the rich and the proud," Child wrote, "let it not arrogate to itself the name of a *benevolent* institution."[4] Susan Paul wrote with equal indignation of her plight as a black woman in Boston, condemning the "spirit which persecutes us on account of our color—that cruel prejudice which deprives us of every privilege whereby we might elevate ourselves— and then condemns us because we are not more refined and intelligent."[5]

Members of the Boston Female Anti-Slavery Society also organized the Samaritan Asylum, a home for orphaned and indigent black children. But though the Boston Female Anti-Slavery Society allocated a portion of its earnings to sustain the orphanage and its members constituted the governing board, the society carefully disavowed any formal connection with the asylum or, for that matter, other projects to benefit local blacks. "In relation to the colored population in our own land," wrote recording secretary Martha Ball in the society's first annual report, "we have endeavored to do what we could during the past year, *as individuals, though not in the capacity of a society*" (italics hers).[6]

In early 1835 Boston's female abolitionists ventured beyond these fairly customary female charitable activities to join their male colleagues' efforts to discredit organizations promoting alternative solutions to the problem of slavery. The abolitionists' initial target was the American Colonization Society, whose program of "deportation" embodied the prevalent and "hateful spirit of colorphobia."[7] Hoping to make Garrison's "immediate emancipation" the only antislavery philosophy in Boston, women infiltrated meetings of the American Colonization Society and its offshoot, the American Union,[8] with a critical eye toward the proceedings and ready applause for the refutations their male associates shouted from the audience. Boston Female Anti-Slavery Society member Deborah Weston described a typical encounter in her diary: "Went to the Temple in the evening to a Colonization meeting. Alexander Everett in the Chair. Mr. Gurley spoke and Mr. May answered him. It was delightful. Mr. May 'funned' him so well." At another of these meetings, Weston sat next to Lydia Maria Child, who was in a "great fury" the entire time. It was, Weston wrote, "the best fun I ever *saw* in my life."[9]

Such boisterous behavior among women elicited criticism from the Boston press and clergy, who complained that members of the female antislavery society were behaving in a manner unbecoming to their sex. "We hope that Anti-Slavery Ladies will cease so far to forget the dignity and delicacy which should mark the deportment of their sex, as to join in such obstreperous expressions of feeling in promiscuous public assemblies," observed the Reverend Joseph Tracy. "Perhaps they will say that they cannot *see* why clapping and hissing in public meeting is any more unbecoming in them than in men; to which our only reply is, that if they cannot *feel* the difference, we are very sorry for them."[10] When these same women promoted the lecture tour of English abolitionist George Thompson, daring to invite him on three different occasions to speak before them, they attracted even sharper comment from local authorities and, ultimately, provoked the mob assault on their 1835 annual meeting. As early as 1835, then, controversy arose concerning women's public behavior and their proper role in benevolent and reform movements. At the time, male abolitionists came to their defense, arguing that women had the right and responsibility to do whatever was necessary to destroy slavery.[11]

The "Garrison Mob" stunned Boston's abolitionist community and temporarily threw the movement into disarray. "There *is great fear among the brethren,*" wrote Anne Weston a week after the riot, "and all the leaders are gone." Some male abolitionists, according to Weston, had "flinched altogether . . . not daring to keep these times."[12] The Boston Female Anti-Slavery Society, however, refused to be defeated. Disappointed by the weakness of the male leadership, the women urged a more assertive course. So when the Massachusetts Anti-Slavery Society suspended its monthly "concert for the slave" to forestall renewed rioting and further damage to the antislavery offices, Anne Weston was indignant. "I think this was very wrong in them," she complained. "I would have removed the most valuable of the books & run the risque."[13] Displaying similar defiance of popular opinion, Weston's sister, Maria Weston Chapman, convinced the Reverend Henry Ware, Jr., to announce the society's upcoming meeting during the services at William Ellery Channing's Federal Street Church. The notice, reported Deborah Weston, caused "great excitement" among the Unitarians:

> Mrs. [Abby] Alcott lingered in the porch to hear what was said. One man said no one but Mrs. Chapman would have the impudence to do this. Another said, if Mrs. Chapman will insult this congregation, she must expect to be insulted herself. . . . Zebedee Cook, it is said, doubled up his fist at the rector & asked him how he dared to do such a thing.[14]

Male activists seemed genuinely impressed with the Boston women's courage and "indomitable spirit of perseverance," to quote the *Boston Daily Advocate*. As the *Boston Reformer* lauded, "The ladies of this society appear to be as firm as Roman matrons in the maintenance of their principles." The society's 1835 annual report, written by Maria Weston Chapman as a history of the riot, was accorded similar acclaim: "There is almost moral excellence enough in such a production to atone for the brutality of a whole city," read one review. "The riot has already enhanced the strength and popularity of the anti-slavery cause," this reviewer continued, "but this report, we have faith to believe, will make more converts than there were persons engaged in the tumult." The president of the Worcester County Female Anti-Slavery Society expressed the feelings of many when she wrote to the *Liberator:* "We feel that we are far behind our sisters of Boston, and numerous other places, who have borne the burden and heat of the day, but we hope to emulate their worthy example."[15]

Spiritually united, increasingly confident, and enjoying widespread attention, the Boston Female Anti-Slavery Society was rapidly transforming itself into a powerful, dynamic organization, and the activities they undertook during the year following the riot accelerated their shift away from traditional female benevolence toward political action. Their first effort came in March 1836, when the Massachusetts state legislature granted eight Massachusetts Anti-Slavery Society representatives a hearing before a subcommittee to account for the public disturbances their abolition meetings had precipitated. A large contingent of Boston Female Anti-Slavery Society members sat in the audience to lend support to their male colleagues, attracting comment in the local newspapers that "an array of beauty and fashion" now graced the State House halls.[16]

Political antislavery activity in Boston intensified during the summer and fall of that year, as local authorities began searching private residences for runaway slaves. Pointing to another constitutional right suspended to appease the South, Garrison urged Bostonians to "lock their doors and refuse admittance to every officer who seeks for runaway slaves."[17] The Boston Female Anti-Slavery Society, now 200 strong, was particularly moved by the plight of an escaped female slave and promptly offered its assistance. In July the society took an interest in two black women wrongly detained as runaway slaves, visiting them in jail and attending their hearings before the Massachusetts Supreme Court. When Chief Justice Lemuel Shaw ruled that the black women had been falsely imprisoned and must be released, the society was exultant.

The very next month, the society again entered the courtroom, this time in defense of a slave child allegedly brought to Boston illegally by her southern owner. Posing as Sunday school teachers, several members visited the Thomas Aves household to ascertain if a slave was being detained in the residence. They verified the girl's presence in the city and then attempted to have her removed from the household and placed in the Samaritan Asylum. Failing in this, the society then used money donated by wealthy member Mary Chapman to hire lawyers Rufus Choate, Ellis Gray Loring, and Samuel Sewell to file a suit against Thomas Aves and the slave owner, Samuel Slater, for unlawfully "imprisoning" the girl.

During the ensuing trial, counsel for Aves and Slater argued that their clients had a legal right to retain property while visiting the North. The lawyers were "full of sophistry and eloquence," wrote Lydia Maria Child of the courtroom scene. "One of them really wiped his own eyes at the thought that the poor little slave might be separated from its mother by mistaken benevolence. His pathos was a little marred by my friend E. G. Loring, who arose and stated that it was distinctly understood that little Med was to be sold on her way back to New Orleans, to pay the expenses of her mistress's journey to the North."[18] Boston Female Anti-Slavery Society lawyers declared that because slavery was illegal in Massachusetts the child, upon entering the state, was free. "Our laws do not authorize it," Loring expounded, "our principles revolt against it—our citizens will not tolerate its existence among them." Chief Justice Shaw again delivered the court's opinion, declaring that since in Massachusetts it was illegal to detain any person against his or her will the slave child must be set free.[19]

"The Boston Female Anti-Slavery Society may be excused for their rejoicing at this event," wrote the organization's committee as they paid the lawyers' fees to Loring. [20] Indeed, the Med slave case was a landmark in the cause of black freedom. It both denied southerners the right to bring slaves into Massachusetts and, by implication, confirmed that blacks were state citizens entitled to equal legal protection. Twenty years later, the Dred Scott decision by the United States Supreme Court would nullify the Med verdict, but by then Bostonians had come to honor Justice Shaw's opinion as a symbol of their own state's rights. Even at the time, the *Boston Courier* bristled in response to southerners decrying the court's decision: "We suffered ourselves to be frightened out of our rights, by that scare-crow *nullification*, and now we are to have the same bugbear or that other, *dissolution of the union*, whenever we dare to speak or think for ourselves? Let us throw off this spirit and meet them face to face on their own ground."[21]

Of less dramatic impact, but of enduring significance, was the petition campaign that the Boston Female Anti-Slavery Society, in conjunction with antislavery societies throughout the North, embarked upon in early 1836. Abolitionists petitioned for a variety of causes: to protest the admittance of Arkansas as a slave state, to demand the repeal of laws prohibiting interracial marriage, and to insist that slavery be banned in Texas, to name but a few. Anne Weston oversaw the distribution and collection of these petitions for the society, assigning different individuals the responsibility for their dispersal in each of Boston's wards as well as in every town in the state. Weston attached to each petition an address by the society urging all Massachusetts women to protest the existence of slavery in Washington, D.C., which made the nation's capital "a disgrace to the earth . . . for which no other spot on earth affords a parallel."[22]

The Boston Female Anti-Slavery Society's petition campaign displayed the women's growing organizational competence as well as the extent and effectiveness of women's networks throughout New England. In 1836 Massachusetts women sent twice as many petitions to Congress as their male colleagues, with women in towns like Lowell and Lynn circulating over 1,000 each while in Fall River, New Bedford, and Springfield they sent more than 500 petitions apiece. New England women sent an estimated 33,000 signatures to Congress to protest slavery in the nation's capital alone. As for the Boston Female Anti-Slavery Society, members collected over 3,100 names on their petitions, nearly equaling the combined effort of all other New England towns. [23]

Leaders of the society were convinced by the success of their petition campaign that female activities, like male, now required national organization. A convention had been proposed for May 1837, and although the Philadelphia Female Anti-Slavery Society was reluctant to participate in a separate women's conference (preferring instead to send delegates to men's conventions), many female antislavery societies eagerly promised their support. Angelina and Sarah Grimké, who at the time were working with the Ladies' New York City Anti-Slavery Society, joined efforts with the Boston women, and the two organizations, assisted by Philadelphia abolitionists, arranged for the meeting to be held in New York. Organizers fully appreciated the significance of what they were planning, for they believed this would be the first nationwide convention of women held in the United States. "All who reflect on the subject with the seriousness it requires must feel that our meeting together as a national convention is a step of great importance," Sarah Grimké wrote to Anne Weston in Boston. "The eyes of many will be fixed upon us, watching for our halting, & it is exceedingly to be desired that all the strength we have should be concentrated at that time."[24]

The Boston Female Anti-Slavery Society selected four delegates—two whites and two blacks—to represent them at the convention: President Mary Parker, Recording Secretary Martha Ball, Counselor Susan Paul, and Julia Williams. In a letter to her sister Deborah, Anne Weston explained the rationale behind these choices: "Miss Parker was chosen, of course, for her excellent gifts, Miss Paul because she was a favorable specimen of the coloured race, Julia Williams because the coloured people regard her as one of themselves, a light in which they do *not* regard Susan Paul, and Miss Ball was chosen because Ange [Ammidon] proposed her. Mrs. Child had obstinately refused to go."[25]

All Boston Female Anti-Slavery Society members were encouraged to take part in the convention as "roving delegates," and ultimately the Boston contingent consisted of Mary Parker, Anne Weston, Henrietta Sargent, Eliza Merriam, Julia Williams, Lydia Fuller, and Lydia Maria Child. To the satisfaction of the Bostonians, their own Mary Parker was chosen president of the convention so that "the same voice which for a moment allayed the fury of a portion of the Boston Mob," wrote an admiring delegate, "threw a sanctity over this consecrated assembly."[26]

Despite her initial opposition, Lydia Child joined with the Grimké sisters as the prime movers of the convention. Offering resolutions to fight for freedom without compromise, they encouraged female activists to denounce churches refusing to condemn slavery, to use free-labor products, and to continue petitioning state and local governments to enact antislavery legislation. Convention participants also heard testimony from black delegates about the pernicious effects of racism in the North, after which Angelina Grimké urged that they, as abolitionists and Christians, associate with black neighbors "as though the color of the skin was of no more consequence than that of the hair or the eyes."[27] Aside from this type of ideological pronouncement, the convention also produced several important documents pertaining to the role of women in organized reform as well as a promise to reconvene in Philadelphia the following year.[28]

This first Anti-Slavery Convention of American Women served as a capstone to the achievements of the Boston Female Anti-Slavery Society during the year and a half subsequent to the Boston riot. The society had won two important legal cases, submitted to Congress more petitions than any other antislavery society in New England, published several books of poetry and readings, and organized a profitable antislavery fair. "Many have done nobly," extolled the American Anti-Slavery Society's *Human Rights*, "but it seems to us just now that the ladies of Boston have exceeded them all."[29]

The adventures of the Boston Female Anti-Slavery Society, however, drew increasingly negative comment from other Bostonians. That "our females should have come forth from their retirement—from the holiness of the fireside, the protection of their household goods—to mingle in scenes like this," complained the *Boston Courier* of the women's courtroom behavior. "It is, it must be, but a dream. Oh deliver me from its agony." The *Boston Commercial Gazette* similarly dismissed them as a "parcel of silly women" and "petticoat politicians" who spent their days not attending to domestic duties but "prowling about stirring up discord and dissension."[30]

Although most in the society were offended by these accusations and criticisms, members were at this point not prepared to challenge the cultural assumptions the comments conveyed. Thus, in self-defense, women abolitionists stressed these same feminine stereotypes, cleverly manipulating women's images and roles to justify their public behavior. "May not women take an interest in the abolition of slavery without losing the modesty and gentleness that are her most appropriate ornament?" asked President Mary Parker, Vice-President Catherine Sullivan, and other officers of the society. "May not the ornament of a meek and quiet spirit exist with an upright mind and enlightened intellect, and must a woman necessarily be less gentle because her heart is open to the claims of humanity or less modest because she feels for the degradation of her enslaved sisters and would stretch forth her hand for their rescue?"[31] Thus it was as outraged wives and mothers that they fought slavery, an institution that openly disregarded and often defiled domestic arrangements. "The more closely our hearts cling to our altars and our homes," the Boston women maintained, "the more fervent are our aspirations that every inhabitant of our land may be protected in his fireside enjoyments by just and equal laws." Their antislavery activity, then, had to do with the "DUTY not the RIGHTS of women."[32]

Within the Boston Female Anti-Slavery Society, however, a more radical viewpoint was beginning to develop among some of its more prominent members. These women—including Maria Weston Chapman and her sisters, Henrietta and Catherine Sargent, Thankful Southwick and her daughters, and Lydia Maria Child—seldom served as officers in the society, but they were the prime movers and policy makers for the group. They were proud of their demonstrated competence and the success of projects like petitioning and the fairs. Indeed, when Theodore Weld offered his services at the women's convention, Anne Weston instructed Angelina Grimké to inform him "that when the women got together, they found they had *minds* of their own, and could transact their business *without* his directions."[33]

As social activists, these women experienced firsthand the pervasive sexism that permeated urban society in the 1830s and began to notice the extent to which women themselves participated in these limiting gender stereotypes. For instance, society members were annoyed with those women who refused to sign their petitions not out of moral conviction but because their husbands would disapprove. The abolitionists were upset further when women would lecture them for doing such an "odd, unladylike thing."[34] Some even began to scrutinize the signatures they secured, such as when Anne Weston mused, "Mrs. Rufus Choate gave me her name, and gave it too just as I have written it, Mrs. Rufus."[35] Weston also noticed how family relationships and responsibilities influenced members' freedom to participate fully in the petition campaign. "Mrs. Merriam has taken a ward, which as she is a bride, is to her glory."[36]

In short, in the midst of the Boston Female Anti-Slavery Society's success, there began to develop two divergent philosophies regarding women's roles within reform work. One group interpreted female abolition as part of women's customary benevolent and domestic responsibilities; the other considered social activism as evidence of what women, given the opportunity, could accomplish. In early 1837 these differences were more tendencies than fully considered ideologies, but subsequent controversies over women's rights, nonresistance, and the relationship of the church to organized reform would transform these sympathies into competing factions.

Strains within the antislavery movement surfaced in a serious way during the Massachusetts lecture tour of Sarah and Angelina Grimké. The appearances by the southern women in the summer and fall of 1837 helped fill the void created by George Thompson's departure. Their speeches attracted hundreds of women and, eventually, men. The turnout for their debut in Dorchester was so large that organizers moved the meeting site from a private residence to the town hall. At Roxbury, the Grimkés spoke to nearly 300 women and men, at Lowell over 1,500, and their three lectures in Salem drew 2,400 listeners. At Amesbury, on 17 July 1837, Angelina argued with two local men on slavery and the Bible, an event considered to be the first public debate between the sexes. [37]

The Boston Female Anti-Slavery Society enthusiastically promoted the Grimkés' tour and sponsored several lectures themselves. In addition, the society issued an address that urged other female abolitionists to attend the Grimkés' public presentations to demonstrate that women must take action in matters of grave moral significance. In "spiritual things," Corresponding Secretary Maria Chapman insisted, the role of women and men are "identical," for every individual is obliged to "obey the commands of God as responsible to him alone." In adopting this position, Chapman transformed a customary introductory letter into what today would be considered a feminist tract. [38]

When in July 1837 Sarah Grimké published her opinions on sexual equality in a series of open letters addressed to Mary Parker, president of the Boston Female Anti-Slavery Society, the society further linked itself with the "woman question." In fifteen essays published in the *New England Spectator* over the next three months, Grimké proclaimed that God created women "in perfect equality," not to be "governed by the views of any man, or set of men." All women asked was that men "take their feet from off our necks, and permit us to stand upright on that ground which God designed us to occupy."[39] The more progressive Boston Female Anti-Slavery Society members avidly received Grimké's advanced ideas. "I had a long talk with the brethren on the rights of women," Angelina Grimké wrote Theodore Weld after a social evening at the Chapmans, "and found a very general sentiment prevailing that it is time our fetters were broken. L. M. Child and Maria Chapman strongly supported this view; indeed very many seem to think a new order of things is very desirable in this respect."[40]

Other New England abolitionists, however, were opposed to associating women's rights with the antislavery movement and were often embarrassed by the argument and language. Following a condemnatory "Pastoral Letter" issued by the General Association of the Massachusetts Congregational Churches which denounced women reformers and lecturers as "unnatural" and their activities as "a shame and a scandalous offense against propriety and decency," some abolitionist ministers expressed their own concerns. Outlining their grievances in an "Appeal of Clerical Abolitionists on Anti-Slavery Measures," they lamented the direction the movement seemed to be taking. Many especially feared the other reforms that the radicals were attaching to antislavery. As the Reverend J. T. Woodbury complained, "We are not willing, in overthrowing slavery, to overthrow government, civil and domestic, the Sabbath, and the church and ministry."[41]

To fight this defection, Garrison used the same tactics with which he fought all enemies—untempered accusation and denunciation. In a two-page diatribe, he condemned the clergy as the greatest stumbling block in the way of emancipation. "It is becoming more and more apparent, that they are nothing better than hirelings," he raged, "blind leaders of the blind, dumb dogs that cannot bark . . . [that] love the fleece better than the flock." If the authors of the Clerical Appeal really understood the true character of antislavery in New England, contended Garrison, they would not have wrapped themselves in their clerical robes and presumed to dictate the course of the movement. "Abolitionism," he maintained, "brings ministers and laymen upon the same dead level of equality and repudiates all clerical assumption, all spiritual supremacy."[42]

The national American Anti-Slavery Society executives took a hands-off position toward these attacks and counterattacks, emphasizing that this was simply a "Boston controversy." Privately, however, the New York–based abolitionists sympathized with the general tenor of the Clerical Appeal. "As to the Boston controversy, my heart is sick," confided Gamaliel Bailey to James G. Birney. "I believe in my soul that we have all over valued Garrison. And as to himself, pride has driven him mad." Elizur Wright regarded Garrison's attacks upon the clergy as sinful. "You exalt yourself too much," he admonished the fiery editor, while James Birney felt that Garrison's departure might be the best thing for the antislavery cause.[43]

While many women's abolition groups, including the Philadelphia, Fall River, and Lynn societies, supported Garrison, the Boston Female Anti-Slavery Society was strangely silent, finding themselves unable to achieve a consensus. Many in the society firmly believed that the Grimkés had the right to preach their antislavery testimony. Maria Weston Chapman, Henrietta Sargent, and Lydia Maria Child went so far as to propose organizing a women's rights lecture and establishing a women's newspaper but ultimately decided against what might be construed as perpetuating the custom of separating the sexes.[44] As for taking Garrison's side against the abolitionist ministers, the Boston women were deeply divided.

Maria Chapman's annual report for the Boston Female Anti-Slavery Society that year forced the membership to confront their differences regarding these issues. Entitled *Right and Wrong in Boston,* Chapman's report became an exposé of the New England clergy. "We find that at almost every step we have taken towards the slave, our progress has been impeded by the same obstacle," Chapman fumed. "As church members, we have been hindered by the ministry:—as women, we are hindered by the ministry:—as abolitionists, still comes a 'clerical abolitionist' to prevent, as far as in him lies, the vigorous prosecution of our efforts." To Chapman, church doors were prison doors, and slavery would never "be abolished till the protecting influence of ministers and churches is removed." Even Anne Weston allowed that her sister's annual report was "a very spicy affair."[45]

Because of Chapman's unsparing criticism of local ministers, the Boston Female Anti-Slavery Society board of officers refused to endorse the report's publication. "We were an antislavery society," reminded Vice-President Catherine Sullivan, and Secretary Martha Ball complained that "our report ought to consist of our doings." Yet despite the board's protestations, Chapman refused to alter her report. "Spiritual despots" were suppressing free speech within local abolition circles, she exclaimed, "and now I fear they are influencing the B.F.A.S.S.!" Ignoring the reservations concerning her report, Chapman proceeded with its publication.[46]

"I suppose you think us priest-ridden," commented Catherine Sullivan as she and the other officers insisted upon placing a disclaimer in the front of what had become the society's unauthorized annual report. "While we give our cordial approbation to many of the sentiments of this Report," the insert read, "the love of freedom and justice constrain us to state that to some portions of it we cherish the most serious objections."[47] In response, Chapman penned a curt letter to President Parker, requesting that her resignation as corresponding secretary be announced at the society's next meeting.[48]

Thereafter, the Boston Female Anti-Slavery Society was engulfed in a bitter power struggle. The organization's elected officers—particularly Mary Parker (and her sister Lucy), Catherine Sullivan, Lucy and Martha Ball, and Judith Shipley—composed the proclergy faction, while the radicals included Maria Chapman, her sisters (Anne, Deborah, and Caroline), Lydia Maria Child, Ann Phillips, Henrietta and Catherine Sargent, and Thankful Southwick, some of the most active women in the society. Tradition was against the board of managers, for the Boston women had often acted individually, seeking the society's endorsement of their endeavors after the fact. So, despite the officers' protests, these radical members persisted in sponsoring women's lectures to mixed audiences, publishing feminist tracts, and attacking the local clergy, all in the name of the Boston Female Anti-Slavery Society. When the board attempted to exercise control, they found themselves quite powerless. As Maria Weston Chapman baldly stated, "I shall never submit to any custom of any society that interferes with my righteous freedom."[49]

The demise of the Boston Female Anti-Slavery Society took nearly two years. Prefiguring its dissolution, male abolitionists themselves divided in the spring of 1839 because, as opposition leader Amos Phelps complained, the Massachusetts Anti-Slavery Society was "no longer an *Anti-Slavery* Society *simply*, but in principles and modes of action, has become a *woman's-rights, non-government anti-slavery society*." Baptist minister Nathaniel Colver concurred: The Garrisonians had perverted the original aims of the movement by attaching to it "filthy" and "new-fangled" schemes that would lead to "anarchy, Jacobinism, infidelity, and atheism."[50] As a result, disgruntled anti-Garrisonians, with the blessing of the American Anti-Slavery Society, organized an alternative association, the Massachusetts Abolition Society.

As a consequence of this split among male abolitionists, the Boston Female Anti-Slavery Society board (whose ministers were Phelps and Colver) redoubled their efforts to align themselves with the "New Organization." To accomplish this fully, the officers still had to wrest control of the women's society from Maria Chapman and her allies. First, the proclergy faction successfully voted all Garrisonians, save Thankful Southwick and Mary Ann Johnson, out of office. The newly constituted board then assumed responsibility for the society's main fund-raising event, the annual fair, an enterprise traditionally managed by Chapman and her sisters. The officers also refused to allocate funds to support Garrison's *Liberator*, donating the money instead to the now anti-Garrison American Anti-Slavery Society. Mary Parker "begins to feel she must manage the Soc. by herself," complained Deborah Weston of the changes in the organization's direction, "& she grows gray very fast upon it."[51]

A good example of the tactics employed by the society's board occurred in March 1839, when radicals asked the officers to call a special meeting of the society in support of Garrison and his Massachusetts Anti-Slavery Society. Chapman and others circulated a petition calling for such a gathering, and, according to Anne Weston, "it was signed by the Sargents, Sewells, Manns, Louges, Ann Terry [Phillips] & in short the strength of the cause in the Soc." But she was forced to admit that "there is no probability that they will allow a meeting to be held." As Weston predicted, the officers denied the request to convene, explaining that "no reasons were assigned which appeared to them of *sufficient importance* to warrant the calling of a meeting of the society." Moaned Caroline Weston: "We are all gagged here. Padlocks are in our mouths, fetters on our limbs, free discussion *cloven* down in our midst."[52]

Radical members of the Boston Female Anti-Slavery Society were not ones to be defeated by bureaucratic obstacles. For example, when the officers resolved to collect petitions for Phelps's Massachusetts Abolition Society as part of a wider campaign to repeal state laws prohibiting interracial marriage, Chapmanites insisted upon submitting their petitions to Garrison's Massachusetts Anti-Slavery Society.[53] On another occasion, when a majority of women in the society were convinced by an impassioned appeal from black members to renew the annual subscription to the *Liberator*, Maria Chapman editorialized triumphantly but without authorization: "I have great pleasure in stating, for the information of all who may have supposed that this faithful and valuable Society was infected with clerical Abolition, that a crowd of witnesses [the Boston Female Anti-Slavery Society] stood up on this occasion to testify their sense of the importance of the Liberator to the holy cause for whose service they labor."[54]

In April 1839, when the Boston Female Anti-Slavery Society voted to use fair earnings to sustain the American Anti-Slavery Society rather than the Massachusetts Anti-Slavery Society, Chapman and her supporters countered by the organizing a "Fair of Individuals" to benefit Garrison's group. To promote the sale, Chapman published a letter in the *Liberator* directly adjacent to the announcement of the official Boston Female Anti-Slavery Society fair, exposing the "treachery" of the officers of the women's society. "It has been evident ever since the attempt to break up the Massachusetts Society in 1837, known by the name of the Clerical Appeal," the article read, "that a very wide difference of opinion and feeling exists in the Boston Female A. S. Society as to the means and manner of conducting the Anti-Slavery cause." Chapman then proceeded to urge New England women to attend her separate fair to demonstrate support for the Massachusetts Anti-Slavery Society in its struggle for "freedom" against the "domination" of clerical abolitionists.[55]

This type of one-upmanship continued throughout 1839. By the society's October annual meeting, the situation had so deteriorated that members were incapable of selecting a new slate of officers. Thereafter, in special meeting after special meeting, radicals contested the vote for each new officer, claiming that the acting recording secretary, Lucy Ball, miscounted the votes to insure victory for New Organization sympathizers. Shouts of "I doubt the vote" again and again disrupted the proceedings, until in frustration Mary Parker, whose reelection was the first to be contested, cried, "Then you may doubt it to the day of your death!" Ultimately, the disputed board chose to ignore the radicals' protests and attempted to conduct the society's business by speaking over the dissenting voices. Meanwhile, radicals continued to maintain that nothing the society did was legal because the officers had not been officially elected.[56]

Finally, at the April 1840 meeting, Vice-President Catherine Sullivan broke into Anne Weston's now familiar tirade about the illegality of the proceedings, to move that

> Whereas, for some time past, the harmony of this society has been disturbed and its usefulness impeded by differences of opinion and feeling resulting from causes not anticipated in its formation;
>
> And, moreover . . ., as these differences being formulated in the sense of duty of both sides, no compromise, concession, or change can be expected;
>
> And as this state of things is painful to us as individuals, as friends of the slave, and as co-workers in his behalf; therefore
>
> Resolved, That the Boston Female Anti-Slavery Society, be by the act of adjourning, *Dissolved.*[57]

In emotional appeals, radicals insisted that this ploy, kept secret until that moment, was not only dishonest but designed to mask the board's true intention: to "accompany their brothers and go off to the New Organization." A shaken Maria Weston Chapman proclaimed that she was forever "united with the society." There were so many women present, she exclaimed, from whom "she could not by human possibility be disjoined."[58]

Unmoved, Parker instructed those in favor, respectively, of adjournment and dissolution, to stand. Then, according to Chapman, without counting she declared the society dissolved, and the women left the hall.

Within the week both factions had regrouped. Those who had supported the society's officers constituted themselves as the Massachusetts Female Emancipation Society and became an auxiliary to the Massachusetts Abolition Society. Declaring that the Boston Female Anti-Slavery Society's dissolution was illegal and therefore invalid, Chapman and her supporters resuscitated it. For the next several years both groups continued to vie for leadership of the women's antislavery movement in Boston and throughout the region.

During its brief history, the Boston Female Anti-Slavery Society progressed from a modest charity to one of the most notorious, if not most influential, women's organizations in the country. Yet at its pinnacle of fame and prominence the organization virtually ceased to function as a unified group. By 1838 the Boston Female Anti-Slavery Society had become, in reality, two organizations whose concerns and priorities were not only different from but wholly unacceptable to each other. Moreover, each faction accused the other of creating the dissension and discord that had culminated in the society's destruction. According to the Chapmanites, church-controlled members of the board were "at once ignorant, servile, tyrannical, and fraudulent," and "paralyzed" the organization with their attempts to associate the society with the anti-Garrison clergy.[59] According to the officers, the radicals were a "turbulent, noisy, querulous faction" who had "opposed with desperation every thing the society attempted to do for the last year," making "all its meetings disgraceful scenes of riot and uproar."[60]

To fully make sense of the division, however, one must look beyond the immediate complaints and accusations of these Boston Female Anti-Slavery Society members and consider the wider transformations and tensions in Boston society at the time. In the following chapters, I will outline the political and economic situation in 1830s Boston and then attempt to locate women within its changing sociopolitical structure. As will be shown, the demise of the Boston Female Anti-Slavery Society was not simply a territorial dispute among a small group of female activists but part of the larger process of class formation and conflict in antebellum Boston.

28

CHAPTER 2

Boston in 1835

"SO THIS IS BOSTON! WHAT A BEAUTIFUL PROSPECT!" EXCLAIMED A CORRE-
spondent to the *New England Magazine* who, like Harriet Martineau, was
visiting the city in 1835. Newcomers sailing on a packet through the
narrow channel into Boston Harbor would have been impressed as their
boat threaded its way among a "fleet of ocean steam Leviathans" and
headed toward the "huge and stately docks of stone and steel and brick."
The nation's third-largest port was a "forest of masts and spars" and "snowy
canvas" as domestic and foreign vessels—laden with textiles, shoes, fish,
and paper from New England, nails from England, leather from Russia,
sugar and hemp from Brazil and the Philippines, tea from China, and silk,
indigo, and opium from India—entered and departed the channel. Beyond stretched the city of Boston, with its "spires pointing to the sky," its
"glittering roofs reflecting the rays of the sun," and its "green lawn [of the
Common] midst the streets and surrounding blocks," while the copper
dome of the State House "rises and crowns the whole."[1]

Packet lines from New York and points farther south like Baltimore,
Savannah, and New Orleans docked at Central Wharf, the city's most
important pier in the 1830s. Lined with brick stores and warehouses four
stories high, it was the "most conspicuous and the most attractive" of the
city's wharves and boasted of the "largest continuous block of warehouses

in the country."[2] An impressive observation tower arose from the dock's center and afforded a panoramic view of the harbor, while seven marine flags (sometimes called conversation flags) flew from its top to signal the local population of incoming vessels, arriving mail, and nearby fires. Disembarking and traversing Central Wharf's 413-yard length, passengers would pass no fewer than fifty-four businesses, including grocery stores, flour merchants, ship chandlers, and fish dealers, as well as specialty shops trading in brimstone, steel, coal, iron, hops, and, in season, oranges, lemons, figs, and raisins.

Those spending the evening in Boston might take lodgings in the Tremont House, located on the corner of Tremont and Beacon streets. From its Athenian porticos to its private dining and reading rooms, the seven-year-old hotel was "not surpassed, if equalled, by any similar establishment in the world."[3] In the past, visitors might have preferred the Marlboro' Hotel on Washington Street for its convenience as a stage stop. But recently a social reformer named Willard Sears had purchased the hotel and converted it into a temperance house that greeted guests with a list of rules to observe during their sojourn in the city. Sears's activist proprietor, Nathaniel P. Rogers, not only prohibited drinking and smoking on the hotel's premises but also expected guests to attend chapel twice daily and to use free-labor products.

Luckily, a visitor might think, the stately Tremont House was equally well situated, located in the heart of Boston's commercial/government district and adjacent to the Tremont Theatre, one of the city's most popular halls. In 1835 equestrian performances were the rage in most Boston theaters. However, the cultured guest—if well connected—had the option of spending the evening listening to music at the Handel and Haydn Society or the Boston Academy of Music or indulging in some quiet reading and conversation at any number of exclusive Boston libraries such as the Athenaeum, the Massachusetts Historical Society, or the Academy of Arts and Sciences.

The finest view of the city in 1835 could be found at the Massachusetts State House. Built by Charles Bulfinch in 1795, this impressive edifice on Beacon Hill occupied the highest physical position of any structure in Boston. Guidebooks of the period urged sightseers to give this "consecrated place for the delegated wisdom of the State" their immediate attention, for from the lookout atop its dome the stranger could enjoy the entire expanse of the city as it stretched below toward the sea. Looking away from the harbor past the wandering ribbon of the Charles River, the visitor also could glimpse the brick buildings of Harvard College in Cambridge as well as the city's neighboring towns, their "white houses and country seats, amidst groves and luxuriant fields," creating a scene considered by many to be "one of the most delightful panoramas that the world affords."[4]

Looking eastward from the State House toward the harbor, one could survey Boston's financial and commercial district. As the eye traveled down State Street from Washington Street to the waterfront, one could identify more than fifty bank and insurance offices, the Old State House, Faneuil Hall, the four-storied granite commercial building popularly called Quincy Market, the Custom House at the head of Central Wharf, and finally the harbor dotted with its many islands and "fine, handsome ships . . . their royal skysail yards aloft."[5]

A tangle of commercial streets ringed Boston's financial district along State Street, and here residents were able to purchase goods and luxuries to match those available in any major metropolis. Already in 1835, Boston shopping was organized into discernible districts—leather goods on North Market and Broad streets; silks on Kilby; mirrors, glass, and books on Cornhill; and stationers, printers, and fine goods shops along Washington—though most shops remained owner-operated specialty stores bearing the proprietor's name. At Charles B. Lloyd's, for instance, one bought "looking glasses of every description," while William P. Tenny dealt in carpets and Timothy Gilbert sold pianofortes.[6]

Longtime visitors to Boston would have witnessed substantial alterations in the appearance of this financial/commercial district over the past twenty-five years. The first of these "improvements" occurred along the waterfront, as local entrepreneurs widened streets, expanded wharf facilities, and erected imposing warehouses to meet the requirements of the region's prospering foreign and domestic trade. This transformation of the city's business district was the physical manifestation of an economic boom that Boston had enjoyed since the turn of the century. Indeed, the opening of the China trade in the late 1700s had revived Boston's sagging shipping industry and generated considerable new wealth for Boston's established mercantile elite.

After the War of 1812, these same entrepreneurs began to invest profits from foreign and domestic trade into manufacturing, commerce, and real estate. Boston merchants built textile mills in Lowell and Fall River and shoe factories in Lynn, while in the city they established profitable banking and insurance companies. Merchants also invested in the construction of toll roads, bridges, and canals as well as in new housing tracts, marketplaces, and hotels. In fact, the aforementioned Tremont House was among the many successful real estate ventures of merchant-capitalists Harrison Gray Otis, Josiah Quincy, Robert Shaw, and Samuel Appleton.[7] Bridge tolls alone netted merchant-investors over $200,000 annually. As a result of this extensive speculative activity, by 1845 Boston merchants owned 20 percent of New England's mills, 30 percent of Massachusetts's railroads, 40 percent of the state's insurance companies, and 40 percent of the local banks, amounting to over one-half of the state's wealth.[8]

Because of their financial position and prominence, local merchants and bankers enjoyed an abiding prestige and respect in 1830s Boston. As one admirer of these early capitalists recalled, "Fifty years ago the average citizen, clerk, schoolboy and laborer could distinguish the merchant who did business on the wharf from any other class" as he strode through the city on his way to the post office and then to Topliff's Reading Room. To "receive a bow or a Good-morning salute" from one of these Brahmins as "he walked down State Street and along Commercial Street to his counting-room," recalled another, "was something not to be despised by anyone."[9]

The post office and Topliff's Reading Room were located in the Old State House, which still stands at the head of State Street, in the heart of Boston's business district. Topliff's was an exclusive gathering place for local businessmen, and for their convenience the proprietors subscribed to major domestic and foreign newspapers and provided up-to-date ledger books that recorded all arrivals and departures in the harbor, their cargoes, and vessel personnel. At Topliff's, the Boston merchant could always find current shipping information, many maps, and a good clock.

In addition to providing space for the post office and Topliff's Reading Room, the venerable structure, since 1830, also housed the city's administrative offices. Boston had not incorporated until 1822, since for many decades Bostonians were loath to modify their traditional town-meeting style of governance. However, after the turn of the century, economic, social, and demographic change rendered Boston's time-honored paternalistic political system increasingly ineffective, and despite outward expressions of respect and deference, mercantile elites found they no longer could depend upon the Boston populace to endorse automatically their political and developmental programs. For example, in the 1820s, the middling economic groups began to protest laws they considered preferential to the upper class, condemn exclusive political and social associations of the rich, and resist compulsory volunteer civic responsibilities like fire fighting and policing duties. About this same time, local artisans staged

Boston's first large-scale labor strike, while among the poor mob rule seemed to have replaced customary deference to established authorities. As a result of this increasing class tension, the Boston oligarchy turned to incorporation as a means of protecting their personal and property rights and to meet the escalating demand for municipal services.

After incorporation, primarily due to the vision and energy of third mayor Josiah Quincy (1823–29), Boston's municipal government was thoroughly modernized. Quincy was the ideal individual to guide Boston's move away from a traditional, deferential authority system toward one that was more professional and bureaucratic, for he was a transitional figure himself. The son of Josiah Quincy, Sr., a prominent lawyer and diplomat, the younger Quincy was a respected statesman and leader. Yet, in his style of governance, the future Harvard president was a quintessential capitalist—"progressive," "fearless and aggressive," and not afraid of investing unprecedented sums of money in city-run enterprises. Determined to rationalize municipal operations, Quincy professionalized the city's police and fire departments, installed sewer and water systems, undertook major redevelopment projects, and established new correctional and welfare institutions. The mayor's crowning achievement was Quincy Hall, a "bold and noble plan" whereby the city replaced a number of "disorderly buildings" on Market Street with an ornamental, two-story brick structure with enough space to accommodate 128 shops. [10]

Modernization of Boston's government did not entail the corresponding changes in the city's political structure that occurred in other large metropolises. As historians Frederic Jaher and Ronald Formisano have demonstrated, Boston's wealthy merchants distinguished themselves from other preindustrial elites in their ability to adapt to new economic opportunities and so retain their traditional political preeminence. [11] Thus, throughout the antebellum period, Boston Brahmins not only dominated the region's manufacturing and commercial development but also continued to control the mayor's office, the common council, and the appointment of top city officials. At the state level, the Boston establishment continued to wield its political power through the exclusive Whig party.

Boston's mercantile class maintained their cultural unity and social cohesiveness through prestigious educational and cultural institutions such as Harvard College, the Boston Athenaeum, and most importantly the Unitarian church. This elite religion drew its membership largely from local merchants, professionals, and government officials. In fact, by 1820 artisans accounted for only 28.4 percent of the new admissions to Boston

Unitarian churches, whereas fully two-thirds of Boston's wealthy residents were connected to the denomination.[12] As Harriet Beecher Stowe, daughter of evangelist Lyman Beecher, had complained in 1825 when her father arrived in Boston to effect a religious revival among the beleaguered orthodox Congregationalists: "All the literary men of Massachusetts were Unitarian. All the trustees and professors of Harvard College were Unitarians. All the elite of wealth and fashion crowded Unitarian churches."[13]

While the social philosophy and exclusiveness of the Boston Unitarians served as an important component in the self-definition of local elites,[14] Boston's increasingly segmented residential patterns helped further distinguish the upper from the lower classes. In the first few decades of the nineteenth century, wealthy Unitarians commissioned Charles Bulfinch and other architects to build splendid mansions as monuments to their prosperity and power. These sturdy brick edifices were secluded in exclusive neighborhoods surrounding the Boston Common and in residential enclaves like Essex and Pearl streets, Bedford Place, and Bowdoin Square. The most "favored seat of respectability," as one Boston guidebook put it, was Beacon Hill. Within this district directly adjacent to the new Massachusetts State House stood some of the "most elegant houses and most eligible residences in the city"—family homes of entrepreneurs like the Appletons, Lowells, and Shaws, statesmen like the Phillipses, Quincys, and Adamses, and intellectuals like the Channings and Prescotts. Other wealthy Bostonians preferred Summer Street, which in the 1830s was "admired for its glory of trees and aristocratic residences." The Chapmans, Emersons, and Websters, to name a few families, lived in elegant homes there, and with its gardens, lawns, and towering trees Summer was "decidedly the most handsome street in Boston."[15]

In the eighteenth century, merchants had preferred to live in Boston's commercial district, closer to their waterfront stores and warehouses. Now clerks, salesmen, and lower professionals resided in these financial zones, staying in boardinghouses and small private dwellings in areas adjacent to State Street and on the south side of Beacon Hill. Between 1830 and 1850, this segment of the Boston's population was growing faster than any other economic group, save unskilled labor. In fact, it has been estimated that the number of clerks and salesmen increased by 35 percent in the 1830s and by an incredible 225 percent in the next decade.[16]

During the antebellum period, this burgeoning new middle class enjoyed increasing political and cultural influence in Boston. They first flexed their political muscle in the controversies surrounding the city's incorporation. Known then as the "Middling Interest," this loose-knit group of clerks, small businessmen, upwardly mobile artisans, and prominent newcomers, demanded—and won—several important concessions from the elites before incorporation succeeded. For example, the Middling Interest obtained ward voting in local elections so that population concentrations would be reflected in city government. They also successfully lobbied against the local prohibition against the use of wood in the construction of tall buildings and established the public's right to one free bridge leading in and out of town. Finally, this middle-class coalition prevented the mayoral nomination of real estate developer Harrison Gray Otis, forcing the election of a compromise candidate, John Phillips, as the city's first mayor.[17]

Organized religion offered another source of social organization and political power for Boston's nascent middle class. Studies of other antebellum cities have demonstrated that evangelical denominations—particularly Congregational, Baptist, and Methodist—were extremely useful to small proprietors, lower professionals, artisans, and new residents in establishing a common identity and viable class goals,[18] and this pattern pertains to Boston as well. Between 1820 and 1840 at least twenty-five new evangelical churches were organized in Boston, and the bulk of the membership was drawn from the new middle class. For example, in 1834 converts to the Federal Street Baptist Church included a clerk, flour dealer, housewright, teamster, boatman, and brass founder. Of the four identifiable women who joined the church, three ran boardinghouses and the fourth sold groceries.[19] Similarly, in 1835 Lyman Beecher's Bowdoin Street Congregational Church counted three clerks and two merchants, as well as a tailor, school principal, and engraver among its new members, with all but the two merchants indicating that they were Boston newcomers. As for the female converts that year, three were the daughters of merchant Philip Ammidon, two were widowed, and one ran a boardinghouse. Recruiting patterns of the Franklin Street Congregational Church followed the same pattern. Four of the seven new male converts in 1836 were recent Boston arrivals. Three had established small businesses, and the others were employed as a clerk, teacher, minister, and artist. Only two female members were included in the Boston directory that year—one was a milliner, the other an innkeeper.[20]

Middle-class Bostonians, it seems, found evangelical Congregational and Baptist churches more structurally and ideologically democratic, more participatory, and more expressive than the Unitarian church of the upper class. Church membership was determined through an interrogation and vote by the entire congregation, and as a body the congregation could, and did, excommunicate deviant members. Many evangelical churches required a temperance pledge and expected communicants to contribute time and money to church-sponsored charities and "voluntary" associations. Evangelical religion thus demanded a moral accountability from its adherents that was based upon the Word of God, not the dictates of the local aristocracy.[21] As a result, middle-class Baptist and Congregational churches, like middle-class political parties, challenged age-old assumptions that authority resided with the traditional elites and provided an institutional alternative through which Boston's emerging middle class could express its own values and political agenda.

Just as Boston's nascent bourgeoisie was obtaining heightened visibility, the city's working classes were making their presence felt as well. In the 1830s, local artisans dominated Boston's West End, residing in the area between Beacon Hill and the Charles River and in newly developed housing tracts in South Boston. However, this socioeconomic group was faring less well than their upper- and middle-class cohorts, as evidenced by their dwindling numbers throughout this period. Peter R. Knights has estimated that skilled artisanal labor declined steadily during the decades before the Civil War, whereas the number of unskilled workers in the city rose by 85 percent. By 1850 Knights figures that over half of the city's workforce was composed of unskilled and semiskilled laborers.[22]

This deterioration of artisanal labor was due in large part to the capitalization of Boston's economy, as merchant-investors increasingly assumed control over manufacturing and construction. As historian Lisa Beth Lubow explains:

> Land was no longer viewed simply as a resource purchased for use by ordinary citizens. . . . The "builder" or "developer," in a growing number of situations, was a merchant middleman, who in unprecedented fashion intervened between the craftsman and the customer, took over the administration of the project, and ultimately appropriated the profits realized from the enterprise. The consequences of these developments, for the artisanal housewright, were profound.[23]

Some artisans were able to become members of the upwardly mobile middle class, no longer simple craftsmen but now contractors and middlemen with substantial annual incomes. The less fortunate either left the city or fell into the ranks of Boston's working poor. The economic position of

Boston's artisans declined further after 1840 as the migration of unskilled Irish into the city depressed wages, overcrowded low-income housing, and taxed municipal services.

The mass migration of poor Irish into the city was not unique in the city's history, for Boston traditionally received displaced people, ranging from refugees of colonial wars to individuals forced to abandon declining family farms in rural New England and sell their labor in the city marketplace. In fact, as historian Gary Nash points out, as early as 1750 Boston was simultaneously New England's commercial, cultural, and intellectual capital and its center of indebtedness, widowhood, and poverty.[24] James Henretta substantiates this depiction of the steady impoverishment of Boston, estimating that the number of propertyless adult males in Boston rose from 14 percent in the late seventeenth century to 29 percent by the Revolution.[25]

Many of the local poor crowded into Boston's North End, the oldest section of the city, where luminaries like Cotton Mather and Paul Revere once lived. It remained the most populous area in Boston in the 1830s, but now the destitute and desperate huddled in its dilapidated old buildings. "I always enter your city with my mouth open, and I always leave it with my eyes shut," wrote the correspondent to the *New England Magazine* of Boston slums. "So much outward happiness, and so much real misery! There are pale cheeks, sunken eyes and broken hearts! . . . They die by poverty with opulence all around them."[26]

Boston contained a district even more desolate than the old North End. Located on the north side of Beacon Hill, on the streets bordering Belknap (now Joy) and Cambridge, was "Nigger Hill," where the majority of the city's 1,750 African Americans were confined. Slavery was abolished in Massachusetts in 1783, yet Boston remained inhospitable to free blacks throughout the first half of the nineteenth century. As a consequence, the black population residing in this section of the city never rose above 2,000 before the Civil War.

The list of hardships endured by antebellum free blacks is a familiar one. As victims of persistent poverty and open discrimination, they were employed in jobs society defined as most menial—chimney sweep, waiter, domestic, laundry worker, and day laborer. Blacks were excluded from Boston hotels, restaurants, and theaters and were restricted to segregated areas on public conveyances. Boston charity, regularly used by the urban poor as supplemental income, was denied to blacks, while custom and law kept them out of most schools, churches, orphanages, and hospitals.

Yet, as historians like James and Lois Horton and George Levesque have demonstrated, racial discrimination did not result in social disorganization among Boston's blacks; instead, racial segregation promoted community solidarity, self-sufficiency, and mutual aid among them.[27] By 1835 black Boston had a well-defined social hierarchy, community leaders, at least two churches (Baptist and Methodist), one public and several private schools, as well as active social and reform organizations. The community even boasted of its own forty-year-old Masonic Lodge. Thus, while white Bostonians viewed black poverty and deprivation (which was real enough) with horror, local African Americans enjoyed a strong community life revolving around church and family.

Outsiders, however, habitually conflated poverty with immorality and failed to distinguish between the homes of respectable poor families and the disreputable dance houses that were the haunt of "very low white women" and "the resort of the worst kind of people."[28] Already in 1835, bourgeois Bostonians worried about the "Irish mob" and the permanent poor. Citing their "propensity to drink to excess" and "habits of dependence," the upper and middle classes condemned North and West End "rabble" who periodically outraged respectable Boston with violent and destructive behavior.[29] Indeed, the Garrison Mob was only one of many popular uprisings that exploded in the mid 1830s. In fact, two days after the attack on the Boston Female Anti-Slavery Society several working-class youths from South Boston set fire to a wooden structure on South Street occupied by eighteen Irish families. The most notorious riot occurred in August 1834 when members of the non-Catholic working class torched the Ursuline Convent, which at the time served as a private school for upper-class Boston girls but had of late been rumored to hide sexual perversions behind its walls.[30]

Historians have analyzed these episodes of public violence and have found them neither unpredictable nor irrational but structured and purposeful, serving as political devices for unrepresented groups.[31] To early-nineteenth-century Bostonians, though, residents of the North and West Ends were not less fortunate, politically powerless neighbors but inhabitants of a separate world ruled by raucous, vulgar, and dangerous ruffians and foreigners. As one resident described it, "By a strange anomaly, in one of the most orderly and decorous cities in the world, another Alsatia, on a small scale, had been suffered to grow up."[32] In Boston slums, admitted Mayor Quincy as well, there existed a "struggle for the supremacy of the laws" between the law-abiding and "that class of vicious population."[33]

Just as the upper and middle classes were learning to channel class tensions and social dissatisfactions into new forms of political organization and expression, they also found ways to cope with a Boston's increasingly aggressive lower class. Professionalized police and fire departments helped curtail the worst public offenses among the North and West Enders. The city also demolished the old almshouse, workhouse, and granary (all originally built on Park Street by the Common) and constructed a House of Corrections, a House of Industry, a so-called Lunatic Asylum, and a new city jail outside of town.

Local benevolent organizations and city administrators also began to distinguish between what they viewed as the innocent poor—the orphan, widow, disabled, and elderly—and the vicious poor who were considered capable of work but who preferred idleness and vice. The city and charities then allocated public assistance to the deserving poor and withheld funds from those judged unfit as a form of coercion and punishment.[34] Elites did not expect to purge Boston of its "audacious" and "notorious" population, for, to quote Mayor Quincy, "in great cities, the existence of vice is inevitable." Civic leaders did hope to remove the appearance of immorality and poverty so that it should, again to quote Quincy, remain "secret, like other filth, in drains and in darkness; not obtrusive; not powerful; prowling publicly in the streets for the innocent and unwary."[35]

No tour of Boston is complete without a visit to "the most intimately Bostonian tract of land," the Common. Stretching beyond the new State House, the "dear old Common," with its venerable trees, broad lawns, and noble statues, was full of symbolic and sentimental significance for the city's inhabitants.[36] Located adjacent to Boston's expanding commercial and residential districts, the park connected past to present, keeping the people in touch with their not-so-distant rural heritage and values. In contrast to the teeming slums of the West and North Ends, nineteenth-century guidebooks and literary giftbooks described the grounds as natural, peaceful, and healthy, using words like frolic, promenade, and rendezvous to express the Common's timeless virtue. Lithographs likewise depicted visitors to the Common as well dressed and orderly, casually conversing as they walked its paths. Even when 150,000 celebrants converged on the park to enjoy Fourth of July fireworks, boasted one Bostonian, "not a single oath or an improper word did I hear, and there was nowhere to be seen an ill-dressed person. . . . Everybody was his own policeman and the duty was exceedingly well performed." Such a peaceful gathering, the writer maintained, would have been impossible in England. As for such an orderly event coming about among the Irish, "I need not say that *some* disturbance must have ensued."[37]

The Common represented democracy in practice. Citizens were frequently reminded that the property was "indeed common to rich and poor," owned by all, and local authors lovingly evoked images of revolutionary heroes walking the malls shoulder to shoulder with fellow Bostonians. However, by 1835 the Common was already surrounded on three sides by the splendid brick mansions of Boston merchant-capitalists, who were no doubt drawn by the Common's beauty and prestige. Moreover, that year these upper-class neighbors began collecting money to build an "imposing" and "substantial" iron fence to enclose the park. Evidently, even in the Common democracy had its limits.

Boston in 1835 was experiencing a period of profound change. The fourth-largest city in the United States, Boston's population would triple by the Civil War. Residents were extremely mobile, moving in and out and around the city at a rate of about 80 percent per decade. Over this same period, Boston's ethnic composition experienced a permanent shift, going from a 95 percent native-born citizenry in 1830 to one composed of 50 percent foreign-born and their offspring in 1850.[38]

These demographic patterns were reflected in Boston's changing physical environment. The leveling of hills to fill in marshes and tidal lands altered the size and terrain of the city significantly. Meanwhile, urban renewal and real estate development transformed the city's appearance, as multistoried brick and granite markets, banks, warehouses, and mansions replaced deteriorating wooden structures in the downtown area. New building trends and tastes revealed an increasing differentiation between commercial and residential areas, as well as a segmentation of neighborhoods by class and ethnicity.

Far-reaching economic development also played a significant role in the transformation of Boston in the 1830s. Much of this economic growth occurred outside of the city, in places like Lowell, Lynn, and Fall River where textile mills and shoe manufactories flourished in the 1830s and 1840s. However, Boston entrepreneurs financed these ventures as well as invested in the construction of the railroads, canals, turnpikes, bridges, and shipping facilities necessary to transport these manufactured goods to domestic and foreign markets.

Unlike other metropolitan areas undergoing similar socioeconomic development, Boston's preindustrial elites were able to retain their control over much of the city's political, economic, and cultural resources. However, rapid population growth combined with significant economic and social change did seriously undermine Boston's deferential authority system, making consensual town meetings, cooperative and mutual policing, and even the established Congregational church obsolete. To cope with these changes, Boston's merchant-capitalists sought and eventually succeeded in incorporating the city and developing government-run institutions to handle the multiplying urban problems. Prominent families also joined with the Protestant clergy to organize benevolent and reform associations to provide additional welfare and social assistance as well as to proselytize bourgeois values like temperance, hard work, and chastity among the city's increasingly heterogeneous population.[39] Finally, the Boston upper class protected itself from what they considered to be an increasingly vicious lower class by building jails and welfare institutions outside the city and sequestering themselves in wealthy neighborhoods, private clubs, and exclusive gathering places.

The transition from domestic and artisanal production to large-scale, capitalist manufacturing had a significant impact upon Boston's nonelite population as well. As the financial, commercial, and shipping center of the region, Boston became the destination for New England and European migrants seeking employment in the city's thriving economy. Newcomers found their way into two distinct occupational sectors, either in the city's burgeoning clerical, service, and professional positions or as unskilled and semiskilled wage and day laborers. Because of the continuing solidarity and exclusiveness of Boston's aristocracy, local middle and lower classes were obliged to create alternative institutions and customs through which they established separate sources of power and identity. The middle class, in particular, channeled its ambitious restlessness into grassroots political parties, religious revivals, and social reform, while the lower classes relied upon workingmen's associations, popular demonstration, and flagrant disregard for accepted social mores. Despite the creation of alternative institutions and values, these socioeconomic groups would not assume power commensurate with their numbers until well after the Civil War.

By the 1870s, however, longtime residents would be lamenting, with barely disguised bigotry, the passing of this era of the merchant-capitalist. Describing the 1830s as those "palmy days of yore," Aaron Sargent wistfully wrote that those "solid men of Boston" like "those tall-masted ships have passed away forever." When in 1874 some ancient trees were "cruelly" felled by city officials, another oldtimer swore that former Brahmin leaders "never would have voted to have those old elms cut down." As he concluded, "Those were the days when Boston was governed by Boston born men."[40]

But what of Boston-born women? Women would not have been welcome in Boston's countinghouses, government offices, or Topliff's Reading Room. Moreover, statistics on skilled, unskilled, and service workers minimally reflect female participation in the labor force. How did women in Boston fit into these male worlds of work and politics? How did they carve out spheres of their own in religion, charity, and the household? Chapter 3 will attempt to locate women within the transformative world of 1830s Boston.

⌐✐(C H A P T E R 3)✐⌐

Women of Antebellum Boston

"THERE IS A STRONG AND RECOGNIZABLE TYPE OF BOSTON WOMEN WHOSE characteristics are clear and enduring," gushed Ednah Cheney in the early 1880s. Of English stock, well bred and educated, the Boston dame was "more intellectual than passionate" and displayed a "morality" both "stern and exacting."[1] This effusive description has been the standard image for the Boston matron. Yet, contrary to Cheney's stereotype, recent historiography and common sense have demonstrated that the public and private lives of antebellum women, even those in Boston, varied according to their economic status, racial, ethnic, and sociocultural backgrounds.[2]

Unfortunately, information about these divergent women within Boston's socioeconomic hierarchy is elusive. Not only are demographic figures, employment rates, and official reports skewed, unreliable, and incomplete, the records that do exist for Boston women are virtually untapped and those including African-American women are almost nonexistent. Consequently, the following discussion, gleaned from censuses, directories, promotional and reform literature, and personal manuscripts, is intended to be suggestive, not definitive. Its purpose is not to give a comprehensive or systematic history of women in 1830s Boston but to show the social context within which those in the Boston Female Anti-Slavery Society lived. As such, this chapter's focus will be on white upper- and

43

middle-class women, and it will concentrate upon those areas particularly influencing their reform activities and personal lives.

While Harriet Martineau was staying in Boston, she had access to people and places closed to most American women—or men for that matter. During her two-year American sojourn, she was "Lafayetted" by the country's most distinguished persons of letters and politics, including James Madison, John Calhoun, Henry Clay, and Andrew Jackson. In Boston, she was entertained by local luminaries of the stature of Senator Daniel Webster, Harvard professors Jared Sparks and Nathaniel Bowditch, and Unitarian minister William Ellery Channing. Martineau's Boston excursions, however, did not often lead her to the new State House, the wharves, or Topliff's Reading Room. Neither did she frequent local hotels, restaurants, and theaters. Instead, Martineau and her female traveling companion were housed and escorted by local Unitarian clergymen and other representatives of the city's upper crust, and the dramas of their Boston days, as with most affluent New England women, were played out in churches, charitable institutions, and private drawing rooms.

Because Martineau was a practiced social analyst, her descriptions of American society and politics at that time have had lasting value. Moreover, as a self-supporting woman traveling independently within domestic circles, her observations regarding America's private world are equally instructive. Despite the royal treatment she received in Boston, Martineau's judgments of the booming metropolis, particularly attitudes toward and treatment of the lower classes, women, and blacks, were harsh. In *Society in America* (1837), *Retrospect of Western Travel* (1838), and assorted essays appearing in English journals in the late 1830s and 1840s, Martineau expressed her disgust that, "among a people whose profession is social equality . . . [and] universal self-government," there existed "assumptions of class" that one would more expect to find in England or Russia than in the United States. Wealthy Bostonians, she complained, commonly regarded power and property as "eternally together," while they impugned the lower class as universally "ignorant" and "opposed to law." The Englishwoman also found distasteful the widespread references to class warfare, a struggle that the rich portrayed among themselves as the "power of the mind . . . arrayed against [the] brute force" of the lower classes.[3]

As for women, Martineau believed them treated much worse in the United States than in Europe. In America, she observed, "woman's intellect is confined, her morals crushed, her health ruined, her weaknesses encouraged, and her strength punished." All the while, she "is told that her lot is cast in the paradise of women." Martineau located the source of women's plight in their inability to earn a living wage. In this country, she wrote, "women can earn a maintenance only by teaching, sewing, employment in factories, keeping boarding-houses, and domestic service." Yet earnings in every one of these occupations, save factory work and some teaching positions, were so wretched that women were forced into precipitous marriages—or worse. Because marriage was seen as woman's "one worldly objective in life," Martineau felt that the institution was "debased," domestic harmony destroyed. Yet, because women were politically "nonexistent" within an "unjust," nonrepresentative governmental system, they were helpless to remedy their situation.[4]

In her writings, Harriet Martineau identified the key issues facing women in the 1830s: the persistence of "old feudal notions" toward women; women's political and economic impotence; and women's virtual imprisonment within the domestic sphere. It is a tribute to Martineau's perspicacity that contemporary historians of nineteenth-century women continue to address the very same issues today that she raised over 150 years ago.

Women's status, roles, and images in 1830s Boston were influenced by the widespread socioeconomic transformations accompanying New England's transition from an economy based on domestic production of goods and subsistence farming to one of commercial manufacture. American and foreign factories could make cloth, shoes, and many household goods faster, cheaper, and often better than individual families, thus relieving many households, especially the women in them, of the full burden of providing these necessities themselves. However, as production moved out of the home and into the factories and commercial centers, the men followed. Increasingly, work became a public role assumed by males, while women remained behind to tend home and children. As essayist-educator Catharine Beecher wrote, "The Americans have applied to the sexes the great principle of political economy which governs the manufactories of our age by carefully dividing the duties of man from those of woman, in order that the great work of society may be the better carried on."[5] Thus the development of commercial manufacturing intensified the division of labor based upon gender, demarcating the lines between men's public world of work and politics and women's private sphere of home and family.

Although the changing organization of work released many women from production and some domestic chores, it did not liberate them entirely from economic responsibility. Drawing upon traditional expectations that all family members contribute to the household economy, young, unmarried women, like their male cohorts, streamed from rural New England and upstate New York to find work in mill towns like Lowell and Troy or wage employment in commercial centers like Boston. These young women often lived on their own for the first time, supporting themselves as well as sending money home to assist with family finances.[6]

Many of these farm girls were hired as domestics and seamstresses by affluent urban housewives. In fact, by the late 1830s cities like Boston contained specialized employment agencies that provided domestic training for single women and located employment for them in respectable families. Such arrangements created unaccustomed leisure for upper- and middle-class women, and many used this free time to become involved in different religious and charitable organizations, activities deemed by antebellum society as most suitably performed by women. Some went so far as to participate in antislavery and women's rights societies; these latter activities were less favorably regarded by their friends and neighbors.

Historians differ in their interpretation of the consequences of these changes in women's work and leisure. To some, it is a story of decline as women were dispossessed of their political and economic responsibilities. Mary Ryan, for example, has contended that, "by mid-century, woman had been escorted to a definitive place" in the home "while the great common man conquered the West, built the railroads, and championed democracy." Gerda Lerner, too, has shown how women's situation "in many respects deteriorated" as they were "by tacit consensus excluded from the new democracy." Other historians have told of women's declining economic possibilities as their economic function in the household diminished and most occupations and proprietorships were taken over by male "professionals." What work women did continue to find was in areas traditionally relegated to underpaid female hands—sewing, laundry, nursing, and domestic work—while the best-paying jobs, such as teaching and factory work, still paid women far less than what their male counterparts earned.[7]

As Martineau had reasoned, restricted economic opportunity meant women had few alternatives to marriage. Trapped within the ideological and physical confines of the "cult of true womanhood,"[8] early-nineteenth-century women gradually lost not only their economic roles but also the protection inherent in traditional communal life. Mobility and the gradual privatization of the nuclear family weakened the mediating role of kin and community in marital relations, depriving women and children of this form of protection from an irresponsible or abusive husband. Moreover, widows and orphans ceased being the responsibility of civic and religious authorities and were forced to seek charity within an increasingly anonymous and punitive welfare system. Many historians conclude that sentimental declarations about women's special mission as moral and physical guardians of the family merely disguised the failure of American government and society to grant them legitimate rights and freedoms.

On the other hand, historians studying women's life styles and self-images within their domestic context conclude that nineteenth-century women actually enjoyed increasing power and autonomy. Pointing to the slow but eventual changes in laws regulating marriage, divorce, property ownership, wages, and authority over children, these historians contend that over the course of the nineteenth century women's status improved. Furthermore, within the domestic setting women developed life styles and values distinct from their husbands and brothers that provided them with new avenues of self-fulfillment and self-esteem. At the same time, intense relationships between women gave them deeply satisfying emotional lives.[9]

Scholars also have found that prescriptive ideology regarding women's character and capabilities was not as restrictive as it might appear. For example, in antebellum New England the number of unmarried, self-supporting women increased dramatically. Some historians interpret this to be a consequence of new educational, economic, and ideological opportunities afforded them, another example of the improvement of women's lot. As one so-called spinster was eulogized: "Though she never married, she dignified maidenhood, and commanded the respect of all who knew her. . . . There was a place in [the] community for her to occupy; that place she found and filled with grace and dignity."[10]

Antebellum women were also adept at using Victorian ideology to expand their spheres of activity to include public and political functions. As Carroll Smith-Rosenberg has pointed out, "During the very years when the new bourgeois men began to proselytize for the confining Cult of True Womanhood, wild, religious women created a public and powerful role for themselves as a female conscience and moral voice crying in a wilderness of male corruption." So, by assuming a significant part in religious revivals and benevolent causes, women claimed a political role, however unofficial, in antebellum America. The nineteenth-century women's rights movement, some conclude, was a direct outcome of women's involvement in these religious and benevolent activities as well as evidence of women's increasing status in American society.[11]

Historians also explain changes in the behavior of and attitudes toward antebellum women in terms of wider transformations in the American social structure, particularly in the development of a class society and class consciousness. Accordingly, the emergence of a distinct urban middle class depended upon a redefinition of the gender system and the creation of an ideology based upon separate spheres and female domesticity.[12] This analytical framework has proved useful in the interpretation of women's participation in benevolent and reform organizations. As historians such as Nancy Hewitt and Lori Ginzberg have found, many middle- and upper-class women who became activists did so not simply because of sexual stereotypes and expectations but also as a way of working with their husbands in promoting social change in accordance with their particular class values.[13]

Generalizations regarding upper- and middle-class women's roles and values have proven less useful in explaining the lives of working-class and African-American women. Increasingly, historians have found that attitudes and expectations regarding status, behavior, and work were very much contingent upon class, racial, and ethnic backgrounds. Claudia Goldin, for example, has examined the occupational patterns of Philadelphia women between 1790 and 1860 and discovered that women's participation in the labor force was determined by wealth, ethnicity, age, and family size. Similarly, Suzanne Lebsock has shown that black as well as lower-class white women in Petersburg, Virginia, were often a permanent part of the local workforce, unlike their married, middle-class cohorts. Black and white working-class women coped with economic insecurity, exploitation, and powerlessness, Christine Stansell and Jacqueline Jones have observed, by operating within self-defined value systems that, though different from each other, were more appropriate to life in urban slums. Indeed, for these women, white, middle-class standards governing women's responsibilities and deportment were largely inappropriate and thus often disregarded.[14]

These studies illustrate the complexities involved in generalizing about antebellum women, particularly in assessing advancement, decline, and continuity. Moreover, the evaluation of women's autonomy, status, and power depends not only upon class, racial, and ethnic circumstances but also upon the criteria used for investigation—that is, economic opportunity, political rights, family roles, or personal life style. Any model, then, must be explicit about who and what is under investigation when describing the lives of early-nineteenth-century women.

But, again, what of Boston women? The demographic data available on Boston in the 1830s provide a starting point. Federal and city census figures reveal that in 1830 women composed 53 percent of the city's 61,400 population, a figure somewhat higher than the 51 percent that women represented in Massachusetts generally. Over the next ten years, women would become a minority in Boston, their numbers declining to 47 percent of the city's 93,000 residents. Statewide, the proportion of women remained stable at 51 percent.

In the 1830s and 1840s, the United States Census categorized inhabitants by race and cohort group, and this information is suggestive of more subtle changes occurring in Boston's composition and character during this time. The bulk of white men and women in the city were between the ages of twenty and forty. This trend was particularly evident among males in that age group who, in 1830, made up 42 percent of the white male population and 52 percent ten years later. In contrast, white males between twenty and forty in Massachusetts declined overall, their numbers amounting to only 36 percent in 1840. Age groupings of local females appear more stable. White women between twenty and forty accounted for 40 percent of Boston's white female population in 1830 and 41 percent in 1840. Statewide, however, figures for this age group declined, with the percentage of women twenty to forty decreasing from 40 percent in 1830 to 33 percent in 1840. Census data thus suggest that Boston, as compared to Massachusetts, was the destination of white working-age men and women. In fact, while the state's overall population rose by 21 percent between 1830 and 1840, Boston's population increased by 52 percent during that same period.[15]

The 1830 and 1840 federal censuses also provide aggregate statistics on occupations in Boston. For example, in 1840 nearly 11,000 residents indicated that they were involved in some type of navigation; 5,300 were in manufacturing and trade (artisans); 2,000 were in commerce; and almost 600 were employed in learned or professional occupations.[16] However, these figures reveal little about women's work, which customarily was intermittent or hidden within the household. As Thomas Dublin warns, historians must always keep in mind the special nature of women's work, which was often transient because of competing family obligations.[17]

Boston's widowed population, which accounted for over 1,000 of the 2,000 white women listed in the 1835 *Boston Directory*, provides a good example of this hidden world of female employment. Little is known about the circumstances of these women, though Gary Nash has written of the "widowing" of Boston's population as a result of deadly colonial wars and epidemics. In fact, Nash estimates that in 1742 30 percent of the city's married women were actually widowed.[18] However, only 10 percent of the widows listed in the 1835 directory had any employment indicated: Thirteen were nurses, eight ran boardinghouses, while others were small proprietors, laundresses, and seamstresses. That taking in lodgers was particularly commonplace among widows is suggested by the fact that the phrase "apartments to let" became a slang term for widows. Widows frequently lived with and were supported by working children, usually unmarried daughters. The widow Susanna Baker, for instance, lived with daughter Susan B. Baker, a seamstress. Similarly, Mary Bell shared a home with Mary Ann Bell, a dressmaker. Historian Lee Chambers-Schiller writes of how even independent, enlightened women did not always escape cultural dictates and family assumptions that single daughters were responsible for aging or ailing relatives.[19]

The bulk of women wage earners in Boston were employed as domestics, although not a single domestic is listed in the 1835 directory. However, the 1845 city census did list 4,046 women employed as house servants, a figure that was higher than all other categories of women's work combined.[20] Before 1800, domestic employment was part of a larger apprenticeship system whereby young rural or orphaned girls were taken in by affluent families who educated and provided for them in return for domestic labor. Casual remarks about domestics suggest that during the early part of the century Boston domestics were still an accepted part of the household scene, comfortable and predictable. "All of the Dr.['s] housekeepers are cut out of the same model," one observer commented, "kind, neat, trusty sort of people, just enough pinned to the ministry to be shocked considerably at his talk."[21]

By the 1830s, however, the nature of domestic service was undergoing substantial change. In many ways, female servants experienced the degradation in working conditions that artisans suffered as a result of the development of commercial manufacturing in New England. Increasingly, native-born girls found employment in mills and other emerging female occupations that were more attractive and lucrative than domestic work, which paid weekly salaries ranging from $2.50 for cooking to as little as $1.25 for housekeeping. Female Irish immigrants filled the void, no longer as permanent household members but now as hired help. One conservative oldtimer gave voice to the transformation that took place in domestic service during his lifetime and Bostonians' reaction to it. "Seventy-two years ago there was not a single Irish servant girl in Boston; no not one," he wrote in 1883. "All the 'help' was native-born American. . . . The recollection of this blessed condition of domestic life is one of the greatest comforts in my old age. Happy, happy days!"[22]

Aside from domestic work, sewing was the major source of income for women in antebellum Boston. The 1835 directory indicates that 35.3 percent of employed white women earned a living by their needle—working as corset and truss makers, dressmakers, milliners, tailoresses, and upholstresses. By 1860, nearly 40 percent of working women were listed in the business directory as earning their livelihood through sewing. These statistics probably reflect a fraction of seamstresses working in the city, for most seamstresses sewed anonymously in their homes and were paid by the piece.

A seamstress was among the worst-paid women in the country: In New York City she earned about $1.25 a week, $5.00 a month, while in Boston she earned a mere eight cents per shirt. In her study of working-class women in New York City, Christine Stansell evokes the misery and desperation of sewing women in early-nineteenth-century cities. Dispersed in squalid tenements, underpaid and overworked, seamstresses were easily exploited by unscrupulous employers who took advantage of women's limited employment alternatives and family responsibilities that tied them to the household.[23] One can assume that conditions were much the same in Boston. An exposé in a local women's magazine, the *Friend of Virtue*, for example, told of a local tailor "in the habit of employing young women to work in his shop," who was guilty of sexual harassment and rape of his female employees.[24]

In contrast to the impoverishment of domestics and seamstresses, upper- and middle-class women were beginning to find more lucrative, professional employment opportunities in urban centers like Boston. Of the white working women listed in the 1835 directory, 6.2 percent were identified as teachers. Traditionally, teaching was an important part of female childrearing responsibilities, and educational reformers and government officials were quick to point out that women were temperamentally well suited to deal with children. There were practical reasons as well to employ female teachers who would work for half the salary of men.[25] In the 1840s, male teachers in Boston earned between $1,500 and $2,400 annually, depending upon the level of employment, whereas women were paid $300, with a $25 room allowance.[26] This differential pay scale was based largely on the fact that in Boston teaching positions were assigned according to gender. Public high schools and grammar schools restricted teaching positions to males only, while women taught in primary schools (children under eight) or worked as teaching assistants in the higher grades. So, in effect, low-paying teaching jobs and female school employment were synonymous.

Yet, despite comparatively low pay, little mobility, and working conditions that subjected women to "many and great evils," teaching was the aristocracy of women's occupations in Boston, paying more than any other position, save factory work.[27] In addition, many women teachers were self-employed or worked in female-run schools, which allowed them the flexibility to adjust their teaching assignments with their family and household schedules. Teaching proved so popular among educated middle-class women that by 1860 77.8 percent of the state's teachers were female.[28]

Other professional positions, especially those in the social services, were also opening up to white Boston women in the 1830s. Nursing and doctoring, which like teaching were traditionally female functions, witnessed a dramatic increase in paid employment. In 1835, 18.3 percent of Boston's employed women indicated they were involved in health care—as nurses, midwives, and leechers. There were no female physicians in the city at that time. By the 1850s, 32 percent of the city's working women were employed in health care. This figure includes eighteen women listed as doctors, including Mrs. Mott, who advertised that she was "ready to attend to all diseases incident to the Human Frame, in Men, Women, and Children, *except those arising from immorality.*"[29]

Other female professions were developing as well. Already in 1835 Boston, two women were employed as librarians, and a number of women worked in intelligence offices (employment agencies) arranging safe, suitable jobs for girls newly arrived in the city. Some middle-class women secured paid positions as social workers, helping destitute and homeless women and unwed mothers. In 1835 social workers earned two dollars per week, about twice the wages paid seamstresses and domestics.[30]

Finally, the 1835 *Boston Directory* listings for white women suggest that a significant number of women were employed in jobs requiring property ownership or some capital. One hundred and fifty women (25 percent) operated boardinghouses, while fifty-one (8.5 percent) were proprietors, running fancy goods and import shops, as well as grocery, dry goods, and clothing stores. Two female clerks also were listed in the directory, one of whom was employed by a female-owned establishment. Finally, there were four female artisans—an ink master, a silk dyer, a paperhanger, and a "mechanic." Oddly, the 1835 directory included no women in the printing and binding trades, although the city census for that year indicated that 437 women worked in book production, ranking that occupation third in number of women employed, trailing only domestic service and sewing.

Of course, most women's names never appeared in the local business directory or city census. Although many women did earn money, they did so within a separate female economy wherein they sold items from their kitchens, gardens, and sewing rooms.[31] Others worked as behind-the-scenes partners with their husbands. For example, in the 1836 Boston *Merchant's and Trader's Guide*, J. F. Foster promoted his personalized trusses. Small print at the bottom of the notice read, "Ladies wishing for any of these instruments will be waited upon by Mrs. Foster, at any of their homes or at her residence."[32] By 1851 Mrs. Foster's female trusses had advertising space of their own in the Boston business directory.

Even women at the upper end of Boston's social spectrum filled important functions vis-à-vis their husbands' positions. For instance, when Lafayette came to Boston, Susan Quincy, wife of the mayor, publicly welcomed the statesman with an "elegant and appropriate speech."[33] Mrs. Harrison Gray Otis was also involved in political and civic projects, and she assumed a leading role in the creation of the Bunker Hill Monument and the establishment of Washington's birthday as a national holiday.

In sum, Boston women continued to participate in the local economy, despite the decline of domestic production. Most women's work was done within the household, while others converted traditional female functions—housekeeping, sewing, nursing, and teaching—into paying occupations. Only the elite of Boston's working women made their way into the city directories: women with education, property, or special skills salable in the urban marketplace. The situation of black women underscores this fact. Free black women routinely worked outside of the home as self-supporting heads of households or as working wives.[34] Yet the 1835 directory lists only four employed black women: a cigar maker, a doctor, a milliner, and a boardinghouse keeper.[35] Little change occurred in the types of jobs available for women in Boston during the following thirty years, although women, white and black, increasingly were segregated into low-paying, female-defined jobs, "that kind of work," wrote a woman at the time, "which consists in rendering services, not in producing results."[36] Aside from domestic service, the bulk of wage-earning women continued to be employed as seamstresses or as health-care providers.

Women's participation in other occupational categories declined. In

TABLE 1. White Women's Occupations, Boston, 1835

Occupation	# Women	% Wk. Wom. (N = 598)
Widows	1,121	NA
Sewing trades	211	35.3
Boardinghouse operators	150	25.1
Nurses	109	18.3
Proprietors	51	8.5
Teachers	37	6.2
Laundresses	21	3.5
Social workers	6	1.0
Artisans	4	0.7
Librarians	2	0.3
Clerks	2	0.3
Actresses	2	0.3
Artists	2	0.3
Ladies' hairdresser	1	0.2
No occupation listed	319	

Source: *Boston Directory, . . . 1835* (Boston: Charles Stimpson, 1835).

1857, for example, there were no female artisans or tailors, and the number of women working in employment offices had been halved. Between 1830 and 1860 the division between retail sales and manufacture increased, a trend that excluded women from more profitable proprietorships.[37] Accordingly, between 1835 and 1857 female proprietorships declined from fifty-one to sixteen. All "carpet makers" listed in the 1857 *Boston Directory* were female; all retailers of "carpetings" were male. Similarly, every dressmaker was female, yet only one woman was listed as running a clothing store. Of the 115 milliners, 32 were women, yet not one woman's name appeared among the 20 wholesale dealers of millinery goods. By the Civil War, women could be found in only 30 of the 506 job categories encompassed in the city business directory. These changes were not simply changes in the female labor force but reflected more significant transformations in the organization of work in Boston. As the home workshop gradually was replaced by manufacturing concerns and the family store was coopted by impressive commercial establishments, women, like men, became wage employees, their names hidden from the historical record.

TABLE 2.   *Women's Occupations, Boston, 1857*

Occupation	# Employed	# Women	% Wom. in Occ.	%Wk. Wom. (N = 283)
Sewing trades	254	113	44.5	39.9
Nurses/leechers	57	57	100.0	20.1
Boardinghouse operators	64	27	42.1	9.5
Teachers (gen.)	54	20	37.0	7.1
Physicians	285	18	6.3	6.4
Proprietors	447	16	3.6	5.7
Midwives	14	14	100.0	4.9
Restaurants, etc.	208	4	1.9	1.4
Employment office	13	3	23.0	1.0
Hairdressers	132	3	2.3	1.0
Bakers/confect'rs	106	2	1.9	0.7
Medicines	30	2	6.7	0.7
Artists (portrait)	43	1	2.3	0.4
Teachers (spec.)	138	1	0.7	0.4
Booksellers/publ.	128	1	0.8	0.4
Shoemakers	105	1	1.0	0.4

Source: William Damrell et al., *Boston Almanac for the Year 1857* (Boston: John P. Jewett, 1857).

The changing organization of work, especially the separation of workplace from home, work time from leisure, and employer from employee, had a significant impact upon the personal lives of Boston women. Those of the upper and middle classes withdrew from what was once a family economy, and how they allocated this new leisure time became an important component of bourgeois society. Working-class women also developed leisure-time activities, often in contradistinction to urban bourgeois culture. In effect, leisure as much as work helped delineate class in antebellum Boston, especially among women.

Nonworking women organized their daily lives around family, friends, church, and charity, spending significant time paying and receiving social calls. "After school in the morning Miss Dodge and Miss Percival called," wrote Caroline Weston in her diary in September 1835, and shortly thereafter two additional women friends arrived. "Then came Mrs. Johnson and then a Mr. King to call upon Eugenia, who by the way came to us on Monday." During the afternoon, Weston continued, "We have sent for

Mary and Anne to tea—and the Danas announced their intention of coming—& Ammidons. Sarah Cowing came in the stage, so we shall have a good housefull."[38]

Historians have emphasized the homosocial aspects of female visiting, arguing that these daily social rounds enabled idle women to weave personal ties among themselves that lessened their isolation within the home. Intimate female–female relationships contrasted with male–female relationships, which were strained and formal, even those between husband and wife. In fact, Carl Degler had discovered situations in which a visiting female friend displaced the husband from his wife's bed.[39] However, extensive social intercourse among urban women was not simply a manifestation of female culture or a compensatory activity that made up for women's exclusion from public sources of prestige and power. Through such social rituals women strengthened personal ties among Boston's elite families and cultivated social networks that reinforced class bonding.[40] These social occasions were particularly valued by women since they provided one way in which they participated in upper-class networking.

In addition to representing the family at social functions, the leisured Boston woman had religious and moral responsibilities to fulfill. As Massachusetts minister Jonathan Stearns remarked, "The religion of Christ is chiefly prevalent among women, and chiefly indebted to them for its spread."[41] Local church membership lists substantiate Stearns's observation, for statistics derived from Baptist and Congregational church records indicate that women accounted for nearly 70 percent of new converts during the 1820s and 1830s. The Federal Street Baptist Church, for example, was founded in 1827 by forty-one women and twenty-four men. Of the sixty-six converts in 1830, forty-six were women. Over the next decade 417 women joined the church, whereas only 191 males converted during this same period. Similarly, when Lyman Beecher arrived at the Bowdoin Street Congregational Church in 1826, it contained twenty-five males and twelve females. By the time he left in late 1832, 342 females as compared to 195 males had converted. This same disparity in conversions was true for the Union Congregational Church. Between 1822 and 1839, 602 women and only 229 men were among its new admissions.

Female church converts also showed remarkable fluidity in church affiliation, as they moved back and forth between churches of the same and occasionally different denominations.[42] The Union Congregational Church, for instance, gained 35 percent of its new members from other churches, while 35 percent of its own flock left to join other churches. At the nearby Federal Street Baptist Church, only one of its sixty-five original members became a permanent fixture in the pews. Although, in 1838, 101 individuals converted to the church, by 1872 only seven of these remained. Of the rest, sixty-two were dismissed to other Baptist churches, fourteen died, seven stopped attending, six (women) joined other evangelical denominations, and five (three men, two women) were excommunicated. In short, women showed marked independence and experimentation in their church activity. They joined churches independently from their husbands and families and changed affiliations often. Traditionally, religion provided New England women a legitimate outlet for public activity that was separate from their husbands and fathers. In the 1830s women made the most of the opportunity.

Female benevolence was the most important manifestation of women's religious commitment in the 1830s. As Ednah Cheney once remarked, "A lady hardly thinks her life complete, unless she is directly aiding in some work of reform or charity."[43] Only a handful of charities existed in Boston before 1800: the Boston Marine Society (1762), the Boston Humane Society (1791), the Boston Dispensary (1795), and the Massachusetts Charitable Fire Society (1794), to name the most prominent. After the turn of the century, the number of charitable and cultural institutions in the city rose dramatically. Indeed, between 1800 and 1845 Bostonians donated more than $5 million to organized philanthropy.[44] "Certainly," observed the *New England Magazine* in 1834, "no age has been so remarkable for societies for the improvement of mankind as the present."[45]

Reasons for this growth in organized charity are many and complex. As discussed earlier, religious revival and accompanying social activism were in large measure an outgrowth of economic change in Boston. In fact, Peter Dobkin Hall directly correlates the creation of charitable institutions with the emergence of corporate capitalism in the city and demonstrates how both charities and corporations were vital to the continued socioeconomic hegemony of local elites. For one thing, large institutions, like the Massachusetts General Hospital, the Athenaeum, and the Perkins Institute for the Education of the Blind, as well as scores of lesser philanthropic societies, provided respectable, professional positions for the sons of Boston merchants without diverting economic resources now necessary for capitalist investment. Hall also discovered that donations to major philanthropic organizations (placed in Boston banks and insurance companies) were the means by which merchants accumulated capital sufficient to undertake railroad and real estate ventures. Charities operated not off of the principal of these "donations" but off of the interest. Hall concludes that benevolent institutions furthered the economic interests of Boston's upper class and at the same time enabled elites to continue fulfilling personal and societal expectations of noblesse oblige.[46]

Bostonians also considered charity an effective solution to the problems arising from rapid social change. Living within what was still fundamentally a religious culture, Bostonians understood slums, poverty, and crime in theological and moral terms. They sought to alleviate some of the human suffering around them through numerous religious and benevolent organizations. Although Boston's upper class controlled the large welfare institutions, middle-class Congregationalists and Baptists did their part as well in organizing benevolent societies to help assist the needy. As a result of this social concern, Boston counted at least fifty-nine organizations devoted to different causes in 1835; by the Civil War this number increased to more than 160.

Because charity was, at root, a religious enterprise, women soon assumed an important voice within organized reform. Customarily, these were female-only organizations that addressed "women's" concerns: poor widows and orphans, prostitutes, missionaries, and theological students. The Boston Female Asylum was the first large, cross-denominational Protestant female benevolent society in Boston. Established in 1800 and devoted to the care of orphaned girls, the asylum continued its operations well into the twentieth century. The Boston Female Society for Missionary Purposes was also established in 1800 to support religious missions as long as the "needle can be instrumental of spreading the knowledge of a Savior's name."[47] Other female groups soon followed their example: the Corban Society to aid theological students (1811), the Fragment Society to provide assistance to poor women (1816), and the Penitent Female's Refuge to rehabilitate prostitutes (1818).

Males were equally philanthropic in turn-of-the-century Boston. Encouraged by the success of the Boston Female Asylum, a group of gentlemen established the Boston Asylum for Indigent Boys shortly thereafter. Local men also contributed time and money to professional and cultural organizations such as the Boston Dispensary, which was essentially a free clinic, the Boston Debating Society, and the Boston Lyceum. Women often formed auxiliaries to male-only organizations, meeting separately but contributing their earnings to the original society. Still other benevolent causes, like the Penitent Female's Refuge, were begun by men but run by women.

Organized benevolence in Boston, then, represented an extensive, cooperative effort among women and men to deal with pressing social problems. In 1834 a coordinating committee was formed to devise a more systematic way of dispensing to the poor funds collected by these assorted philanthropic groups. Composed of delegates from the different executive boards of the city's charitable societies, this coordinating committee consisted of five men and three women. Apparently no general outcry accompanied the creation of this "promiscuous" group.[48]

Aside from the impressive Boston Female Asylum, most women's benevolent groups were quite small and affiliated with local churches. The Baptists were particularly enthusiastic in creating societies, and Baptist church covenants customarily mandated that members support church-sponsored charities. As unpaid assistant to her husband, often the minister's wife headed the congregation's benevolent groups.[49] For example, the Boston Female Asylum began as the brainchild of Samuel Stillman, popular minister of Boston's First Baptist Church. The society's direction, however, fell to Hannah Stillman. As the historian of the Female Asylum reported, "Mrs. Stillman, the daughter of Dr. John Morgan, a distinguished surgeon and professor of Philadelphia, appears to have been a worthy helpmate to this good man [Samuel Stillman] . . . interesting herself deeply in all the charities and good works in which he was engaged."[50] Lucy Malcom, whose husband served as minister of the Clarendon Street Baptist Church, fulfilled a similar role. Her death was a "severe loss to both Pastor and Church," for it would be hard to replace her "energy and ability" in overseeing the Sabbath school, running the church's infant and maternal associations, and working for the blind.[51]

Church-based women's groups were usually small, with fifteen to thirty women participating on a regular basis. Meetings were held once or twice a month, usually at the sponsoring minister's or president's home. The gathering opened with a prayer by the minister or a woman officer and closed with religious singing. In between, women sat together sewing and conversing. That these occasions were valued as much for their social as for their religious dimensions is apparent in their beautifully lettered minutebooks. Very little included in these meeting records is of a religious or spiritual nature, for the societies were more practical than philosophical in orientation. "This society has no definite object in view," wrote the secretary of the Watertown Female Charitable Sewing Society, "its aim being to perform such acts of benevolence as may be brought before the society and considered worthy."[52] Boston's Bethel Sewing Circle, under the direction of

Baptist minister Phineas Stow, reported its meetings in this way: "October 28, 1846—A stormy *eve* without, but pleasant within the precincts of our society." Of another meeting the secretary wrote: "The afternoon and evening were delightfully passed in sewing and knitting for the poor mariner. For the most part profitable conversation employed the lips of all."[53]

Admonitions that found their way into minutebooks also reveal that sociability was an integral part of women's benevolent activities. The secretary of the Bethel Sewing Circle worried, "It is to be feared that such occasions [meetings] favor generally too much of trifling and vanity." On another occasion, the secretary observed, "It is to be sincerely regretted that such occasions, consecrated as they are to works of charity, are not oftener the means of moral and intellectual culture to those present."[54] The Ladies' Benevolent Society of Roxbury was sufficiently concerned about the character of their conversation during the meetings that they banned gossip in their constitution. "We will not speak directly or indirectly against the character of any, but by our conduct and conversation during the meetings seek to leave a good impression on the minds of all present."[55]

Female benevolent societies' primary function was to earn money or make usable items for the city's poor. Much of their income derived from annual membership subscriptions and periodic donations and bequests. Women's groups, especially the larger organizations like the Boston Female Asylum and the Penitent Female's Refuge, expected sizable donations from male relatives as well. The wives of William Prescott (lawyer), Amos Lawrence (merchant), Thomas Perkins (merchant), and Samuel Eliot (mayor and statesman), for example, were prominent members of the Boston Female Asylum, and their husbands regularly gave large sums of money to the institution. After just seven years in operation, the asylum had accumulated more than $21,000 in Boston banks. Interestingly, the Boston Female Asylum also raised money through the indenture of many of the girls in their care. Other smaller, less prestigious women's groups earned money by publishing religious and moral pamphlets and selling their own handmade clothing, bedding, cushions, and quilts. More enterprising societies held fairs or bazaars at which they sold their goods directly to the public.

Some of Boston's female charitable groups were interdenominational. The Boston Female Asylum, for example, was initiated by Baptists, but soon its subscribers included prominent Unitarians and Congregationalists. The Boston Female Society for Missionary Purposes was open to all women of "good moral character," and officers endeavored to keep track of whether donations were intended to support Congregational or Baptist missions.[56] After 1820, however, there developed a hierarchy of associations as Boston's benevolence increasingly became differentiated by denominational affiliation and, more importantly, socioeconomic status. By the 1830s it was understood that the "most wealthy and influential ladies of the city" managed the Boston Female Asylum, while their husbands served on other exclusive boards and commissions.[57] Similarly, the wives of Boston elites including Nathan Appleton (merchant), Abel Adams (merchant), Robert G. Shaw (merchant), and Lemuel Shaw (chief justice of the Massachusetts Supreme Court) dominated the Fragment Society; their husbands headed the Bunker Hill Monument Association. Samuel May (secretary, Marine Insurance Company), John Codman (lawyer), and Pliney Cutler (president, Atlantic Bank) served as trustees for the Unitarian Massachusetts Bible Society and as board members of the Harvard Corporation, the university's governing body; their wives participated in the Boston Female Asylum and the Fragment Society.[58] Thus, as indicated earlier, public charity in Boston increasingly became the collective endeavor of the city's upper class, both as a means of promoting social bonding and as monuments to their enduring wealth and power.

Still, small reform and benevolent groups persisted alongside these larger institutions, especially societies connected with the local Baptist churches. These organizations remained more traditional in nature, less formal and bureaucratic. Well into the 1840s, church women continued to spend an afternoon a month sewing and conversing. Their products and goals remained small—a shirt, a pillowcase, or a dress so a child would be suitably clothed to attend Sabbath school. Often these women's groups helped known individuals meet specific needs, and at meetings officers would read aloud notes of gratitude from the recipients of their beneficence.[59] Thus the benevolence of middle-class groups was, perhaps, more personal and direct than the charity dispensed by the large welfare institutions run by Boston's elites.

Both upper- and middle-class charity was directed toward white lower-class, even "fallen" women living in Boston's North and West Ends. As observers of the goings-on in the local slums, respectable women worried about the fate of innocent female residents there who seemed likely to fall victim to male "depravity" and "high-handed profligacy."[60] Working-class girls were particularly at risk because of the way they spent their leisure time. Instead of joining churches and charity groups, they were known to engage in the "undecent practice" of meeting unattached males after work and on Sundays, spending their free time "in a manner not pleasing to Jehovah." Such familiarity between the sexes, respectable Bostonians believed, was wrong and inevitably led to "licentious conduct." The decent youth filled his or her leisure time with profitable activity. "Be at your place all night," one women's writer advised, and "let the whole time be filled with useful employment," added another.[61]

Lower-class women consciously distinguished themselves from the Boston matron through dress as well as deportment. No lady would wear "more than seven distinct colors in her dress," appear in a pink bonnet, or show her ankles, yet lower-class girls delighted in wearing a combination of colors "in utter defiance of those conventional laws of harmony and taste." Whereas respectable women felt that one's dress should be "neat, dignified, and chaste," lower-class women insisted upon calling attention to themselves by wearing elaborate hats and other ornaments.[62]

Probably few young white women were as entirely free from family authority and social scrutiny as upper- and middle-class critics would have us believe, yet the urban slum environment did provide an unprecedented opportunity for young people to spend unsupervised time together. This informal intermingling of the sexes was part of a distinctive working-class culture that emerged in the 1830s and 1840s. Although working-class culture was aggressively male in orientation, it revolved around leisure-time activities rather than the workplace, which allowed for the inclusion of women. To upper- and middle-class outsiders, North and West Enders were rude, audacious, and obtrusive, a collection of "lewd, idle, and disorderly persons."[63] In actuality, lower-class individuals functioned within a self-constructed, coherent, cultural milieu that corresponded to the needs and conditions of slum life. Whether gathering in groups of boisterous girls, strolling on the arm of a bowery tough, or hanging out in a local sweetshop, lower-class women established, through dress and deportment, the separate identity that so offended their Victorian counterparts.

In conclusion, women in antebellum Boston were, for the most part, restricted to gender-specific roles inside and outside the home. In the workplace, they were segregated into female-only jobs with low pay, little mobility, and minimal security. Between 1830 and 1850 employment opportunities declined so that by the Civil War over 90 percent of working women (excluding domestics) held positions as seamstresses, nurses, teachers, and boardinghouse operators. Although economic options were limited, within the women's employment sector there existed a hierarchy of jobs based upon class and ethnicity. For white middle- and upper-class women, new sources of employment were opening up in teaching, social work, and writing, allowing some to maintain themselves as independent and self-supporting women in the city. The bulk of working women, however, were the poor, the black, and the Irish, who were trapped in the lowest-paid, most menial jobs.

Leisure activities also reflected the increasing segmentation of women along class, racial, and ethnic lines. While poor black and white women continued to work, upper- and middle-class women directed their energy into social, religious, and benevolent activities. During the 1830s women joined churches at three times the rate of men, and women played a prominent role in the city's many charitable institutions. On the other hand, lower-class females, especially the young and unattached, frequently rejected bourgeois leisure pursuits and instead amused themselves in the streets and cafes of the city's North and West Ends. In either case, leisure-time activities, like work, performed an important role in the delineation of class in antebellum Boston.

~~✍(C H A P T E R   4)~~

Women in the Boston Female
Anti-Slavery Society

WOMEN INVOLVED IN ANTISLAVERY ACTIVITIES PRIDED THEMSELVES ON what they termed the "nonsectarian" nature of their movement. The horrors of southern slavery, Caroline Weston explained, "raised the fear and indignation of all classes" and brought diverse women together to fight for its abolition.[1] Lydia Maria Child took great pains at the first national women's antislavery convention in 1837 to underscore their heterogeneity, declaring that female abolitionists had successfully laid aside "sectarian views and private opinions" in pursuit of their "holy object."[2] Sarah Grimké again gratefully acknowledged at the next year's gathering that in the cause of freedom all "sectarian feeling" had been abandoned as Christian women joined forces to fight for the slaves.[3] The Boston Female Anti-Slavery Society was prototypical of this heterogeneity, though ironically this prized diversity eventually devolved into the bitter sectarianism that would destroy it.

The society began with only twelve members, but during the next several years its membership grew to over 250. When it disbanded in 1840, nearly 600 women had at one time or another added their names to the society's rolls. Although most of Boston's women abolitionists were white and New England–born, their organization contained at least twenty-five active African-American members; and although the society was predominantly Congregationalist and Baptist, it included Unitarians, Quakers, Episcopalians, Methodists, and Universalists as well. Finally, Boston's female abolitionists were drawn from all levels of society, ranging from the wives and daughters of wealthy merchants and lawyers to single working women and free blacks.

Like most organizations, the Boston Female Anti-Slavery Society had a floating membership, with women moving in and out of its active ranks as personal circumstances warranted. Many names on the rolls represented honorary life memberships awarded to individuals like George and Anne Thompson and Sarah and Angelina Grimké in recognition of their contributions to the cause. The society also gave memberships to the wives of local civic and religious leaders such as Baptist clergyman Baron Stow, Massachusetts governor Edward Everett, and state Supreme Court chief justice Lemuel Shaw. These honorary memberships were intended to enhance the society's respectability and promote abolition but rarely resulted in the active involvement of the recipient.

Often membership in the Boston Female Anti-Slavery Society was a symbolic gesture rather than a commitment to participating in organized programs or projects. In the 1830s adding one's name to a membership roll was a significant act, a public statement of support for the objects of the organization and a way of contributing money. The Boston Female Anti-Slavery Society received scores of letters from women throughout New England asking that their names be added to the membership roll, such as the simple note Henry David Thoreau's younger sister, then living in Concord, penned to Maria Weston Chapman in 1839. "My mother and myself desire to add our mite to the Anti-Slavery subscription at this season. I enclose five dollars." The missive concluded, "With much esteem, believe me, yours very truly, Sophia E. Thoreau."[4] At any given time, then, there were probably no more than 150 or 200 women who attended meetings regularly and voted upon policy issues. Only about half of these were legitimately active members who passed out petitions and antislavery tracts, made items for sale at fairs, or helped in society-sponsored schools and orphanages.

The following prosopographic analysis of the Boston Female Anti-Slavery Society is based upon biographical material located for 293 women active in the organization between 1833 and 1840.[5] As discussed earlier, demographic information on antebellum Boston women is sketchy and uneven, and women abolitionists provide few exceptions. However, some of the society's notable members, such as Lydia Maria Child and Abby

May Alcott, have received full-length biographical treatment, while others, like Maria Weston Chapman, Ann Phillips, and Eliza Follen, have been accorded some scholarly attention.[6] In addition, some of the male relatives of these women achieved sufficient fame so that biographical and genealogical information about them and their families is available as well.[7]

Yet most of the women on the Boston Female Anti-Slavery Society rolls remain obscure, forgotten names from the past penned on faded and worn membership lists. Biographical data about these once active and committed individuals are now fragmentary but can be pieced together from city directories, church records, organizational histories, Suffolk County birth and death reports, probate and tax records, federal and city censuses, and the occasional reference in reform newspapers and personal correspondence. Again, it must be emphasized that generalizations and observations based upon this data are tentative and speculative. Yet, despite the fragmentary nature of this evidence, significant patterns do emerge about the complex social composition of the Boston Female Anti-Slavery Society, and these patterns help explain the bitter sectarianism that surfaced after 1837.

Again, diversity seems to be the key in generalizing about the original membership of the Boston Female Anti-Slavery Society. It was not a particularly young group of women; in 1835 the average age was thirty-three (N = 71). However, the organization contained a wide range of ages, spanning from Anna Southwick, Lucia Weston, and Sarah Southwick, aged twelve, thirteen, and fourteen in 1835, to Henrietta Sargent and Abigail Cummings in their fifties, and Mary Ball, Ann Mann, and Catherine Sargent in their sixties.

This diversity of ages was due primarily to the involvement of family groupings in the society. Members from the Ball family, for example, included widowed mother Mary (61) and her three unmarried daughters, Lucy (27), Martha (24), and Hannah (21). Similarly, Thankful Southwick (42) joined with her daughters Abby, Anna, Elizabeth, and Sarah, as did Rebecca Eaton (47) and her daughter Elizabeth (19). The largest family contingent was the Chapman–Weston bloc, consisting of Maria Weston Chapman (29), her sisters Caroline (27), Anne (23), Deborah (21), Lucia (13), and Emma (?), as well as her mother-in-law Sarah Greene Chapman (?), sisters-in-law Mary Gray Chapman (37) and Ann Greene Chapman (33), and cousin by marriage Ann Terry Greene Phillips (22). The Westons were also related to Mary and Susan Grew, original members who moved to Philadelphia after 1833 and were active in abolition there.

Many sisters became involved in abolitionism together, such as Janette and Rebecca Louge and Angelina, Melania, and Sylvia Ammidon, all childhood friends of the Westons. Boston Female Anti-Slavery Society president Mary Parker (34) moved to Boston from Jaffrey, New Hampshire, with her three sisters, Abigail (38), Lucy (37), and Eliza (32), in the early 1830s, and jointly they opened a boardinghouse and became involved in local reform. Four Blasland women offer an interesting variation on this sister theme. Mehitable, Mary, and Mary Ann were sisters-in-law, the wives of Thomas, William, and the late Gideon Blasland, respectively. A G. Blasland also appeared on the society's rolls.

Other family constellations present in the society, though, are more difficult to trace. African Americans Anna Lawton, Eliza Logan, and Anna Logan were sisters-in-law; Eliza Follen and Susan Cabot were sisters. Sarah Shaw was the mother of Anna Shaw, and Sarah Shaw Russell was Anna's aunt. Other relationships are even more complex. Mary Ann Allen and Catharine Spear, for example, were sisters; Louisa Sewell and Abby Alcott were cousins by marriage. Susan Jackson and Eliza Merriam also were sisters; their aunt was Ruth Copeland. The aforementioned South-wicks were related to Emily and Abby Winslow (Thankful Southwick's daughter) as well as to Eliza and Anna Philbrick, all of whom were in the society. Louisa Sewell was born a Winslow, and thus she too was a member of the Southwick–Philbrick–Winslow family group. Extending this even further, Hannah Robie was Louisa Sewell's husband's aunt. In all, 120 of the 293 women studied had a *known* relative (male or female) involved in antislavery. Another eighty-two members had the same surname as other women in the society or individuals known in local abolition circles. It is possible, then, that at least 70 percent of the women in the society joined as part of a family unit.

Among themselves, Boston abolitionists looked upon each other as representatives of larger family constellations and unselfconsciously associated individuals with their family connections. "To-day has been the day for the Ladies' Fair," reported William Lloyd Garrison to his wife, Helen, in late 1835. "There were several tables, as usual, which were under the superintendence of the Misses Weston, the Misses Ammidon, Miss Paul, Miss Chapman, and Miss Sargent (who by the way spoke in the kindest manner of you) and one or two others whom I did not know." Sarah

Southwick's reminiscences of society members are in the same familial vein. "Mr. [Henry G.] Chapman's sister, Ann G. Chapman, was also a much-valued member," Southwick wrote in 1893, as were Chapman's other sister, Mary, the "Misses Ammidon," Lucy Parker, "sister of the president," and so forth.[8] During the disputes within the society, families always voted as a bloc, which underscores the essentially familial, rather than generational, basis of the society.

The marital status of Boston Female Anti-Slavery Society members again suggests diversity. The organization was composed of more married than unmarried women; in fact, at least 153 women are known to have been married (often to a male abolitionist) at the time of their involvement in the antislavery movement. Helen Garrison, for example, was a regular at the society's meetings. Pregnant with her first child, she had been among those who, on 21 October 1835, had been prevented by the crowd from attending the annual meeting. She later described to Caroline Weston her experiences on the afternoon the rioters vented their fury against her husband, William:

> I put on my things with a full determination of seeing him [Garrison], and ascertaining for a certainty how much injury he had received; but before I reached the [antislavery] office, I met with several friends, who dissuaded me from attempting it; and not thinking it expedient myself, when I was apprized of the multitude that had assembled, I concluded to tarry with my kind friend Mrs. [Lydia] Fuller, to await the result. About five, I learned he was safely carried to jail for safe keeping. How my heart swelled with gratitude to the Preserver of our being, for having enabled him to pass through the hands of a mob without receiving the slightest injury.[9]

Like Lydia Fuller, the wives of some of Garrison's closest friends and allies—Henry G. Chapman, Wendell Phillips, and Nathan Winslow, to name a few—were members of the Boston Female Anti-Slavery Society. In fact, husbands of Lydia Maria Child, Mary Ann Johnson, Louisa Loring, Louisa Sewell, and Lydia Fuller were among the twelve founders of the New England Anti-Slavery Society. On the other hand, a large contingent of society members were connected to men who would become outspoken critics of Garrison. Ministers married to Sarah Colver, Eliza St. Clair, Mrs. Fitch, and Elizabeth Torrey were prime forces in the clerical defection in 1838, and the husbands of Eliza Cushman, Mrs. Brackett, Mary Dexter, Mrs. Chamberlain, and Nancy King were strong supporters of the anti-Garrison Massachusetts Abolition Society. In 1839 Boston Female

Anti-Slavery Society husbands Josiah Brackett, H. M. Chamberlain, John Fuller, and others came out as "voting abolitionists" and publicly repudiated nonresistance, women's rights, and the rest of the "kindred absurdities" the Garrisonians espoused.[10]

Although a majority of Boston Female Anti-Slavery Society members were married, those composing its elected board customarily were not. In 1836, for example, all officers and counselors except for Maria Weston Chapman and Mrs. Robinson were single, and the slate of officers in the disputed 1840 election was composed entirely of unmarried women.[11]

Of the eighty-one identifiably single women in the Boston Female Anti-Slavery Society, about half, as far as can be discerned, would never marry. Interestingly, many of those women who remained single were among the most active in the society; indeed, the organization's president, vice-president, secretary, and treasurer would all remain single. For example, Secretary Martha Ball and her treasurer sister, Lucy, passed their lives as spinster schoolteachers, as did Maria Ray, Elizabeth Eaton, Mary Ann Collier, and Sarah Southwick. The society's perennial president, Mary Parker, died unmarried at thirty-nine, and not one of her three sisters ever married. Of the women in the Chapman–Weston contingent, other than Maria, only Ann Phillips and Caroline Weston married; Maria Chapman, whose husband, Henry, died in 1841, never remarried.

The Boston Female Anti-Slavery Society was notably diverse in terms of social class and included the wives and daughters of an assortment of merchants, lawyers, proprietors, clergymen, clerks, and artisans.[12] Income levels ranged from enormous wealth to modest means, though none of the women in the organization were entirely destitute.[13] Even the impecunious Garrison household included a domestic or two as well as a cat named Mr. Gray, and Mehitable Blasland, the widow of a housewright and matron at the New England Female Moral Reform Society's temporary home for women, died leaving assets of over $14,000.[14]

The wealthiest and most prestigious women in the Boston Female Anti-Slavery Society were those married or related to Boston merchants, lawyers, politicians, and manufacturers. At least twenty-five members were connected to Boston's mercantile class, and Maria Weston Chapman was, perhaps, the most influential among them. Her husband, Henry G. Chapman, earned a substantial income as a shipping merchant, and they lived comfortably with their children and servants on West Street, near Elizabeth Peabody's bookstore and A. Bronson Alcott's experimental school. Chapman's father-in-law, Henry Chapman, Sr., was considered one of the

TABLE 3.   *Boston Female Anti-Slavery Society Occupations*

Women		Male Relatives	
Teacher	16	Artisan	34
Boardinghouse keeper	9	Merchant	25
Author/editor	6	Minister	23
Social worker	6	Proprietor	17
Proprietor	5	Lawyer	10
Seamstress	5	Physician	10
Domestic	2	Gov't official	7
Reform-related empl.	23	Manufacturer	6
		Clerk	4

Note: Some women were employed in more than one occupation. Also, some women had male relatives in more than one occupational category.

richest men in Massachusetts, and he was also an active abolitionist as were his wife Sarah Greene, unmarried daughters Ann and Mary, and niece Ann Greene (later Phillips). This wealthy, activist family lived on exclusive Chauncy Place and afterward in a mansion on Summer Street near the residence of Governor Edward Everett.

Eliza Cabot Follen and Abby May Alcott also came from mercantile wealth, enabling them to grow up in the best of Boston society. Both married men whom relatives considered beneath them—in Eliza's case German expatriate Charles Follen, in Abby's social philosopher A. Bronson Alcott. Abby Alcott's father, Samuel May, had earned his fortune during the Revolution but spent a good deal of his time and money in philanthropic endeavors, such as the establishment of Massachusetts General Hospital. Eliza Follen's father, Samuel Cabot, was also a respected merchant who, in 1796, was appointed a United States representative to Great Britain. Follen's brother, Samuel Cabot, Jr., became a successful businessman as well; indeed, in 1850 his wealth was estimated at more than $500,000.

Unlike Abby Alcott and Eliza Cabot Follen who, because of their social and personal commitments lived in reduced circumstances during the time of their interest in the Boston Female Anti-Slavery Society, the Sargents, Jacksons, and Shaws were among the wealthiest women in the city, if not the state. From Massachusetts' famous Sargent family, Henrietta and Catherine were the daughters of Epes Sargent, a delegate to the Massachusetts Constitutional Convention who later became the president of the Suffolk Insurance Company. Susan and Eliza Jackson's father, Francis, was a wealthy merchant and city official who bequeathed $10,000 to freedmen's aid and $5,000 to women's rights organizations upon his death in 1861. Sarah Shaw Russell, Sarah Shaw, and Anna Shaw, the daughter, daughter-in-law, and granddaughter of merchant-capitalist Robert Gould Shaw, were also listed on the society's rolls. Sarah Shaw's husband, Francis, also was a prosperous merchant. Considered one of the richest men in the state, he paid taxes in 1855 on over $400,000 in assets.

Other women in the Boston Female Anti-Slavery Society associated with wealthy and prestigious New England families were married to successful lawyers and high government officials. Ann Greene Phillips, of course, was married to the movement's best-known lawyer-abolitionist, Wendell Phillips. Although it was said that Wendell's mother "behaved like a perfect dragon" at their wedding,[15] Ann was well connected herself, the daughter of wealthy shipping merchant Benjamin Greene, who left her a $93,000 trust when he died in 1823. Mary F. Rogers was married to John Peabody Rogers, who had apprenticed with Richard Fletcher, another influential Boston lawyer and Whig congressman. Louisa Sewell and Louisa Loring were married to lawyers Samuel Sewell and Ellis Gray Loring, and the inherited wealth and successful legal practices of both the Sewells and the Lorings placed them among the richest couples in Boston. In fact, in 1844 the Lorings paid taxes on over $83,000 worth of real estate and personal property. In addition to their advantageous marriages, the two Louisas were from prominent families themselves. Louisa Sewell was the daughter of Nathan Winslow, a prosperous hardware merchant whose liberal endowments to Garrison often kept the *Liberator* afloat. Louisa Loring was born a Gilman, and her relatives included a former Massachusetts governor; her brother Samuel was a noted Unitarian minister and author.

In addition to lawyers and merchants, Boston Female Anti-Slavery Society members were also the wives and daughters of some prominent physicians. Henry Weston, brother of Maria Weston Chapman, for example, became a respected doctor in Weymouth, though he was a student at Harvard College during the late 1830s. Mary and Sarah Fifield were also Boston Female Anti-Slavery Society members related to a Weymouth physician, Noah Fifield. Lucinda Otis was the sister of George Alexander Otis who in later years distinguished himself for the medical service he

71

performed during the Civil War. Finally, both Charles Hildreth, an established Boston doctor, and his wife, a society member, were very much interested in local reform.

Women and men from these influential, moneyed New England families lent prestige to the local abolition movement and helped bankroll various projects and programs. In 1835, for example, the combined contributions to the Massachusetts Anti-Slavery Society by the Chapman, Phillips, Jackson, Loring, and Winslow families amounted to $340. Over the next three years these families donated over $2,500 to that organization alone.[16] As time passed, their donations increased even further, and their influence in the antislavery movement mounted accordingly.

Although often overshadowed by their more socially prominent colleagues, women from the city's emerging class of entrepreneurs were also very interested in abolition. Some were married to local businessmen and builders who profited from Boston's financial boom, earning fortunes that soon rivaled the aforementioned Brahmins. For example, Judith Shipley's husband, Simon, was a baker whose net worth increased by almost $15,000 between 1844 and 1850. Another husband, Francis Whiston, was a real estate agent and government official who parlayed his property holdings from $20,000 to $34,000 during the same period. Ebenezer Smith, husband or father of Emma, was a modest proprietor turned real estate investor. By 1850 he was considered one of the wealthiest men in Massachusetts with personal assets valued at over $300,000. The husbands of Mrs. Rayner and Susan Sears also established lucrative businesses in the city's building industry. By 1844, both Thomas Rayner, a slater, and Willard Sears, a housewright, amassed real estate valued at $41,000. Over the next half-decade, Sears would multiply his assets fourfold, so that by 1850 his property holdings totaled over $160,000.

Other Boston Female Anti-Slavery Society husbands gained wealth through manufacturing and sales. John Rogers, husband of Lucy, was beginning to earn a sizable income in the shoe industry at the time both entered the movement. By 1850 Rogers owned property worth well over $46,000. Janette and Rebecca Louge were related to Hugh B. Louge, owner of a Boston soda manufactory in the 1830s, and Hannah Tufts's husband, Charles, was a Medford steam engine manufacturer and investor who used his riches to found Tufts College in 1852. Boston Female Anti-Slavery Society husbands David Foster and Timothy Gilbert were prosperous piano manufacturers and dealers. When Foster died in 1882, he left almost $90,000 in personal and real property. Gilbert's financial success was even more phenomenal. In the 1840s his piano company was worth $50,000. By 1850 his assets were valued at more than $160,000.

About half of the women in the Boston Female Anti-Slavery Society were wives and daughters of Boston's rising middle class—city employees, clerks, small businessmen, and proprietors—whose income and property in many instances were sufficient to rank them among the city's taxed residents ($6,000 or more). Several women abolitionists were related to men employed in newly created municipal positions, such as Mary Ann Clough whose father, Ebenezer, was the city weigher and Mrs. Francis Whiston whose husband served as the superintendent of the local house of corrections and as deputy city marshal. Mrs. Dodd, Mrs. Eayrs, M. B. Carpenter, and Eunice Safford were married to clerks; in fact, the latter two (Orin Carpenter and Henry Safford) were employed by fellow abolitionist and piano manufacturer Timothy Gilbert.[17]

The society included at least seventeen women related to local proprietors, while another thirty-four were married to artisans. Josiah Brackett, Samuel Philbrick, and Joseph Southwick all dealt in leather, while Rufus Mosman sold coal. Gideon Blasland and James Loring had been apothecaries, Charles Briggs was a bookseller, F. F. Wheelock was in dry goods, and John Gove sold clothes. As for the artisans, there were at least six printers, five housewrights, four tailors, and two bakers, as well as a jeweler, a mason, a cordwainer, an upholsterer, a cooper, and a sailmaker. William Damrell was both an artisan and a proprietor. A Boston printer with no formal education, his work in the 1830s came mostly from local reform organizations. Over the next decade the enterprising Damrell became a major supplier of stationery goods in the city, and when he died in 1860 he was serving in the United States House of Representatives.

These middle-class abolitionists rarely owned property valued at more than $20,000, but many showed increasing prosperity during the time they were involved in abolition. Coal dealer Rufus Mosman, for example, raised his assets from $10,000 to $16,300 between 1844 and 1850. Eunice Safford's husband, the clerk in Timothy Gilbert's piano manufactory, was assessed taxes on $9,000 in property in 1850. Prescott Dickinson and his abolitionist wife also paid taxes that year, as proprietors of Dickinson and Company, a woodenware store valued at $15,000. Hannah Walker's husband, Amasa, was perhaps the most successful of this rising middle-class group of abolitionists. During the 1840s Walker's net worth rose from $14,000 to $20,000, providing sufficient income for him to abandon business to become an economics professor and subsequently a state senator.

The African-American women in the society could also be classified among this middle-class contingent, though they represented the elite among the community's black population as a whole. Of those women whose husbands' occupations could be identified, three were married to ministers, another three to hairdressers, while still others were married to blacksmiths, boardinghouse operators, tailors, and waiters. These women were thus individuals of prominence and economic standing in Boston's African-American society, where most blacks were consigned to the most menial and insecure occupations.[18]

Finally, the Boston Female Anti-Slavery Society of the 1830s included the wives, sisters, or daughters of more than twenty clergymen: at least six Baptists, six Congregationalists, three Unitarians, three African Baptists, perhaps two Methodists and two Episcopalians, and a Presbyterian. In their background and station, these abolitionist ministers ranged the social spectrum. Several were Harvard graduates, such as the brothers of Abby Alcott, Lydia Maria Child, and Louisa Loring and the son of Mary Loring Young. Caroline Clark's husband, Thomas, was a Princeton graduate, while Melissa Neale's husband, Rollin, was among the first students at Andover Theological Seminary. Other minister husbands like Baptist Nathaniel Colver and Episcopalian (and later Seventh-Day Adventist) Joshua V. Himes had little formal education, having been poor craftsmen before receiving the call to the ministry.

Some of these abolitionist ministers served in Boston pulpits, such as Neale who was the pastor of the First Baptist Church for many years and Mary Young's husband, Alexander, minister of the Unitarian New South Church. Several were employed in radical or at least socially conscious churches. For example, when Charles Follen, German-born husband of Eliza Lee Cabot, lost his teaching position at Harvard and several pulpits because of his political opinions, he finally found employment in a liberal Unitarian church in Lexington. Mrs. Fitch's husband, Charles, became the first pastor of the Free Congregational Church, a religious institution established by local reformers in 1835. Two years later Fitch was replaced by Amos Phelps, husband of first Boston Female Anti-Slavery Society president Charlotte. Sarah Colver's husband, Nathaniel, was the first pastor of the Baptist's Tremont Temple, another reform-based church established in the city.

Other activist ministers did not have permanent positions within Boston's religious establishment. Often these activist ministers receive economic support from the local reform community, working as agents, lecturers, publishers, and organization secretaries or operating special schools and homes for the city's needy. For instance, Dexter King, Methodist husband of Boston Female Anti-Slavery Society member Nancy, ran a book and printing shop in rooms below the Massachusetts Abolition Society offices. After the Civil War, King established a school for the deaf (which employed a young Alexander Graham Bell). William Collier, father of Mary Ann, was also a "minister-at-large" in Boston and active in the city's mission and temperance movements. Collier supported his family by editing the *Baptist Preacher* and the *National Philanthropist*, a temperance weekly. Collier and his wife also took in boarders to make ends meet, and their lodgers included fellow abolitionists John Greenleaf Whittier, Isaac Knapp, Stephen Foster, and William Lloyd Garrison.

Preoccupation with male employment, though necessary in charting women's economic status during the years of their involvement in abolition, ignores the existence of many unmarried and widowed women in the Boston Female Anti-Slavery Society living independently or semiindependently in the city. Some like Henrietta and Catherine Sargent, Relief Loring (widowed mother of Ellis Gray Loring), and Mary Young enjoyed private annual incomes ranging from $12,000 to $30,000. At thirty-five, Ann Greene Chapman was already quite well off at the time of her sudden death in 1836. In her will, Chapman left $1,000 to the American Anti-Slavery Society and smaller legacies to the Boston Female Anti-Slavery Society and the Samaritan Asylum. Her sister Mary was equally wealthy and was generous to various social causes, as well as to her less moneyed relatives. In fact, in the 1870s Mary distributed $40,000 among her sister-in-law Maria Weston Chapman's family. At her death in 1876, she left $66,000 in assets.

Most self-supporting women abolitionists, however, did not have large private incomes to sustain them. In fact, many of these women were part of the migration of young men and women to Boston in the 1830s and hailed from rural towns like Binghamton and Exeter, New York; Westmoreland, Jaffrey, and Dunbarton, New Hampshire; and Hallowell, Maine. It was not uncommon for these women to be buried in their Massachusetts hometowns—the Westons in Weymouth, the Blaslands in Needham, Charlotte Phelps in Waltham, and so on.

As newcomers, Boston Female Anti-Slavery Society members often expressed concern over the plight of young women who, like themselves, were looking for work in the Boston marketplace. "The subject of labor, as connected with woman," remarked Mary Ann Clough some years later, "is one that is now taxing the wisdom of our wisest and best minds." Clough and others in the Boston Female Anti-Slavery Society believed that the lack of safe and suitable employment for lone women in Boston was the source of many social evils, especially prostitution and crime.[19] Actually, society members were not among those unemployed females lured into prostitution by unscrupulous city dwellers. But the stories of seduction, false imprisonment in brothels, and abandonment that they wrote of and read about expressed their economic, social, and probably psychic vulnerability. Through reform, they made the distinction between themselves and society's victims, becoming, as it were, the conscience of the city.

The occupations of forty-six Boston Female Anti-Slavery Society members could be established. Most were employed in the elite occupations available to women in antebellum Boston, positions that implied education, property, or connections. Only two domestics were in the organization: Phillis Salem, a black woman living with the Southwick family, and Eliza Garnaut, a Welsh immigrant employed by the Phillipses. There also might have been as many as five seamstresses in the group,[20] but as a general rule domestics and seamstresses did not become involved in the local abolition movement.

At least sixteen of the society's working women were teachers. Maria Weston Chapman, for example, taught and at the time of her marriage in 1830 was serving as principal of Boston's short-lived high school for girls.[21] Lydia Maria Child and Eliza Follen taught before their marriages as well. Deborah Weston taught for several years in an abolitionist-run school in New Bedford, and when her sisters Anne and Caroline came to Boston around 1834 to set up housekeeping near sister Maria, they also opened a school. By spring of 1835 the Westons had ten "scholars," including the two daughters of Maria's former employer Ebenezer Bailey and the young Quaker abolitionist Sarah Southwick. "I went to school to Caroline Weston, the oldest sister," Southwick later recalled. "She resided and kept school on Boylston Street where the Public Library now stands. I look back to her as a teacher and life long friend with love and gratitude—a sensible, cultivated, unaffected, warm-hearted woman, whom everybody respected. How much I owe to her in the way of education I can never express."[22] In later years Southwick became a teacher, too.

Several individuals in the women's antislavery organization were employed in the city's segregated schools for African-American children. Susan Paul taught in the Smith School (also called the African School), an educational facility jointly funded by the city and donations from local philanthropist Abiel Smith. Paul was the daughter of prominent black minister Thomas Paul, the late founder of the African Baptist church, and after Thomas's death in 1831, Susan's teaching salary supported her widowed mother.[23] Julia Williams was another African-American schoolteacher in the Boston Female Anti-Slavery Society. A former student in Prudence Crandall's integrated school for girls, in the late 1830s she taught in the school established by white abolitionists Martha and Lucy Ball. She eventually married abolitionist Henry Highland Garnet.[24]

Women who ran black schools were able to combine social concern with paid employment. Others, especially those working in schools outside their homes, found it taxing to work and continue to take part in female benevolence. In 1839, Anne Weston was employed in a Dorchester school, and a letter to her sister Deborah suggests the grueling schedule. "I am for a wonder writing in school," she wrote; "that is, school is just finishing and the rain's pouring down so that I can't go home." She continues, detailing the difficulty in combining paid work with social commitment:

> Monday I came out of town and kept [school] all day as usual. . . . Tuesday I came from school, oh, so tired, I did not see how I could keep the term out. I laid down long before dark & there I laid till 9, vainly trying to get the strength to undress. Wednesday you will remember was the day of the Boston Female. I had previously arranged with Mr. Tilden that I should teach my classes in the morning . . . so as to go to Boston in the afternoon. I staid at school till 1 & then hurried home, bolted my dinner, & a little after 1 I found myself in the omnibus. I had a warm, uncomfortable ride, & reached Maria's about 2. I found Mrs. Child, Caroline, Lucia, & Emma all on the ground. M. Chapman soon came & we proceeded to the Marlboro' [Chapel].[25]

Despite its respectability, teaching was an exhausting, often unreliable source of income, but it was a job that could be taken up and abandoned as economic and family needs dictated. Eliza Follen, for example, resumed teaching after her husband was killed in a steamship accident in 1840. Abby Alcott intermittently taught as finances required. Anne, Caroline, and Deborah Weston all worked off and on as teachers, taking turns supporting their Boston household.

Women abolitionists (particularly the teachers) often supplemented their income by writing and editing. For example, society member Rebecca Eaton edited the New England Female Moral Reform Society's journal, the *Friend of Virtue*, for almost thirty years; her successor was teacher-abolitionist Martha Ball. Both Lydia Maria Child and Eliza Follen added to the support of their families by writing fiction and nonfiction as well as editing journals, and Maria Chapman regularly assumed the reins of the *Liberator* and the *Non-Resistant*, though probably not for pay.

As many as nine working women in the Boston Female Anti-Slavery Society operated boardinghouses. For twenty years Keziah Grant took boarders into her Atkinson Street home, and John and Lydia Fuller offered "genteel board" in their residence near the Odeon Theatre, the lecture hall where the Grimké sisters drew their largest crowds. The Fullers' home boasted of a "quiet, central, and pleasant" location, a "large yard, and plenty of good aqueduct and well water, bathing rooms, shower bath, etc."[26] The Garrison family, Samuel May, Amos Phelps, and many other itinerant abolitionists resided at the boardinghouse at 5 Hayward Place run by society president Mary Parker and her sisters Lucy, Eliza, and Abigail.

Five or six women abolitionists in Boston owned small businesses. Mary Ann Blasland, widow of an apothecary, ran a dry goods store. Abigail Ordway pieced together an income as a milliner and traveling antislavery agent. Unmarried Hannah Farrar, who hailed from rural New Hampshire, supported herself by selling English goods in her shop on Washington Street, and Ann Mann sold "fancy goods" in or near her Summer Street home.

Women activists, like many other urban wives, probably participated in family businesses far more than the historical record documents. As noted earlier, casual references in correspondence, advertisements, and the like suggest a hidden world of women's work, and this was no less true of Boston Female Anti-Slavery Society members. For example, Abigail Ordway postponed an antislavery organizing tour sponsored by the Salem Female Anti-Slavery Society because of other financial commitments. "Mr. and Mrs. Blodgett left Boston this morning for a journey of about fifty miles, and has during their absence entrusted their business to my charge," she explained.[27] Louisa Blodgett was also in the Boston Female Anti-Slavery Society, and this letter suggests that Ordway considered the "warm sulphur bath" business operated out of the Marlboro' Hotel to be an enterprise of both husband and wife. The Blodgetts, for their part, seemed to feel that it was entirely appropriate for a woman to manage their affairs while they were out of town. In the same vein, another society member, Emma Smith, once suggested to Caroline Weston that since the society's fairs had been so lucrative the women might open a shop filled with articles made by local abolitionists. "A variety store," Smith elaborated, "where the old ladies might send their knitting and plain sewing and the young ladies their embroidery & fancy articles, & mechanics, shoemakers, etc. whatever that had to dispose of in *their* line."[28] Again, it did not strike Smith that a female-run boutique was unusual or inappropriate.

The Parker boardinghouse, the Balls' school for African-American girls, and the proposed abolition store are all examples of the ways in which working women in the Boston Female Anti-Slavery Society used connections and activities associated with their benevolent work to support themselves in the city. In fact, nearly one-half of the women in the society who worked for wages did so under the umbrella of social reform. The circumstances surrounding the closure of Martha and Lucy Ball's school illustrate the close relationship between women's paid work and charitable activities. The Balls opened their school for young black girls in 1833 by taking rooms in the African Church and advertising their plan in the *Liberator.*[29] In addition to nominal tuition, the school received regular donations from the Boston Female Anti-Slavery Society as well as from individual reformers. During the crisis of 1838–39, the Balls lost the support of radical abolitionists and, importantly, the African-American community, which refused to patronize a school connected with the New Organization. Despite continued funding from the increasingly anti-Garrison Boston Female Anti-Slavery Society, the Balls were forced to close their school in late 1839. Martha Ball subsequently was hired as a traveling agent to drum up support for the New Organization among women.[30]

Although teaching, running boardinghouses, and even operating small stores were typical sources of female employment in antebellum Boston, reform movements also opened up new avenues of employment for women. The New England Female Moral Reform Society, organized by a sizable group of women abolitionists in 1835, was particularly adept at creating paid positions for its members.[31] Some, like Abigail Ordway, Martha Ball, and Nancy Low, became traveling agents employed by the moral reform society to promote the cause and solicit subscriptions to its journal, the *Friend of Virtue* (edited by Boston Female Anti-Slavery Society member Rebecca Eaton). These women usually traveled in pairs, staying with reformers in different towns. They did not present public lectures, as did bolder women like Maria Weston Chapman and Abby Kelley. They preferred to meet in homes and churches to converse with sewing circles and other women's groups about the serious problem of licentiousness.

The local moral reform society was involved in female employment in additional ways. In the late 1830s the society established an employment agency managed by abolitionists Maria Holland and Rachel Emerson. A newspaper advertisement detailed its services: "Wanted immediately, at Office No. 2 Chapel Place, American Girls, of good character and habits, to go into good families. No one need apply, who cannot bring *good* recommendations, or furnish *satisfactory* references. *Such* can procure places for service almost according to their own choice."[32] Several years later, the New England Female Moral Reform Society opened the Home Education Society. Run by another abolitionist, Elizabeth Hayward, the Home Education Society was a school that provided domestic training for young American girls looking for work in Boston and then secured for them suitable positions in respectable Boston residences.

In addition to assisting with women's employment needs (theirs as well as other Boston women's), the New England Female Moral Reform Society established several group residences for women. In 1847 the organization sponsored a "Stranger's Retreat," which was sort of an early YWCA designed to provide single women in Boston with a safe and moderately priced place to stay. The retreat was operated by enterprising abolitionist Abigail Ordway. The following year moral reformers, under the directorship of yet another Boston Female Anti-Slavery Society member, Eliza Garnaut, set up a "Temporary Home For Children" to take in those who were orphaned or abused. The moral reform society's most successful venture was a temporary home established in 1842, which offered "the hand of sympathy and kindness to the friendless, homeless, unprotected female."[33] Managed by abolitionist–moral reformer Mehitable Blasland, the home became a halfway house for any woman in trouble—unmarried pregnant girls, prostitutes, battered wives, and the homeless—and served as an asylum for Boston women for many years.

Self-supporting women in the Boston Female Anti-Slavery Society were thus able to use the changing nature of Boston's society and economy to create new and expanded forms of employment for themselves. Many filled teaching posts in the state's educational system, while some ran boardinghouses where they re-created home environments for the city's transient population.[34] Still others served as employment counselors to assist women in finding jobs deemed suitable for "American girls." Finally, female activists were able to transform customary female charity into paid employment by hiring themselves out as lecturers, agents, editors, and social

TABLE 4.   *Boston Female Anti-Slavery Society Denominational Affiliations*

Congregational	62	Episcopalian	4
Baptist	30	Universalist	4
Unitarian	24	Methodist	3
Quaker	11	Zion (black)	2
African Baptist	5		

workers. In so doing they helped change the meaning and uses of female benevolence in antebellum Boston.

When abolitionists spoke of the nonsectarianism in their organizations, they did so largely in terms of religious affiliations. Here again, the Boston Female Anti-Slavery Society was exemplary in the variety of denominations represented by its members. Of the 145 Boston Female Anti-Slavery Society members whose religion could be established 62 (43 percent) were Congregationalist, 30 (21 percent) were Baptist, and as many as 24 (16 percent) were Unitarian. There were also eleven Quakers in the group, thanks primarily to the Southwick family and their cousins, the Winslows and Philbricks.[35] Susan Paul, Lavinia Hilton, C. Barbadoes, and Eunice Davis attended the African Baptist Church on Belknap Street, as did probably many of the blacks in the society, though at least two, Areanna Adams and Anna Logan, went to the Zion Church. There also appear to have been four Episcopalians as well as several Methodists in the organization. One of the Episcopalians, Mary Himes, probably became a Millerite in the 1840s, like her husband, the Reverend Joshua V. Himes. Finally, at least four members were Universalist, most notably Catherine and Henrietta Sargent who were related by marriage to Universalist church founder John Murray.

Congregationalists and Baptists, then, composed about 64 percent of the Boston Female Anti-Slavery Society membership. Most were attracted to Boston's newer, evangelical churches. For example, during the late 1820s seventeen future female abolitionists were admitted into the Union Congregational Church. Organized during the religious revivals of 1822–23, the Union Church was a focal point for the "special effusions of the Holy Spirit" that surfaced in Boston at that time.[36] Another twelve society members were caught up in the religious enthusiasm generated by the arrival of popular evangelist Lyman Beecher and became members of his

Bowdoin Street Congregational Church in the late 1820s. In fact, several of them were married by Beecher, such as Mary Ann Johnson to *Liberator* printer Oliver Johnson, before the minister lost favor among abolitionists.

Most Baptists in the Boston Female Anti-Slavery Society belonged to the Federal Street Baptist Church founded in 1827. The church's first pastor, Howard Malcom, was particularly committed to "training" his congregation "to *work* for the Master" and encouraged his flock to become involved in various church-sponsored benevolent enterprises.[37] Malcom's wife, Lucy, directed the charitable endeavors of female congregation members, and through her efforts the Federal Street Baptist Church was among the first institutions to organize a Sunday school, an infant school, and a maternal association. In August 1828 antislavery pioneer Benjamin Lundy spoke to the congregation, a fitting example of the social commitment of the Federal Street Baptists, though Malcom subsequently repudiated Lundy's fanaticism, an act that alienated many church members (including Garrison) sympathetic to Lundy's views.[38]

As with many female converts to evangelical churches, Congregational and Baptist women in the Boston Female Anti-Slavery Society were experimental in their institutional affiliations as they searched for a pastor and church in sympathy with their personal religious and social concerns. Rachel Emerson, for example, joined the Federal Street Baptist Church in 1833, switched to the First Free Congregational Church several years later, and by 1840 was attending a Southborough Congregational Church. As children, the daughters of merchant Philip Ammidon attended the Unitarian New South Church near their Beacon Hill home. Apparently the Ammidon sisters were discontented with the staid religion of the upper class, so in 1835, about the time they became abolitionists, Sylvia, Angelina, and Melania converted to the Bowdoin Street Congregational Church, then under the pastorate of Hubbard Winslow. Still dissatisfied, Melania switched to the Federal Street Baptist Church the following year. Eventually all three Ammidons married Baptist ministers and committed themselves to the arduous role of minister's wife.

The religious fluidity among women activists was influenced by the political stance and relative orthodoxy of the Boston ministry itself. Abolitionists often followed a favorite pastor to new clerical posts, and they left churches when the minister's theological and political orientation conflicted with their own. For example, Boston Female Anti-Slavery Society members in the Union Congregational Church soon grew disenchanted with the Reverend Nehemiah Adams, who had become pastor in 1834. During the Unitarian crisis, Adams had been a staunch upholder of orthodox Congregationalism. Later, the conservative minister was an out-spoken critic of abolitionists and was particularly venomous toward women activists. As primary author of the "Pastoral Letter to the Massachusetts Congregational Clergy" that appeared in the summer of 1837, Adams likened women to a retiring vine "whose strength and beauty is to lean upon the trellis-work and half conceal its clusters." When women adopt "the independence and the overshadowing nature of the elm," the clergy-man lectured, "it will not only cease to bear fruit, but fall in shame and dishonor into the dust." Within a year, all but five Boston Female Anti-Slavery Society members in Adams's Union Church "removed" to other institutions.[39]

Women in the Bowdoin Street Congregational Church faced a similar crisis when Hubbard Winslow succeeded Lyman Beecher as pastor. An outspoken antiabolitionist, Winslow repeatedly exhorted women in his congregation to remember the sacred "law of female subjugation" and urged them to confine their benevolent energies to "deeds of personal charity and kindness to the destitute and afflicted." As Winslow intoned against the present behavior of local women reformers:

> When females undertake to assume the place of public teachers, *whether to both sexes or only to their own*; when they form societies for the purpose of sitting in judgment and acting upon the affairs of the church and state; when they travel about from place to place as lecturers, teachers, and guides to public sentiment; when they assemble in conventions to discuss questions, pass resolutions, make speeches, and vote upon civil, political, moral and religious matters; when they begin to send up their names to gentlemen holding official stations, gravely declaring their own judgment in regard to what they ought to do; . . . in short, when the distinguishing graces of modesty, deference, delicacy, and sweet charity are in any way displaced by the opposite qualities of boldness, arrogance, rudeness, indelicacy, and the spirit of denunciation . . . they have stretched themselves beyond their measure and violated the inspired injunction that saith: . . . "Let the woman learn in silence with all subjection, but I suffer not a woman to teach, nor to usurp authority over the man, but to be in silence."[40]

Winslow felt so passionately about the "woman question" that he resigned his position with the Bowdoin Street Church in 1844, bought an estate on Beacon Street, and opened the Mount Vernon School for Young Ladies.[41]

But before he left at least nine of the twelve Boston Female Anti-Slavery Society members in his congregation disassociated themselves from the church.

Most Boston Female Anti-Slavery Society Congregationalists eventually joined the First Free Congregational Church of Boston. Known casually as the Free Church, the institution was organized in the spring of 1835 in response to local reformers' disillusionment with the religious establishment in Boston. In forming what could be considered one of the first "come-outer" sects, the Free Congregational Church was based as much on social and moral principles as upon theological strictures. The church had no pew fees and required converts to abstain from alcohol, membership in secret associations, and dealings with slaveholders. As noted earlier, the first pastor of the Free Church was Charles Fitch. His wife was active in the Boston Female Anti-Slavery Society, as were the wives of Free Church deacons John Kilton and Willard Sears. In all, over forty of the sixty-two Congregationalists in the women's society joined the Free Church. In so doing, they were able to reconnect with organized religion and keep a legitimate institutional base for their controversial reform interests.

Baptist women also aligned themselves with ministers supportive of their benevolent and humanitarian concerns. For example, Martha and Lucy Ball, after joining the Charles Street Baptist Church, transferred to the Federal Street Baptist Church, then under activist-minister Malcom. Subsequently, the Balls associated themselves with the Reverend Phineas Stow, whose pastoral labors at Boston's Bethel Church were devoted to the city's seamen—that class of men "beset with stronger temptations to sin" than any other.[42] Others, like Mary Ann Collier, Betsey Mosman, and Emma Smith were members of Rollin Neale's First Baptist Church and spent several decades assisting him in his charitable activities.

Like the Congregationalists, socially conscious Baptists eventually formed a separate religious institution in Boston through which they conducted many benevolent projects. In 1843 the Baptists established the Tremont Temple, brainchild of piano manufacturer Timothy Gilbert, as a Baptist free church open to "the poor and strangers coming to the city."[43] Gilbert and his associates—Thomas Gould, William Damrell, and Simon Shipley—envisioned the Tremont Temple as a religious refuge for the city's homeless that would also be self-supporting. To this end, Gilbert and the others donated $55,000 to purchase the Tremont Theatre in the city center. Investors spent another $22,000 to refurbish the theater and transform it into a 2,000-seat auditorium. They then leased the stores and offices in the building, using the rental income to support their church. Nathaniel Colver was selected as first pastor of the Tremont Temple, a position he held until 1852.[44] The wives and daughters of Gilbert, Shipley, Damrell, Gould, and Colver were all active members in the Boston Female Anti-Slavery Society. As with the Free Congregational Church, the Tremont Temple gave them and other Baptist women activists the institutional support and legitimacy that they needed to continue their efforts to help Boston's fringe and outcast populations.

The Ammidon sisters certainly were not representative of Boston Female Anti-Slavery Society Unitarians when they converted to the Baptist church, although Unitarian women like Lydia Maria Child, Maria Weston Chapman, Abby Alcott, and Louisa Loring were equally disappointed by their spiritual leaders. As Lydia Maria Child once observed, "Unitarianism [is] a mere half-way house, where spiritual travelers find themselves well accommodated for the night, but where they grow weary of spending the day."[45] However, the Unitarians did not act upon their discontent by experimenting with different churches. Instead, these women struggled to convert their ministers and other parishioners to the abolition cause. Most of the society's Unitarians attended William Ellery Channing's Federal Street Church, and despite vehement opposition from other Unitarians, they persevered in having antislavery notices read at services and pressured to have abolition messages included in Sunday sermons.

Much of the Unitarians' evangelical efforts were directed toward Channing, who was an abolitionist in principle but had disassociated himself from the radicals in his congregation. Garrison regularly condemned the clergyman in the reform press for refusing to join their movement, while privately, Maria Weston Chapman, Lydia Maria Child, and Abby Alcott conversed with the respected minister in the hopes of persuading him to their point of view. Child carried on a regular correspondence with Channing, testifying to her abolition ideology. "I understand fully your language when you speak of *reform* as your *work-shop*," Channing patiently responded to Child shortly before his death in 1842. But he still expressed concern over her method of agitation. "We are better reformers because we are calmer and wiser," he advised. "We have more weapons to work with, if we give a wide range to thought, imagination, taste and the affections. We must be cheerful, too, in our war with evil; for gloom is apt to become sullenness, ill-humor and bitterness."[46]

Although Channing never completely aligned himself with the Boston abolitionists, it was a triumph for Unitarians when Channing joined the radicals at an antiabolitionist hearing before the state legislature in 1836. Harriet Martineau was present at the session, and she described the scene in *Martyr Age of the United States:*

> During the suspense the door opened and Dr. Channing entered,—one of the last people who could, on that wintry afternoon, have been expected. He stood a few moments, muffled in his cloak and shawl-handkerchief and then walked the whole length of the room and was immediately seen shaking hands with Garrison. A murmur ran through the gallery and a smile went round the chamber. Mrs. Chapman whispered to her next neighbor, "righteousness and peace have kissed each other!"[47]

In addition to their relationships with Channing and his associate pastor, Henry Ware, Jr., Unitarian women also participated in the New England transcendentalist community. Mary Robbins and her Unitarian minister husband, Samuel, joined Brook Farm in 1842, and the Shaws and Russells were liberal benefactors of the communal experiment. Abby Alcott's intimates (besides her husband Bronson) included Concord neighbors Ralph Waldo Emerson, Henry David Thoreau, and Nathaniel Hawthorne. Lydia Child also enjoyed long-lived friendships with transcendentalists through her brother Convers Francis and dear friend John Sullivan Dwight as well as with other prominent transcendentalists including Emerson and Theodore Parker. In addition, Child and Louisa Loring were among the women who attended Margaret Fuller's "conversations" held at Elizabeth Peabody's library located two doors down from Maria Chapman's home on West Street. The Westons also socialized with Fuller. "Just after I got home, Margaret Fuller called," Anne Weston once wrote to Deborah. "She was more magnificent than usual & held forth at a great rate."[48]

Unitarians in the society were very interested in the controversy over Emerson's 1838 Harvard Divinity School Address, especially as to how it illuminated their own position with Unitarianism. In his lecture before the graduating class, Emerson expressed his conviction that true religious spirit was found through personal introspection and intuition. Emerson discounted the tired teachings of clerical authorities, a sentiment becoming central to radical abolitionists' philosophy as well. Maria Chapman sent a copy of the speech to the Garrisons, explaining that it was "rousing the wrath of the Cambridge 'powers that be' in an astonishing manner! How cowardly are Unitarians generally! They take the alarm at sentiments which differ only in shading from their own (in matters of doctrine I mean)."[49] In a letter to her Harvard professor brother, Lydia Child also commented upon "how absurdly the Unitarians are behaving, after all their talk about liberality, the sacredness of individual freedom, free utterance of thought, etc. If Emerson's thoughts are not their thoughts, can they not reverence them, inasmuch as they are formed and spoken in freedom?"[50]

Whether Congregationalist, Baptist, or Unitarian, many women in the Boston Female Anti-Slavery Society experienced a spiritual crisis during the 1830s. Much of their dissatisfaction stemmed from the refusal of the Boston clergy of all denominations to embrace immediate emancipation. Frustrated abolitionists would spend Sunday traveling from church to church so as to monitor the antislavery sentiments contained in the day's sermons. "Went with Lizzy to the Old South [Congregational Church]," wrote Deborah Weston in her diary in October 1835. "Heard Dr. Codman who pretends to be an abolitionist, pray for everything but the Slaves." Weston found other Boston ministers equally wanting, damning different clergymen as "the worst preacher" she ever heard, and their sermons as "the foolishest" she had endured. In her diary, Caroline Weston reveals how she too was depressed by the "stupid" and "miserable" preaching she encountered in the city.[51]

Sister Anne was particularly upset with the Boston clergy for failing to denounce the mob attack on their women's society in October 1835. Even at the abolitionists' own Free Church, she complained, Deacon Gulliver refused to read a notice for a forthcoming Boston Female Anti-Slavery Society meeting. "The Deacon is, I think, a perfect coward, not daring to keep these times," she wrote. "Debora went to the Free Church part of the day, but was so provoked she could scarcely stay. No notice was taken of the events of the week or any sound abolition preached. To say the truth, I know not where I shall go to church, for *there* I will not go unless they amend. Brother [Henry C.] Wright at the Mission House preached the only suitable sermon that was preached in town."[52] A year later, Anne still expressed disillusionment with Boston's religious establishment. "I wish you would write to me & tell me what you think it my duty to do about joining some church," she confided to her sister in October 1836. "I cannot with all my heart subscribe to all the articles of the Free Church. . . . As for Mr. Winslow, his wickedness on the slavery matter stares me in the face, and probably his whole church are as bad."[53]

Unlike the Congregationalists and Baptists, who reestablished connections with organized religion by joining free churches, Unitarians remained estranged from local religious institutions. To them, theological disputes seemed specious when compared to the important moral and social issues of the day, and they remained committed to converting other Unitarians to their reform principles. Failing in this, some, like Maria Chapman and Caroline Weston, became bitter and cynical, "altogether opposed to every thing that looks like churchdom,"[54] while Ann and Wendell Phillips eschewed organized religion, preferring to worship in their own parlor.

The women in the Boston Female Anti-Slavery Society were a diverse lot, representing the old and the new, tradition and change. The society included many women from the city's established and wealthy merchant and professional class, which historically had assumed moral and financial responsibility for the needy. Joining with them were individuals belonging to the city's rising middle class, wives of proprietors, clerks, and skilled artisans who, in a number of instances, would amass fortunes rivaling that of the Brahmins. Prosperous African Americans also participated in the organization as part of their effort to uplift the local black community. The society included a number of employed women, many of whom were part of the massive migration to Boston that began in the 1830s. But, unlike the majority of female newcomers who became poorly paid seamstresses and domestics, the women in abolition carved out new employment opportunities as teachers, boardinghouse operators, writers, editors, lecturers, and social workers. In terms of religious affiliation, most members were Congregational and Baptist, but the society also included a significant number of Unitarians and Quakers, as well as a scattering of Universalists, Methodists, Episcopalians, and African Baptists. Finding an established religious institution consistent with their social ideals was a challenge that many of these women confronted during the years that they participated in the Boston Female Anti-Slavery Society.

This profile of Boston Female Anti-Slavery Society members is consistent with the depictions of the abolition constituency throughout the Northeast, though some important differences exist. According to the statistical analyses of abolitionists produced by Alan Kraut, Edward Magdol, Gerald Sorin, and others during the last twenty years, the typical antislavery activist was a white, native-born Protestant in his thirties or forties and a member of the middle and working classes.[55] Most abolitionists were propertyless, but they frequently were engaged in upwardly mobile occupations, particularly as manufacturers, skilled artisans, proprietors, and professionals.

Alan Kraut has commented that the "most marked difference" between abolitionists and nonabolitionists was in their employment: As opposed to the agrarian majority, abolitionists were more likely to be in manufacturing, trade, and the professions.[56] Indeed, abolitionists appear to have been among the chief beneficiaries of the transition from an agrarian/mercantile economic system to commercial capitalism and, therefore, fully endorsed the emerging, or "modern" to quote Lawrence Friedman, free-labor system. In their view, slavery was the symbol of a social structure that was fast becoming obsolete.[57]

This basic profile clearly refutes David Donald's earlier, and provocative, thesis that abolitionists were members of New England's traditional mercantile/agrarian elite who joined the antislavery movement because their accustomed status and authority were being challenged by a new and increasingly powerful class of manufacturers and tradesmen.[58] Indeed, Leonard Richards's comparison of antislavery men to those participating in antiabolitionist mobs revealed that it was the rioters, not the abolitionists, who were the descendants of old New England elites.[59]

Although the above socioeconomic breakdowns of the antislavery movement were based on poll records, tax rolls, and lists of rioters—sources that exclude all but white males—the profile applies to women as well. For example, Judith Wellman's work on female petition signers in upstate New York showed that women abolitionists in the 1830s came from towns that were dominated by manufacturing and trade.[60] Nancy Hewitt's forays into Rochester's abolitionism similarly identified members of the local female antislavery society as coming not from the city's "first families" but from "its most dynamic economic sector of shopkeepers and artisans." However, Hewitt also found that the women in the Western New York Anti-Slavery Society (formed in 1842) were a less affluent group of farmers' wives who, unlike the majority of female abolitionists there, were "marginal" to the new commercial social structure of urbanizing Rochester.[61] In a preliminary study of the Ladies' New York City Anti-Slavery Society, Amy Swerdlow determined that her group of female abolitionists consisted of the wives and daughters of prosperous merchants and ministers. Only two New York women abolitionists were employed: one as a teacher, the other as a missionary for the New York Female Moral Reform Society.[62] Finally, though Carolyn Williams does not provide a specific socioeconomic breakdown of the Philadelphia Female Anti-Slavery Society, she too notes that its women "were largely members of merchant and artisan families of the city."[63]

As for religion, Wellman, Swerdlow, Hewitt, and others have found that female abolitionists were predominantly Presbyterian, with a lesser number of Congregationalists, Baptists, Methodists, and Quakers. For example, fifteen of the New York women abolitionists were Presbyterian, four were Methodist, two were Baptist, and there was one Quaker in the group. According to Swerdlow, there were no Congregationalists or Unitarians in the New York society. In Rochester, the female antislavery society also was primarily Presbyterian, whereas the western New York and Philadelphia antislavery societies were almost entirely Hicksite Quaker. Though Wellman does not specifically identify the religious affiliations of the New York petitioners she studied, she does note that abolition towns were dominated by Presbyterians, Baptists, Methodists, and Quakers.

The Boston Female Anti-Slavery Society also was predominantly white, evangelical Protestant, and drew the bulk of its membership from the upwardly mobile middle and working classes. However, the organization presents some interesting variations from this standard profile. For one thing, along with its middle- and working-class constituents, the society also attracted many elite women. In fact, some of the most notable characteristics of the Boston abolitionists were their prestige and power and the enormous wealth they had at their disposal. Whereas the average abolitionist owned property valued at less than $500, Boston abolitionists often paid taxes on assets of $10,000, $25,000, and more. Some enjoyed incomes of over $100,000, quite a significant sum in the 1830s. As the financial, political, and cultural center of New England, it is to be expected that the city's abolitionists would include a higher concentration of merchants, businessmen, professionals, and government officials. Moreover, because of the enduring viability of Boston's traditional mercantile elite, the upper class retained power in the city's political, cultural, and social institutions. Many of these individuals were committed to organized abolition as well.

Boston's distinctiveness is also revealed in the religious makeup of the women's society. In rural New York and New England, Presbyterians predominated (typically accounting for 35 percent or more), followed by Baptists, Methodists, Quakers, and Congregationalists. The same pattern held true in Pennsylvania, except in Philadelphia where Quakers controlled the movement. In Boston the reverse was true. The Presbyterian church contributed few abolitionists to the local movement; indeed, the church had virtually no presence in the city at that time.[64] Instead, the Boston Female Anti-Slavery Society was dominated by Congregationalists and Baptists as well as a substantial number of Unitarians, clearly reflecting the city's unique religious heritage.

Finally, the Boston Female Anti-Slavery Society was integrated from the outset and always included African-American women among its elected officials. Though Boston's black female abolitionists were representative of African-American activists generally, their inclusion in the white society was not typical of other women's societies. The Philadelphia society was integrated successfully, but some women's organizations, including those in Fall River and New York City, specifically excluded blacks from membership. Others, such as the Western New York Anti-Slavery Society, were divided over the admission of blacks to their ranks. As a result of this ambivalence toward them, many African-American women formed separate antislavery organizations. This did not happen in Boston, though black members did participate in other black-only associations in the city.[65]

As useful as collective social profiles are in identifying the abolitionists' motives and goals, by definition they concentrate upon the abolitionists' commonalities rather than the diversity among them.[66] Indeed, to avoid the problem of diversity, social historians have chosen the time period and/or cohort group for their analyses quite judiciously. For example, in order to isolate Utica, New York's antislavery "rank and file," Edward Magdol excluded eighty-three antislavery leaders in developing his social profile, even though, as he later indicates, these locally prominent individuals were generally more prosperous and influential than the group he analyzed.[67] David Donald was equally selective in determining his cohort group, and he purposely looked at pre-1840 antislavery leaders to avoid what he called a "different set of causal problems."[68] By focusing upon feminist-abolitionists, Blanche Glassman Hersh and Ellen Carol Du Bois similarly excluded a large contingent of abolitionists, those opposed to women's rights.[69] Finally, Alan Kraut's and Gerald Sorin's separate studies of Liberty party voters failed to account for nonvoting individuals in the movement.[70] In short, as opposed to political and intellectual historians who have chronicled in detail the differences and controversies among abolitionists, social historians of the movement, with some notable exceptions, have been more interested in what distinguished abolitionists from the general population than in what separated them from one another.[71]

Yet the diversity among abolitionists can also be revealing of who the abolitionists were and what their relationship to antebellum society was. As subsequent chapters will detail, the Boston Female Anti-Slavery Society's heterogeneity, which originally had been pointed out with pride, created a conflict within the organization that was reflective of the social tensions present in Boston society at large. Consequently, as the society began to break apart, it did so along preestablished fault lines with the affluent Unitarians and Quakers forming an alliance on one side and the middle-class Baptists and Congregationalists on the other. After the society disbanded in 1840, these women activists forged new alliances within the city's religious and reform communities, ones which capitalized upon rather than ignored the class divisions within Boston society.

⟨ C H A P T E R 5 ⟩

Divisions in the Boston Female Anti-Slavery Society

"IT WAS ON THE WHOLE THE BLOODIEST BATTLE WE HAVE FOUGHT YET," reported Anne Weston to sister Deborah after the Boston Female Anti-Slavery Society meeting in July 1839. It had been a full session for, following in the wake of the division among male abolitionists, the women's gathering had attracted "peelers" as "punctual as lovers to the moment swoon." Mary Parker "looks fearfully," Weston observed, "all dried up as it were & Catherine [Sullivan] but poorly. The Balls bear things better than any body."[1]

By the time of this meeting, the Westons realized that the Boston Female Anti-Slavery Society was succumbing to the tensions threatening the entire antislavery movement. In their opinion, the women's society had already divided into two hostile camps: the "peelers" who sympathized with clerical abolitionists in the so-called New Organization, their layers of commitment peeling off "just like an onion"; and the "thorough going abolitionists" who continued faithful to what the clericals complained were Garrison's "visionary and foolish schemes."[2] Years later, Caroline Weston recounted to Samuel J. May the circumstances surrounding these divisions in the society:

The clerical appeal had appeared in the summer of 1837 & there was trouble and discontent in the Boston Female Anti-Slavery Society, the members who had "conscientious scruples" about fairs etc. having been tampered with by the disaffected clerical party. . . .

The disaffected members of the Boston F.A.S.S., although as I have said forming a minority of the society, had the advantage of finding most of the officers of the soc. in harmony with themselves. This enabled them to pack the meetings with persons who had no further interest in the soc. than its destruction. They succeeded by fraudulent means[,] such as refusing to receive votes from old members—false counting of votes—altering books & lists, etc., in getting possession of the power.[3]

Maria Weston Chapman agreed that the "afflictions in our Boston Female A.S. Society" resulted from the "grossest dishonesty" of the society's officers, who persuaded "sister church-members" to pack meetings and vote for New Organization resolutions. Lydia Maria Child found the "scenes" during the meetings "exceedingly painful." She, too, was convinced that the "half-and-half abolitionists" were contriving to have society funds given over to support the clericals.

If they would *honestly* come out and say that what appears to us the wrong side seems to [th]em the right one, I should be the last to interfere with their freedom of opinion, or to put obstacles in the way of its free expression. But the difficulty is, many of the *Society* are blinded by the smooth pretenses of the Board and are doing the work of [ministers] Phelps and Torrey, while they know it not.

In Henrietta Sargent's view, it would have been "honester" for the officers "to accompany their brothers, and go off to the new organization" than to constantly impede the initiative of the legitimately active members.[4]

On the other side, New Organization supporters in the women's group, particularly the society's officers, felt Chapman and her allies had deviated from original antislavery precepts by introducing controversial reforms into the movement. As Martha Ball complained to English abolitionist Elizabeth Pease:

Our *no-government* friends being resolved to carry their *peculiar views* along with them *in the Anti-Slavery car* became so annoying in their movements that it was found impracticable to continue united with them & the consequence has been in our Female Society, *dissolution*, and I fear it will be in many others. . . . We find it very important to keep our societies clean and distinct lest they become perverted from their original objects.[5]

An unsigned letter published in the *Liberator* corroborated Ball's interpretation. Because the "Boston F.A.S. Society do not think it right for them, as a body, to adopt the principles and measures of the Non-Resistance Society,—to engage in the discussion of the Woman's Rights question, so called, and to encourage the no-human government doctrines," the correspondent explained, "a few restless, ambitious spirits have determined on our destruction." The proclerical faction, led by the society's officers, thus blamed the Boston Female Anti-Slavery Society's troubles on the Chapmanites who, "without regard to order and propriety," insisted upon introducing their "peculiar" ideas into abolitionist meetings. The board felt that they had proceeded with the "utmost integrity and impartiality." If gatherings had been unproductive or errors made in the counting of votes, Recording Secretary Lucy Ball asserted in self-defense, "censure must rest more on those who annoyed the meeting than on myself."[6]

Many of the organization's problems stemmed from a prolonged power struggle between officers Mary Parker, Catherine Sullivan, and Martha and Lucy Ball on one side and Maria Weston Chapman and her sisters on the other. This competition intensified over whether or not the society would support Garrison in the wake of the Clerical Appeal and the subsequent defection of many abolitionist ministers. Frustrated at the board's apparent neutrality concerning the movement to oust Garrison, Chapman attempted to use her position as corresponding secretary to expose the true character of "those Iscariots, Woodbury & Fitch & co." and the rest of the "black hearted ministry" in her 1837 annual report. As discussed before, the officers were distressed by the tone and content of Chapman's report, which censured the local Congregational and Baptist clergy. "This course is *uncalled* for with regard to the affairs of the Church & will not be expected from us," President Parker protested. Yet despite complaints by many women in the society, Chapman refused to alter her original document. "You would not take it out of the hands of the society in that way?" Parker wondered, to which Chapman replied, "In a case of this kind, the opinions of any society are as immaterial to me as the wind that blows."[7]

Responding to the criticisms of her report, Chapman and her sister Anne resigned their positions on the board in November 1837. Thereafter, Mary Parker and the Balls became the prime movers of the society and proceeded to block Chapman's efforts to direct the organization from the sidelines. For example, when Chapman wanted the society's authorization of a letter to Henry Clay she had drafted, Parker informed her, "We have a secretary competent to do all that the society needs." On another occasion, the Westons sought to have a special meeting called to rally support for Garrison. Martha Ball curtly replied that "no reasons were assigned which appear to them [the board] of *sufficient importance* to warrant the calling of a meeting of the Society." "We are all gagged here," Caroline Weston bemoaned. "We are not permitted to hold a meeting. Miss Parker and the Balls decide it to *be unnecessary.*"[8]

The Westons also suspected that during meetings the officers, particularly Lucy Ball, purposely took erroneous minutes and miscounted votes so that New Organization positions would prevail. Once, when the society voted to contribute money to the Garrison-controlled Massachusetts Anti-Slavery Society, Ball reportedly recorded that the funds were to be sent to the American Anti-Slavery Society instead. On another occasion, word passed among the Chapmanites that the officers refused Garrison money awarded him by the society, first by suggesting that the vote had not been unanimous and then by claiming that the treasury contained insufficient funds.

The Westons also seemed to feel that the officers—most notably Martha and Lucy Ball—were infringing upon their private affairs, intruding upon their social territory. "What a set the Balls are!" exclaimed Anne Weston upon hearing that Martha and Lucy were courting Lydia Maria Child. "Why they are taking all this pain to smooth over and conciliate I hardly know." Maria Chapman was furious to learn that Martha Ball had begun corresponding with Elizabeth Pease, liberal benefactor of American abolitionists. Pease had been Chapman's friend and contact, and she quickly sent word to the Englishwoman warning her of the Balls' "hypocrisy as abolitionists and their want of integrity as women." Fumed Chapman, "These dishonest Misses Ball, by whom we have been so much duped, are the main movers" in the society's dissolution.[9]

An embarrassingly public episode between the Westons and the Balls occurred when Thankful Southwick invited Lucy and Martha to a reception for Lucretia Mott at Maria's West Street home. When the Balls arrived at her doorstep, Chapman flew into a rage and sent them away. Regretting her discourteous behavior, Chapman later penned a note of restrained apology. "Will the Misses Ball receive the assurance of my sincere regret at the painful position they were placed in by the wrong course of my friend Mrs. Southwick in inviting you to *my* house *as abolitionists*," though, she could not resist adding, "I have no hesitation in saying that I consider them [the Balls] *at present* as not occupying the position as helpers of the cause." Lucy and Martha's response was, in turn, designed to rankle the socialite-turned-abolitionist. "We accept your '*regret*' at the unpleasant circumstance that transpired on Friday eve and shall *continue* to pray that God may teach you what are the first principles of the gospel of *Peace*—and that the root of the matter may be implanted in your heart by the adorable Redeemer."[10]

Eventually, the Westons pushed their abolitionist colleagues to choose between themselves and the Balls and were soon gratified as the Balls and others on the board lost favor with Garrison and other male activists. "Oliver's [Johnson] and Garrison's eyes begin to open to Mary Parker's delinquencies—a thing which they have not done before," gloated Deborah Weston in early 1839. Anne happily observed a similar change of attitude. "The Garrisons and Johnsons have become pretty well aware of Mary P's iniquity." However, she was forced to admit, "I fear Phelps' doom is sealed. He has gone to Mary Parker's to board. I hardly think he will marry Mary, but he may Eliza."[11]

These policy disputes and political maneuvering among white Boston Female Anti-Slavery Society members were more than simply personal antagonisms between the Westons and the Balls, though the significance of the society's factionalism has been obscured by their hyperbolic rhetoric. As the coalition of Protestant women unraveled and factions solidified, it soon became clear that the society had divided along class and denominational lines, with the wealthy Unitarians, Episcopalians, and Quakers solidly behind Maria Chapman while the middle-class Baptists and Congregationalists backed the Balls and others on the board. In short, the division of the Boston Female Anti-Slavery Society mirrored the more generally divisive process of class formation occurring in Boston at that time.

With few exceptions, the white women who supported Maria Weston Chapman "bristled with Boston genealogies," to quote Henry James.[12] For example, nearly every woman related by birth or marriage to a merchant or banker endorsed Chapman's efforts to manage the society. Besides those in the immediate Chapman and Weston families, this group included the Sargents, Philbricks, Jacksons, Shaws, and Winslows as well as Susan Cabot and Eliza Cabot Follen, Abby May Alcott, and Frances Robbins. In fact, of the society's merchant women, only Sarah Shaw Russell and the three Ammidon sisters opposed the Chapman–Weston bloc. As mentioned earlier, each of the Ammidon sisters would eventually marry a Baptist minister. As for Sarah Shaw Russell, her husband, George, initially opposed women's admission to male organizations and supported the Massachusetts Abolition Society, while Sarah joined the Massachusetts

Female Emancipation Society. It seems, however, that by the mid 1840s the Russells had reconciled with other upper-class activists.

Boston Female Anti-Slavery Society members connected to Boston lawyers—Louisa Sewell, Ann Phillips, Susan Kingsbury, Louisa Loring, Lydia Maria Child, and Mary F. Rogers—were also strong proponents of the Chapman point of view, as were the women associated with manufacturers and physicians. Among these occupational groups, only Lucinda Otis, daughter of lawyer George A. Otis, and the wives of Dr. Charles Hildreth and piano manufacturers David Foster and Timothy Gilbert sided with the board, and like the Ammidons, these women were Baptists. In fact, Lucinda Otis eventually married a Baptist minister.

The personal circumstances of Maria Chapman and her sisters illustrate the privileged background and social position of many white radicals in the Boston Female Anti-Slavery Society. The Westons were among the earliest settlers in Massachusetts; in fact, Thomas Weston (identified in one local history as formerly "a merchant of good reputation in London") founded their hometown of Weymouth in 1622. The Weston sisters' father, Warren, was a prosperous sea captain and landowner, while brothers Richard and Henry were, respectively, future proprietor of Weston and Grey and Harvard-trained physician. Chapman spent her teenage years living in England with the family of her uncle, Joshua Bates, a banker with London's Baring Brothers. She returned to the United States in the late 1820s and became principal of Ebenezer Bailey's experimental high school for girls. Her marriage to shipping merchant Henry G. Chapman, Jr., in 1830 ended her teaching career, but it represented a propitious merger of two influential families. Meanwhile, Maria's younger sisters, Anne, Caroline, and Deborah, also moved to Boston, where they opened a school in the Boylston area.[13]

Descriptions of Chapman and her sisters by contemporaries stressed their attractiveness, aristocratic demeanor, and intellectual and educational attainments as much as their uncompromising commitment to social causes. According to Harriet Martineau, for example, Chapman was "beautiful as the day, tall in her person, and noble in her carriage," with an intelligence and learning that was "unrivaled." To James Russell Lowell, she was a "noble woman, brave and apt," the "Joan of our arc." Edmund Quincy, son of the early mayor, felt that all of the Westons displayed "the highest education and the first abilities," with "warm hearts, clear heads, wit, human spirit, literature," as well as "the virtue which every woman should have if she possibly can, beauty."[14]

Other wealthy women in the Boston Female Anti-Slavery Society were depicted in similar terms. For example, according to George William Curtis, his mother-in-law, Sarah Shaw, was "the loveliest of women," and her daughter was described elsewhere as the "beautiful Anna Shaw." Henrietta Sargent was remembered by her nephew as "a woman of strong character, cultivated taste in art and poetry, deep sympathies and remarkable power of concentration." Hannah Tufts was equally "earnest and liberal-minded" and "exerted a strong guiding influence" on her husband, Charles, benefactor of Tufts College. Though weak in constitution, Ann Greene Phillips also "abolitionised" her husband Wendell with her "matchless courage and unswerving constancy." Despite her "delicate" health (she was an invalid for many years), Phillips retained her "singular transparent beauty—blue eyes, magnificent long hair, Hebe's complexion, and the form of Juno." Wealthy women activists thus came to represent the idealized Boston dame; if not always beautiful, they were at least powerful and aristocratic, deeply committed to the liberal advancement of human society.[15]

Privileged Boston Female Anti-Slavery Society members enjoyed an urbane life style and took advantage of the cultural, intellectual, and material opportunities available in the city. Their letters and diaries contain numerous references to lyceum series, museums, bookstores, theaters, and other political and cultural institutions and events that they frequented. "In great agony all day about Silliman's lecture before the Natural History Soc.," wrote Deborah Weston in her diary on a snowy day in May 1835. She had feared that the inclement weather would cause the eminent scientist's lecture to be canceled, which it did. Several days later she noted in her diary that sister Maria had called, triumphant that she had been able to gather together seventy-five of the one hundred dollars necessary to purchase a membership in the Athenaeum for Lydia Maria Child.[16]

Upper-class activists were also exceedingly cosmopolitan in their political and intellectual interests and alliances. They read and discussed Carlyle, Coleridge, and other Continental writers then popular among learned circles, and the Westons included Italian and other romance languages in the curriculum of their school. Maria Weston Chapman, Emily Winslow, Ann Greene Phillips, and others traveled extensively in Europe, and Chapman and her sisters spent many years in England and France, as did Eliza Cabot Follen, Susan Cabot, and Eliza Jackson Merriam. Through visits and correspondence, wealthy activists forged strong ties with English and foreign abolitionists that proved extremely valuable in the operation of the antislavery movements on both sides of the Atlantic.[17]

Despite the rigors of running organized female abolitionism in New England, in their personal lives wealthy women in the Boston Female Anti-Slavery Society continued to observe the social forms and conventions of the urban elite. Daily rounds of visiting and elaborate evening parties, for example, still occupied much of their leisure time. In a letter to her aunt, Anne Weston described a fairly typical day of making and receiving social calls.

> Thursday morning Maria and I went out a sky scraping. First we called at Henrietta's [Sargent] and then at Mrs. E[dmund] Quincy's. Mrs. Quincy was out and of this we were glad as this was the first call. We then went to Mary Robbins'. We got home just before dinner time and immediately after we got in Mr. Fairchild, the minister at S. Boston, called. . . . After dinner Mr. Bent called.

Weston goes on to detail a subsequent visit with Catharine Robbins, tea with the Southwicks, two days spent with Maria Mack, and several other social engagements.[18]

As wealthy women, the Westons and others of the upper class devoted considerable attention to their appearance, clothing, jewelry, and other items of personal decoration. For example, after carefully describing the arrangement of a hall for the 1836 Boston Female Anti-Slavery Society fair, Anne reported to Deborah:

> Maria looked like a beauty; her new silk is the colour of your cloak with a small dark figure thereon; she had her hair dressed with great taste & wore on her neck a long beautiful crimson mantle of Mrs. Chapman's. Anne G. [Chapman] looked very well. She wore a cap & part of the time her new cloak; as to myself I wore of course my light silk with a red & black hdk. of Ange's [Ammidon].[19]

In a similar vein, Deborah once noted the contrast between abolitionist gatherings in Boston and one she attended at the home of a New Bedford Methodist minister. "I could not but compare it with the elegant meetings which Mr. Bent holds in his nice drawing rooms," she admitted, "with piano & centre[?] etc., whilst this was in a low uncarpeted scantily furnished *parlour* & no beauty there but the beauty of holiness."[20]

For Boston Female Anti-Slavery Society aristocrats, conversion to abolitionism did not necessitate abandoning social or material pleasures, nor did committing oneself to reform require the renunciation of fine eating, dancing, theatergoing, and other leisure pursuits then popular among the elites. At a party hosted by Louisa and Ellis Gray Loring, whose guest list included the Chapmans, Westons, Follens, Phillipses, and Ripleys, a "magnificent supper" of ices, salads, oysters, cakes, pies, fruits, and ham was served. So much champagne was drunk, Anne Weston remarked, "as quite surprised me."[21] Sister Deborah described another fashionable event that she attended in New Bedford. "The party was like all that are given here [Boston], only there was considerable dancing. The supper table was laid out beautifully. It is something new here to set tables." In short, a commitment to racial and personal freedom did not translate into a more general demand for social leveling, and upper-class women continued to enjoy the advantages and leisure pursuits their wealth allowed. As Maria Chapman once put it, "Do not let us become so bewildered as to call either our virtues or good fortune a sin."[22]

However, upper-class female abolitionists quickly grew dissatisfied with and alienated from the more fatuous aspects of social rounds. "I begin to have great doubts about going to such parties anymore," admitted Deborah Weston after the social evening described above, for the guest of honor proved to be "a dreadful fool" and completely opposed to abolitionism. "If I am going to do any thing, let me go to the theatre," she concluded.[23] To resolve this dilemma women activists adapted customary social conventions and rituals to the demands of political action, infusing elite activities and obligations with new meaning and purpose. Visiting thus became petitioning. "I called at Mrs. Sam Rodman's," reported Deborah Weston after a day of calls, "& found her sick abed but her sister *Aunt Phebe* signed. I had a very pleasant call. . . . I then called at the old lady Rodman's who has been quite ill. She refused to sign—'I'll give my money, my labour & my influence to the cause,' said she, 'but to petition such a set of men as there are in Congress, I will never do it.'"[24]

Partying, like visiting, became politicized, enabling women to use accepted social forms to promote their political message. For example, elite abolitionists used parties to promote racial integration and tolerance in Boston. "Probably 50 people dined at Maria's, table full after table full," wrote Anne Weston of a gathering that followed a Massachusetts Anti-Slavery Society meeting in 1839. She added that there had been "3 coloured people among the rest; 2 men and & a woman." Of another interracial social event hosted by the Chapmans, Caroline Weston declared that "deep was the feeling that a new era was inaugurated & that when these things could be done the hour of the deliverance of the slave was at hand." Chapman publicized the interracial party in her *Liberator* report: "There was no distinction of color; and beautiful it was to see the white man forget his narrow and miserable prejudices and the colored man his wrongs, while their long silenced voices gathered round the same festive board in social and spiritual communion."[25]

Elite women also used formal social occasions, particularly dinner parties, to sustain solidarity among local activists and introduce the yet unconverted to their political agenda. These gatherings often brought dissimilar individuals together in relaxed social settings, as when a call by Garrison at Thankful Southwick's home became an impromptu party that included George Thompson, Charles Burleigh, Anna Grew, Catherine Sullivan, and Mary Parker. "What a collection of raving fanatics and dangerous incendiaries," joked Garrison. "A happy meeting this."[26] Following the Clerical Appeal and the difficulties in the society thereafter, upper-class activists increasingly turned inward, limiting their parties to persons of their own social rank and political sympathies and redoubling their efforts to draw other "fashionables" into the cause. It was in this context that Maria Chapman threw Martha and Lucy Ball out of her home when they dared attend one of her exclusive get-togethers.

Although white elite women's involvement in abolitionism was carried out within a social rather than a denominational context, religion remained an important component of their personal identity. Indeed, in 1830s Boston religious affiliation still was closely aligned with economic status. Consequently, every identifiable Unitarian (save for perhaps two or three) voted with the Chapman–Weston faction, as did all of the Episcopalians, Quakers, and Universalists in the organization. On the other hand, only two identified Baptists and nine known Congregationalists agreed with the positions taken by the Chapman group. Indeed, religious affiliation was so significant that during the society's division crisis the Chapmanites accused Baptists and Congregationalists of conspiring to "put down the Unitarians."[27]

Upper-class women, particularly the Unitarians, had little patience with the social precepts of Old Testament religion. "Calvinism grates and creaks harsher and harsher discord in the ears of my soul," wrote Lydia Maria Child of the orthodox among them. "It is marvelous that they do not see that every enormity under the sun may be sanctioned by the literal sense of the Old Testament."[28] The religious sentiments of the elites dwelled not upon fear, confession, and punishment but upon strength and purpose, serving as a conduit to individual worth and personal accountability. Taking the "bold, uncompromising John" as their mentor, upper-class women filled their writings and speeches with religious phrases and slogans that emphasized their personal power to accomplish social and political goals. At their fairs, for example, radicals emblazoned antislavery banners with slogans such as "God helps the Strong." As Maria Weston Chapman proclaimed in a letter to her sister Deborah, "Let us strike *manful & womanful* for justice and freedom."[29]

The liberal philosophy of Boston Female Anti-Slavery Society elites conjoined independent religious thought with civil and personal freedom in the belief that each person was accountable to God, not man. "We shall none of us relinquish our individual religious opinions," Chapman once declared. "We shall none of us assume each other's responsibilities." Chapman had long surmised that radical abolition concerned the rights of whites as much as the rights of blacks. Therefore, she contended, "We must *strongly assert our right to plea for the blacks*." Thus as "free-born" women, to quote Lydia Maria Child, upper-class activists scorned the "contemptuous treatment" that the "law of chivalry" implied and demanded the attention and respect due "any conscientious . . . member of the community."[30]

Nonsectarianism and anticlericalism were recurring themes in the religious and philosophical writings of the elites. Denominational prejudice represented a conservative, retrogressive mindset, the antithesis of enlightened religious thought. As one editorial argued after the division of the society, "The cause of God and entire humanity is weightier than the cause of any subdivision." Chapman and her allies applauded the "heartiness" with which Unitarians "condemned the sins against freedom committed by their own sect." In fact, when Mary Parker once quoted Chapman's own minister on the limitations imposed upon an individual by involvement in any organization, Chapman retorted, "You know I never consider Dr. Channing as authority." As for the "canting & hypocritical" Baptist and Congregational ministers "calling themselves abolitionists," they were merely using the "poor slave to secure a miserable salary."[31]

In the end, Chapman's upper-class contingent hoped to break the Boston Female Anti-Slavery Society's ties with those "spiritual despots," the local ministry. In particular, they denounced the "bigotry and sectarianism" of the society's Baptists and Congregationalists, accusing them of putting the "peace of one little church"—the Free Congregational Church—"before the peace & happiness of the human race." They condemned their colleagues for continuing to look to the clergy for personal and religious guidance, for in their minds this was tantamount to abdicating independent thought and action and becoming "a tool of the pro-slavery ministry."[32]

Though fervent abolitionists and exacting social critics, upper-class women in the Boston Female Anti-Slavery Society were not especially active in Boston's wider benevolent community. Maria Weston Chapman's obituary noted that when the onetime socialite's fashionably dressed figure first appeared at an antislavery meeting many suspected her of being a slaveholder or a spy. "So unlike was she in external appearance to the group of anti-slavery women-workers," the article read, "that it seemed impossible she could be one with them in sympathy for the slaves. But so it was!"[33]

Such was the case with a number of wealthy women who donated their time and money to the abolition cause in Boston. Many of their mothers and aunts had been prominent in pioneering female benevolent organizations like the Penitent Female's Refuge and the Boston Female Asylum. As a matter of fact, a number of the older relatives of women like Abby May Alcott, Mary Chapman, and Mary Grew served as officers of the venerable Female Asylum in its first years of existence.[34] But the Chapmans, Westons, Sargents, and other elite abolitionists represented a new generation of activists whose social consciousness transcended traditional noblesse oblige to assume an increasingly extreme interpretation of personal and civil liberty. As Maria Weston Chapman put it, "We know that the cause of truth and freedom is periled if a single soul be cramped in the expression of opinion."[35]

In the early 1830s this group did experiment with peace, temperance, and other popular reforms of the day. The Shaws, Russells, and Robbinses, for example, were interested in the communal experiment, Brook Farm. Ann Mann (one of the unsung laborers for Chapman's side) joined Ellis Gray Loring, Francis Jackson, George Curtis, and other Boston intellectuals as patron of the local phrenologist. Anne Weston and Maria Chapman even sampled the Seaman's Aid Society. "It was quite a stupid concern," Weston decided. Ultimately, though, radicals found the apparatus of organized benevolence too restrictive and inherently incompatible with freedom of action and thought, an "old-fashioned, encumbering machine." They continued working within established antislavery societies only because, as Chapman put it, their groups were not really organizations but the "symbol of righteousness and truth on the subject of Freedom."[36]

In 1838 radical males and females formed what was essentially a non-organization, the New England Non-Resistance Society. Repudiating the

Old Testament dictum of an eye for an eye, nonresistants like Chapman, her sisters, the Southwicks, Lydia Maria Child, Mary Ann Johnson, and indeed "all thorough going abolitionists," committed themselves to the ideology that no person or agency should have the power to coerce others. As Garrison explained it, "The assumption that man has a right to exercise dominion over his brother has preceded every form of injustice and oppression with which the earth has been afflicted." At the outset women were admitted as full members to the society, enabling them officially to combine efforts with males of their own class on an equal basis. In effect, the New England Non-Resistance Society was a relatively exclusive vehicle of the radical upper class, serving as an umbrella organization for the entire range of reforms the Boston elite espoused.[37]

Nonresistance also enabled Boston Female Anti-Slavery Society elites to disregard, philosophically and literally, policies imposed by the society's elected officers. During the debates over the 1837 annual report, for example, Chapman announced: "I shall never submit to any custom of any society that interferes with my righteous freedom." So when the society refused to endorse her plans for action, Chapman and her supporters pursued them as independent persons. As Caroline Weston commented after the board failed to issue a statement in support of Garrison, "As individuals, of course, we will do what we can to save the cause."[38]

In the long run, prominent white women proved rather elitist and exclusive in their conception of the abolition movement. Despite their egalitarian rhetoric and experimentation with social and racial integration, they considered Boston abolitionism to be a movement of the upper class, whose participation was central to its progress. Chapman once explained her views to a wealthy English friend: "One of our advantages is, that, if there be here properly any such thing as social rank & respectability . . . the Boston abolitionists are that thing;—some by wealth, as America counts riches;—some by various antecedents;—some by high intellectual gifts." That the society's elites promoted their connections with the local aristocracy was made clear in an 1839 *Liberator* article. Initially, the society had been "weak" and "feeble," the item read, attracting little attention. But "the acquisition to its membership of a Chapman, a Child, a Weston, a Loring, a Sergeant [*sic*], a Southwick and other kindred minds gave it not only a solid dignity of character, but new and quenchless vitality."[39]

As noted earlier, abolitionist elites made a concerted effort to enlist others of their class in the movement, though their proselytizing efforts among local aristocrats met with varying success. Harriet Martineau was an early convert as were Wendell Phillips, Samuel Sewell, and Edmund Quincy, but abolitionists were slower in winning the support of William Ellery Channing and Charles Sumner. Lydia Maria Child sought to enlist her sister-in-law, Laura Dwight Child, whom she described as having "much natural kindness and integrity" but who had "imbibed nothing but aristocratic influences from the hour of her birth to the day of her marriage. Whenever I see her she receives a slight impulse toward abolition," though, Child was forced to admit, she "falls gently back upon her velvet cushions long before I have an opportunity to see her again." With historian George Bancroft they evidently failed entirely, as his diary entry suggests: "I was invited last eve to Henry G. Chapman's, where I found myself in a squad of blue-stockings and abolitionists, both of whom I abhor; so made my exit as quick as possible."[40]

At the same time as upper-class activists courted certain local Brahmins, they severely criticized others who opposed their brand of abolition. Wendell Phillips's dramatic public confrontation with Massachusetts attorney general James Austin over the murder of abolitionist Elijah Lovejoy is legendary. Less well known are Maria Weston Chapman's attack on Mayor Theodore Lyman for his role in the Garrison Mob riot and Lydia Maria Child's heated exchange with Samuel Gridley Howe over Howe's refusal to admit blacks into his institute for the blind. The society's lawsuit to free the slave child Med was directed against other social peers, Thomas Aves and his son-in-law, merchant Samuel Slater.

The mob that disrupted the society's 1835 annual meeting came to symbolize this struggle between Boston's upper-class abolitionists and their proslavery counterparts. Indeed, Maria Weston Chapman and others strongly suspected that local merchants not only instigated the riot but also participated in it. As a result, the mob became immortalized among abolitionists as the "broadcloth mob" or the "mob of gentlemen of property and standing." Wrote Maria Weston Chapman of the intraclass confrontation: "As far as we could look either way the crowd extended—evidently of the so called 'wealthy and respectable'; 'the moral worth'; the 'influence and standing.' We saw the faces of those we had, till now, thought friends;—men who we never before met without giving the hand in friendly salutation;—men who till now we should have called upon for condemnation of ruffianism, with confidence that the appeal would be answered."[41] In short, social standing was an essential component of the collective identity of abolitionist elites, and they charted the movement's progress in terms of its reception among others of their class.

Because Chapman and her wealthy supporters ultimately felt that abolition needed to present an image of respectability and social standing, they often judged fellow abolitionists according to their positions in the community. For example, Maria Weston Chapman considered Boston Female Anti-Slavery Society members Sarah Haskell and Deborah Thacker to be "highly respected," and Catherine Sargent was "a lady as the world counts ladyship."[42] On the other hand, Anne Weston found clergyman Charles Fitch and most of the abolitionists in his Free Congregational Church not her "sort of people," nor was Baptist minister Nathaniel Colver, who was "vulgar beyond description." Moreover, when Weston heard several official letters composed by Boston Female Anti-Slavery Society secretary Abigail Ordway, she declared she nearly "dropped" on the floor. "There was no *peel* about them," she explained, "but they were so incurably vulgar, so miserably written, and altogether so much the product of an uneducated person that I really felt ashamed to have them sent." Caroline Weston perhaps best expressed the elites' opinion of many of their middle-class cohorts when she once dubbed them the "boarding house abolitionists."[43]

The Westons' disdain for the boardinghouse abolitionists in the Boston Female Anti-Slavery Society was exacerbated by the fact that white, middle-class women largely supported the positions of the officers. For example, except for the Quakers, all but three women related to small proprietors, clerks, and artisans voted for the policies that the officers advocated, as did most of the teachers, boardinghouse operators, social workers, and other self-supporting women in the organization. In addition, only three of the twenty-three ministers' wives sided with Chapman, two Unitarians and one Episcopalian. On the other hand, all women associated with Congregational and Baptist ministers aligned themselves with the board.

Although predominantly middle-class in composition, the Parker–Ball faction did include several wealthy individuals. As discussed earlier, the husbands of Judith Shipley, Emma Smith, Adeline Damrell, Mary Gilbert, and Mrs. Foster parlayed modest business and construction firms into large, profitable enterprises, so that by the mid 1840s their taxable wealth rivaled that of the traditional elite. Yet, because of cultural predispositions, institutional and organizational connections, and restricted mobility within the Boston hierarchy, these successful entrepreneurs retained their ties to the local middle class.

In socioeconomic status, religious affiliation, and family background, the Parker and Ball sisters typified white, middle-class abolitionists. Mary, Eliza, Lucy, and Abigail Parker were born in Jaffrey, New Hampshire, the daughters of an undistinguished schoolmaster. Although Jaffrey was a "corporate town" known for its wooden container products, all ten Parker children left New Hampshire in the late 1820s. (The six brothers moved to southern locales—Cuba, Baltimore, and Guiana—though their connection, if any, with slavery is unknown.) The Parker women migrated to Boston, where they opened a boardinghouse on Hayward Place, a district that contained "none of the fashionables," as Anne Weston once observed, "but the decent sort of people."[44] Shortly after their arrival, the Parkers joined the Union Congregational Church, and in 1835 they were among the founding members of the Free Congregational Church. In addition to their antislavery activities the sisters also became involved in several other reform organizations, most notably the Boston Female Anti-Slavery Society's Samaritan Asylum and the Boston Female Moral Reform Society. As a consequence of contacts the Parkers forged within the city's religious and reform communities, many itinerant activists, including the families of William Lloyd Garrison, Samuel May, Jr., and Amos Phelps, patronized their lodginghouse.

Despite Anne Weston's suspicion that widower Phelps was romantically involved with one or another of the Parkers, none of the sisters married. After the original Boston Female Anti-Slavery Society disbanded in April 1840, Mary moved to New York City to become an agent for the American Moral Reform Society. At the time of her death the following year, her younger sisters had returned to Jaffrey and purchased a home on the Baptist green. There they lived with their widowed mother in relative obscurity until their deaths: Abigail at sixty, Eliza at eighty-six, and Lucy at ninety-one.[45]

Martha, Hannah, and Lucy Ball had similar life patterns. Native Bostonians, they were educated in local public schools and converted in local Baptist churches. Their family was of modest means, and when their father, Joseph, died in 1837 they received a $6,000 legacy. Like the Parkers, the Ball sisters were self-supporting, piecing together incomes by teaching, writing and editing, and working for women's organizations. As with the Parkers, too, the Balls never married. Instead, they made their home with their widowed mother, Mary Drew Ball, and devoted their lives to teaching and working for the uplift of Boston's economically and morally needy.

During the 1830s and 1840s, the Balls experimented with several Baptist churches, searching for a religious environment compatible with their personal concerns and moral commitments. After joining the Charles Street Baptist Church in the late 1820s, they converted to the more socially active Federal Street Baptist Church, then to the abolitionists' Tremont Temple, and later to Phineas Stow's Baptist Bethel Church for sailors. In 1858 the Balls rejoined the Federal Street Baptist Church permanently.

The Balls withdrew from organized abolitionism in the mid 1840s in favor of moral reform and missionary causes. For thirty years Martha served as president of the Ladies' Baptist Bethel Society, which was an auxiliary to the Seaman's Aid Society, and for several decades she edited the New England Female Moral Reform Society's periodical, the *Home Guardian*. Lucy also worked for the Seaman's Aid Society and moral reform, but her special interest was in "converting" the Jews. Both Balls continued active in reform and charitable organizations until the early 1890s when Martha resigned her editorial position to care for her then ailing sister. Lucy died in June 1891, Martha in 1894.[46]

In religious affiliation, white, middle-class women in the Boston Female Anti-Slavery Society, like the Parkers and Balls, were almost entirely Congregationalist and Baptist. In fact, of the members whose religious affiliation is known, all but two Baptists and fifty-three of the sixty-two Congregationalists voted with the Parker–Ball faction.[47] As evangelicals, they were alarmed at the radicals' repudiation of religious authority, "filled with horror," to quote Anne Weston, that some of their sisters were no longer "under the watch and care of any minister."[48] At one point, word passed among the society that Maria Chapman had never been converted, leading many evangelicals to wonder "whether any thing she [Chapman] can possibly do in the Society will be blessed to the cause." To this Chapman dryly remarked, "If the slaves condition be the *tragedy* of human life, surely these things are the *farce*."[49]

The language and imagery used in the religious writings of white Baptist and Congregational women in the society often reflect a different set of attitudes and concerns than those of the upper class. For example, whereas the writings of the more affluent Unitarians and Quakers suggest a religious conviction based upon liberalism, independent thought, and worldly concern, the rhetoric of the evangelicals reveals an Old Testament preoccupation with sin and retribution. Slavery was a "direct violation of the law of God," so it was as "trembling Christians" that they endeavored to "cleanse themselves from the sin." Women abolitionists must strike *"terror"* into the hearts of *"evil doers,"* Lucy Ball once wrote to William Lloyd Garrison, and make *"tremble"* those "who dare to make merchandise of the *souls of men*."

To women like the Balls, antislavery was a "heaven-descended" principle through which female abolitionists would alert "our wretched country . . . to a sense of its danger and we hope to repentance."[50]

Despite occasionally assertive language and an alarming chiliastic vision, the religious expression of these latter-day Calvinists more often dwelled upon woman's meekness, unworthiness, and subjugation to moral and religious authority. Martha Ball, for instance, urged women to "leave all to Him." As she once rhymed, "Though friends may turn to bitter foes, leave all to Him, He ever knows." Elsewhere, Ball expounded, "Let us imitate his blessed life of meekness, patience and forgiveness, ever bearing in remembrance that the servant is not greater than the master." Typical of this sort of self-presentation was a letter from a Roxbury activist to Boston Female Anti-Slavery Society member Rebecca Eaton, who at the time was the editor of the *Friend of Virtue*. Before committing herself to a life of reform, the woman confided to Eaton, "I felt myself a poor unworthy worm of the dust and cast myself upon God for wisdom and grace."[51]

Many of the religious beliefs and moral sentiments of middle-class evangelicals were grounded in female martyrdom and self-abnegation, duty combined with self-denial. For example, the women of the Massachusetts Female Emancipation Society considered it a "joy to be deemed worthy to suffer" in the cause of the slave. Although a salaried employee of the Salem Female Anti-Slavery Society, Boston's Abigail Ordway, too, endeavored to make clear her selflessness in carrying out her remunerated tasks. "So far as I know my own heart," she reported in 1839, "self has never entered into part of my policy in arranging my visits in behalf of your society . . . and if at any time there has seemed to be any collision between my own inclination and what seemed to be my duty to you, self has always been sacrificed to what I consider the faithful discharge of my engagements in this cause." Eaton's *Friend of Virtue*, perhaps, best expressed the *mentalité* of middle-class reformers in the reminder, "The pleasure of resisting temptation is the only enjoyment that we can be sure of in this world."[52]

In contrast to the elites' declarations regarding individual rights and personal accountability, pietistic middle-class women justified their reform activities on the grounds of their unique sensibilities and responsibilities as women. As the Massachusetts Female Emancipation Society's first public address proclaimed, "If we prize the blessings and privileges with which we have been favored from our earliest years, shall we not, as mothers, wives, and daughters seek to give these same blessings and privileges to those to whom they are denied?" They simply demanded that black women be granted the "unspeakable sweets of Motherhood," which slavery has "dashed with gall and wormwood." "Who that has the heart of women will not come up to this work with a zeal commensurate to the wants of the desolate Slave?" they wondered.[53]

In appearance, personal habits, and leisure activities, white middle-class reformers continued to encourage morality and restraint and denounced many of the popular diversions of the day. Smoking, for example, was condemned as a "dirty habit"; cigars led to insanity. Because "in the Bible we read nothing about the two sexes dancing together and spending whole nights in rioting and sin," dancing was denounced as "but a step this side of debauchery and infamy." Theatergoing, too, excited "the lower feelings of our nature" and threatened to "kindle the fires of illicit passion," and Boston confectioneries encouraged individuals to spend free time in "unprofitable conversation" and "vicious and unnatural indulgence," both of which led directly to the "house of debauchery."[54]

To cope with the moral pitfalls of urban life, Christian women were encouraged to "take more heed to their own conversation and deportment" and to devote their free time to "industry, prayer, the acquisition of knowledge, doing good," and "keeping good company." No time should be given over "to impurity of thought," one editorial in Rebecca Eaton's *Friend of Virtue* urged, "no not for a moment. Let the whole time be filled up with useful employment." In a similar vein, middle-class women were told to avoid luxury and ornament, for as Eaton posited, "Virtue is in itself a treasure of more value than the wealth of the Indies." Dress, then, should reflect not riches but "the limits of modesty, of chastity, of dignity, and . . . Christian principle."[55]

To white middle-class women activists, the city served as a metaphor for the sin, corruption, and excess that was becoming a normal part of urban life. They believed that Boston was "polluted," inhabited by "spirits of darkness," and filled with "allurements" to "beguile the unwary." Their magazines regularly contrasted the "beautiful scenery," "healthful breeze," and "artless and unaffected" people of the country to the "dirty, narrow lane of the city" and "crowded, filthy dwellings of many a business street." Even after years of good works in Boston, the Ball sisters symbolically rejected their lifelong urban home by choosing the idyllic, still rural Mount Auburn Cemetery as the eternal resting place for themselves and their family, as did several other Boston Female Anti-Slavery Society members, including Lydia Fuller and Mary Gilbert. As a more immediate solution, middle-class women offered the home and family as antidotes for the seaminess of city life, for in their minds the one hope for the future was the children—"the blessed little children."[56]

Finally, if personal attractiveness, social standing, and cosmopolitanism were central to the way in which elites presented themselves, middle-class evangelicals courted images of female piety, morality, and domesticity. Articles about Martha and Lucy Ball, for example, pictured them as "two gentle sisters" and "true Christian" women whose household defined the "exemplary" domestic scene. Similarly, the obituary for Abigail Cummings lauded the former abolitionist and moral reformer for her many years of "labor in the cause of Christ, the Church, the family, the Social Circle, and various operations of the day." Upon her sudden death in 1855, Melissa Neale, wife of the Baptist minister, was eulogized for her "sociability," "cheerfulness," and "Christian deportment," and Boston Female Anti-Slavery Society secretary Lydia Gould was described in reform newspapers as an "amiable young lady" who "possessed in an eminent degree those qualities which adorn the character of the Christian and philanthropist."[57]

Upper-class Boston Female Anti-Slavery Society members were unimpressed with this middle-class admixture of piety, morality, and martyrdom. As Anne Weston complained, the Balls' "overbearingness" and "high missionness" knew "no bounds." Even Harriet Martineau commented that the Scripture Mary Parker read at a Boston Female Anti-Slavery Society meeting "gave out a little vain-glory about the endurance of persecution." On the other hand, Martha Ball and other evangelical women feared that nonresistance and other liberal opinions advanced by Chapman's "no-government friends" were "pulling away the barriers to vice and immorality."[58]

Not surprisingly, middle-class women in the Boston Female Anti-Slavery Society were particularly uncomfortable with the vigorous public style of the elites at the meetings. Preferring consensus, uncritical loyalty, and anonymous benevolence, they were unprepared for and unwilling to engage in free-for-all debates over intellectual freedom, religious opinion, or women's rights. The society had "nothing to do with religious liberty," maintained Mary Parker, while Judith Shipley felt that such subjects were "out of our sphere as women." When the Chapman group published reports of society debates in the *Liberator*, their middle-class associates accused them of trying to "publicly impeach" their "integrity."[59]

Yet, despite strong feelings on the matter, for a long time evangelicals refused to voice their complaints during meetings, some "out of sisterly regard" for the radicals' feelings, others because of inexperience in large public forums. As Lucy Parker explained, she, like many in the society, was "a poor speaker [so] rather than expose herself to ridicule she had been silent." A number of women assumed they would still be able to express their opinions on society policy in smaller, private sessions held afterward, as was the custom with women's groups at that time. Judith Shipley commented that she did not participate in the debates since "it was of no consequence what she thought individually" and she was "willing to give up her feelings about it."[60]

As a result of these irreconcilable differences in reform philosophy and political goals, middle-class Baptists and Congregationalists (men as well as women) resorted to creating alternative reform and benevolent organizations more in keeping with their personal styles and social concerns. In November 1837, for example, a circular appeared calling for the formation of a new antislavery society based on "evangelical principles," signed by the husbands of a number of women in the Boston Female Anti-Slavery Society who supported the board. Other middle-class husbands identified themselves as "voting abolitionists" and proceeded to form the Massachusetts Abolition Society, an organization that included few, if any, of the local elites.[61]

As for middle-class women, they too began forming separate abolition and reform societies after 1837. Not surprisingly, few middle-class women were interested in merging the Boston Female Anti-Slavery Society with the male Massachusetts Anti-Slavery Society but preferred to expand the female abolition movement. To that end, Martha Ball was hired by the women's society in the fall of 1839 as an abolition agent expressly to help form women's sewing circles so that more women's "hearts" would be "enlisted on the side of the oppressed."[62]

Although middle-class women joined the Massachusetts Female Emancipation Society after the Boston Female Anti-Slavery Society divided, increasingly the evangelicals shifted their reform focus to specifically female concerns, such as charities to assist prostitutes and halfway houses for homeless women. They also assumed responsibility for the Samaritan Asylum for Colored Indigent Children, one early Boston Female Anti-Slavery Society–sponsored project they had wholeheartedly endorsed. Martha Ball explained their interest in the antislavery society's fifth annual report: "By taking these children from the abodes of sin and bringing them under the healthful influence of virtue and religion, they are snatched from those paths which lead to the chambers of death, and fitted for usefulness here, and for eternal blessedness in a world of glory."[63]

At least fifteen former Boston Female Anti-Slavery Society members, including Judith Shipley, Betsey Mosman, Emma Smith, and Mary Ann Collier, helped constitute the Baptist Sewing and Social Circle of Rollin Neale's First Baptist Church. Organized within a year of the demise of the Boston Female Anti-Slavery Society, these Baptist women rejected the public activism of upper-class abolitionists, even refused to transfer their allegiance to the clergy-led Massachusetts Female Emancipation Society. They preferred a more traditional form of female benevolence and thus banded together in a sewing and social circle to make "a more general acquaintance with each other" while "aiding the Sabbath School and other benevolent objects." With Mrs. Neale installed as president, the sewing circle kept its goals as modest as they were traditional. The former aboli-tionists prepared garments for their minister and theological students at Neale's alma mater, Andover Theological Seminary, raised money for the Sunday school, supported an orphanage in Canada, and provided money for destitute ministers in the West. The organization was so low key that one year the secretary admitted that "since there has nothing in particular occurred during the past year" there would be no annual report.[64]

The Boston Female Moral Reform Society was, perhaps, the most popular organization among middle-class women abolitionists. Organized in 1835, Baptists and Congregationalists dominated the moral reform society, with Martha and Lucy Ball, Rebecca Eaton, Catharine Kilton, Abigail Ordway, Abigail Cummings, among many others, running it for several decades. Moral reformers were staunch supporters of the Boston Female Anti-Slavery Society board. In fact, of the fifty-six abolitionists belonging to the moral reform group in 1838, only four supported the Chapman faction when the antislavery society divided two years later. After the society's division, moral reformers gradually withdrew from aboli-tionism to concentrate on licentiousness in their community.

In many ways, the Boston Female Moral Reform Society, like the Baptist Sewing and Social Circle, represented a retreat into traditional forms of female benevolence. A women-only association until 1872, the moral reform society continued to look to the local male religious and benevolent establishment for direction. Clergymen were approached to deliver sermons and lectures at meetings, and their wives were encouraged to assume a leading role in the society's operations. The Boston Female

Moral Reform Society shunned fairs and other "frivolous" fund-raising activities, preferring to seek outright financial support from male philanthropists. "Are there not *gentlemen* interested in this cause who will come forward and proffer their aid?" read one early appeal.[65] Yet when males occasionally attended moral reform lectures, it was only "after the gentlemen had retired" that the "ladies were invited to express their minds freely in regard to the subject."[66]

Middle-class abolitionists and moral reformers (again male and female) were also interested in Sylvester Graham's dietary reform movement; in fact, the local American Physiological Society and a Graham boarding-house were both established in Boston by abolitionist David Cambell about 1836. In his analysis of the social composition of Boston Grahamites, Stephen Nissenbaum underscores the fact that they, like middle-class abolitionists, were primarily tradesmen and artisans. As Nissenbaum emphasizes: "Conspicuously absent from the American Physiological Society were the two ends of the economic scale: unskilled laborers and professional men. There were no lawyers, no bankers, no physicians, no commission merchants, no public figures—in short, no members of Boston's elite."[67]

Although women did not reside in the Cambell's Graham boarding-house or become active participants in the American Physiological Society (though many did sign the rolls), in March 1837 they were the beneficiaries of a lecture delivered by Graham himself on "Hygiene, Physiology, and Temperance." Twenty-nine Boston Female Anti-Slavery Society members attended the meeting, twenty-six of whom were supporters of the board during the society's disputes. Moreover, the three Chapmanites in attendance (Helen Garrison, Abigail Ordway, and Mary Himes) were among the few middle-class proponents of Chapman's positions. Interestingly, Graham's lecture was disrupted by a riot, just as the abolitionists' annual meeting had been in 1835. But instead of Chapman's mob of "gentlemen of property and standing," evangelicals were attacked by members of their own class, the local bakers and liquor dealers who felt that the Graham diet threatened business. Even at the time, abolitionists were aware of the social distinctions between the two mobs, the difference, the *Liberator* observed, "being in the *quality of the cloth* worn by the rioters."[68]

The creation of separate middle-class organizations like the American Physiological Society and Boston Female Moral Reform Society and the formulation of moral strictures regarding domesticity, personal deportment, and leisure activities suggest the emergence of a distinct bourgeois culture that consciously distinguished itself from both the lower and upper classes. [69] On the one hand, the benefits of middle-class domestic life were constantly compared to the miserable existence of the poor and homeless. "Think while you are enjoying the comforts and pleasure of your own pure homes," wrote Martha Ball, "how many a wretched girl or woman sits crouched in some desolate attic or cellar without food or fire, perhaps driven to the streets to find that which will keep her from starving."[70] Stories and editorials in women's magazines like Rebecca Eaton's *Friend of Virtue* and Martha Ball's *Home Guardian* impressed upon their readers the precariousness of women's economic and domestic situations and the need for constant moral vigilance. Meanwhile, their solution to the poverty and inhumanity around them was to encourage Boston's lower class and immigrant groups to adopt the moral and behavioral standards exhibited by the city's prospering middle class. At the same time, middle-class activists cautioned women to avoid the pretenses and moral pitfalls of "fashionable society." In comparison to the glamorous Maria Weston Chapman, the true Christian woman was not necessarily "accomplished" or wearing the latest "Parisian mode" but was busy minding "the sanctuary of home" or "at the bedside of suffering."[71]

Implicit in the middle-class critique of the "fashionable dissipation and extravagance of the present age" was a rejection of the prerogatives and authority of Boston's aristocracy. Using licentiousness as a code for excess, immorality, and corruption, women such as abolitionist-turned-moral reformer Susan Frost denounced those "in high places" who considered themselves "beyond the reach of human laws." Rebecca Eaton likewise demanded, "What neglectfulness and indifference are chargeable upon the community when they elect men to office, toast them, flatter them, and give them public dinners, knowing or having reason to believe that these men are constantly in the practice of adultery as well as other grossly immoral habits?" The moral woman, urged abolitionist Lucy Dunnells, must refuse to associate with such men, however "elevated their standing in society." In short, middle-class activists were as concerned about the arrogant abuse of power by Boston elites as they were about poverty-bred immorality rampant in urban slums. Working through female-only church groups and charities, they sought to make Boston "*free* from all *distinction* or *deprivation* of *privilege*," to quote Martha Ball, "on account of *nation, kindred,* or *color.*"[72]

Middle-class female abolitionists thus rebelled against what they considered the presumptuous authority of their upper-class associates and pursued an agenda more in keeping with their own values and goals. This pattern was repeated elsewhere, for often Boston's most successful middle-class entrepreneurs did not convert to the Unitarian church, assume positions on Harvard's board, or contribute to upper-class benevolent and cultural groups. Rather than being subsumed within these establishment institutions, the emerging middle class formed separate, even rival, organizations. Susan Frost's jeweler husband Benjamin expressed this newfound independence and self-confidence when he ventured (tongue-in-cheek, of course) to counter some of the statements contained in Maria Weston Chapman's 1837 report. "As it is in accordance with the spirit of the age, for mechanics' apprentices to take Doctors of Divinity by the nose," he began, "perhaps I shall be pardoned if I attempt to animadvert upon the last Annual Report of your Society."[73]

Elite women abolitionists, on the other hand, continued to operate within traditional forms of status and power. Though women, they were accustomed to established means of social and political action, and their abolition tactics emulated male models like petitioning, lecturing, publishing editorials and tracts, and initiating legal suits.[74] Unlike middle-class women in the Boston Female Anti-Slavery Society, whose benevolent activities were carried out under the aegis of local churches and female charities, elites availed themselves of established upper-class networks, using customary social forms like visiting and parties to further the abolition cause. Relying on traditional modes of authority, Chapman and her supporters had assumed that support for their reform agenda by the middle class would be forthcoming. They were unprepared for the repudiation of their program and the subsequent independent action taken by Mary Parker, the Balls, and others of the Boston Female Anti-Slavery Society middle class.

As Martha Ball predicted, many female antislavery societies suffered some sort of crisis between 1838 and 1842, presumably over the same issues that confounded the Boston Female Anti-Slavery Society. For example, Deborah Bingham Van Broekhoven indicates that after 1840 "the Rhode Island female abolitionist movement declined markedly," with some of the more radical women moving forward to work for women's rights, while others retreated to more traditional female benevolent pursuits.[75] According to Amy Swerdlow, the Ladies' New York City Anti-Slavery Society also disappeared after 1840 because middle-class evangelicals were "unable to move from benevolent Christian action for the less fortunate slave to radical demands for a change in their own status."[76] Judith Wellman found that women in western New York similarly withdrew from organized abolition as a consequence, in her view, of the shift from moral suasion to political action, a move that effectively eliminated women's roles.[77] The Philadelphia Female Anti-Slavery Society, it seems, was one of the few organizations that weathered the schisms intact.[78]

The most comprehensive work on the controversies among and struggle between women abolitionists has been done by Nancy Hewitt. In her article, "The Social Origins of Women's Antislavery Politics in Western New York," and a more recent essay, "On Their Own Terms," Hewitt describes the "profound division" among women abolitionists and attributes their disagreements over strategies and goals to "the social and economic backgrounds" of the various women involved.[79] As in Boston and elsewhere, the women representing Rochester's "new urban bourgeoisie"—the wives of upwardly mobile artisans and proprietors—retreated from the antislavery movement during the 1838–40 crisis. Faithful to their evangelical Presbyterian and Baptist churches, these women returned, at least temporarily, to their church-sanctioned benevolent activities such as sewing circles and moral reform work. Those remaining in abolition were primarily Hicksite Quakers, who founded the alternative Western New York Anti-Slavery Society in 1842 and quickly broadened their reform agenda to include peace and women's rights. However, in stark contrast to Boston's cosmopolitan intellectuals, Rochester's radicals, according to Hewitt, were rural farmers who were marginal to the dominant economy of the region. What these women appear to have had in common with the Boston Brahmins were a liberal religious upbringing and a close connection to their own community's sociopolitical structure, however different these communities were in status and composition.[80]

Although Lori Ginzberg's discussion of female abolitionists' schisms is only a small part of a much broader survey of the transformations of female benevolence during the nineteenth century, her findings provide some fresh insights into the origin and nature of the controversies among women. Ginzberg agrees with Wellman that the development of partisan politics precipitated a crisis among female reformers who were forced to redefine their relationship to politics and the state. According to Ginzberg, evangelical women quickly resolved the problem of reconciling feminine moral suasion with political action by withdrawing from politicized abolition and turning their attention to other benevolent causes. The ultraist women, she continues, similarly disavowed political action but refused to leave the movement. Instead, Maria Chapman and others formed the New England Non-Resistance Society, which repudiated government and politics altogether. Ginzberg's explanation of this apolitical stance coincides with Hewitt's: The ultraists "had fewer material resources" than the women involved in more conservative benevolent organizations like the Boston Female Asylum, and they were far removed from established sources of political power. Their interest in nonresistance was thus a manifestation of this essential powerlessness and enabled them to reject the authority and privilege of the current elite.[81]

Thus Ginzberg shares my and, of course, others' belief that there were important differences among nineteenth-century women and that their reform ideologies and tactics were reflective of their respective class (and generational) assumptions and experiences. As she states in her introduction, "The book asks throughout how the ideology of female benevolence was used differently by women of different social groups and in different social settings."[82] But whereas Ginzberg argues that female ultraists lacked access to local resources and political connections, my research suggests that Boston's radical abolitionists were women of influence and power. Far from being a disenfranchised group, they were prominent members of the city's traditional elite and, like their upper-class counterparts in the Boston Female Asylum, they skillfully used established political networks to pursue their goals.[83]

Despite the significance of Hewitt's work, and Ginzberg's refinements, a more comprehensive picture of the varieties among women activists in terms of region, class, religion, and ideology has yet to be achieved. Several key factors account for this historiographical incompleteness. First, histories of the female abolition movement, including the present study, continue to view each antislavery community in isolation rather than as reflective of more general patterns. We know something about women activists in New York, Rochester, Philadelphia, and, of course, Boston, but the commonalities and differences among these regional groups has not been wholly established.

Second, studies of male abolition, which have been more successful in integrating research findings on a national level, have yet to fully incorporate women into their analyses. These works are suggestive of general trends, but they do not specifically address the situation of women. For example, John R. McKivigan's informative and detailed study of abolitionists' different religious affiliations and beliefs is very significant for women, and his groupings are consistent with those in the Boston Female Anti-

Slavery Society. According to McKivigan, the Garrisonians generally belonged to liberal institutions—primarily Quaker and Unitarian—whereas the anti-Garrisonians were members of evangelical Congregational, Baptist, Presbyterian, and Methodist churches. Yet by limiting his analysis to American Anti-Slavery Society and American and Foreign Anti-Slavery Society leaders, McKivigan has largely excluded women, most notably those supporting the church-oriented faction. Women's relationship to his categories is thus implicit yet unexplored.[84]

Lawrence Friedman's otherwise exemplary look at the various antislavery circles suffers from the same weakness. The different factions he describes have immediate relevance to the Boston Female Anti-Slavery Society situation, particularly his discussions of the "Boston Clique" and the church-oriented abolitionists. According to Friedman, the Boston Clique comprised affluent, educated Unitarians and Quakers who, before converting to abolitionism, "mixed freely and comfortably with the genteel New England urban middle class." This faction, notes Friedman, "took the lead in propagating a more liberalized and appreciative perception of Woman's Sphere." The evangelicals, on the other hand, were predominantly Presbyterian and Congregational and drew their support from shopkeepers and artisans. "Unlike members of the Boston Clique," Friedman explains, the evangelicals "were quite active in the benevolent society movement." As for women's rights, church-based abolitionists "were the most recalcitrant, as they were recalcitrant on most other apparent innovations in missionary goals and practices." Though Friedman does a superb job of analyzing feminists in the movement, he lets them represent the whole of female abolitionism and does not indicate the role evangelical women played in the church-based faction or in antislavery generally.[85]

This disregard of conservative or, more appropriately, nonfeminist women has been even more pronounced among women's historians. As Nancy Hewitt has complained, "If women continue to be marginalized in general histories of abolition, more conservative women continue to be marginalized in women's history of the cause." She rightly attributes this omission to scholars' refusal to "analyze the antislavery movement on its own terms," treating it, instead, "as a prelude to the women's rights movement."[86]

On the positive side, because of this natural concern for the origins of American feminism, we do have a fairly comprehensive picture of the feminist-abolitionist. In addition to Hewitt's agrarian Quakers, radical women, as outlined by Blanche Glassman Hersh in her now standard

Slavery of Sex, were the daughters of middle- and upper-class New England merchant and professional families. As Puritans and Quakers, these social elites were "liberated" from "orthodox dogma, and from their society's evangelical emphasis on sin and damnation."[87]

Though elsewhere Hersh notes that many female abolitionists did not pursue equality but "felt comfortable in their separate female auxiliaries and useful in their work of gathering petitions and holding fund-raising affairs," she does not explore the role conservative women played in the articulation of gender roles or the development of a feminist ideology.[88] In fact, aside from Hewitt's depictions, scant interest has been shown in evangelical female abolitionists. However, because so many evangelical women became moral reformers, social analyses of this reform's composition shed some light here. Marlou Belyea's preliminary work on the Boston Female Moral Reform Society (later becoming the New England Female Moral Reform Society), corroborates my own findings that the bulk of its members were abolitionists in Boston's Free Congregational Church, though the moral reform society included Baptist abolitionists as well. In terms of socioeconomic status, Belyea reports that the moral reformers came from Boston's new middle and upper working classes, with the majority of their husbands owning small businesses or working in the skilled trades. During the Clerical Appeal crisis, the moral reform society professed neutrality, but eventually those society members who opposed the ministers were repudiated by the others in the organization.[89]

Building upon Belyea's unpublished research, Barbara Hobson, in her study of antebellum prostitution, further documents that New England Female Moral Reform Society officers were not upper-class "ladies bountiful" but women married to men in middle- and lower-middle-class occupations—that is, clerks, ministers, shopkeepers, booksellers and printers, housewrights, and masons. The employed women in the society were typically teachers, boardinghouse operators, and reform agents. However, Hobson, I think, mistakenly assumes that these women also were "radical perfectionists" because of Garrison's early association with the Free Congregational Church. Actually, the church became one of Garrison's chief opponents.[90]

Carroll Smith-Rosenberg finds a similar socioeconomic makeup in the New York Female Moral Reform Society and feels, as I do, that both gender and class influenced their motives and actions. "The leadership as well as the rank and file did not come from the oldest, wealthiest and most prestigious families," Smith-Rosenberg reports. Instead, "the societies represented the newly respectable, the recently prosperous—in many cases the families whose roots were not in the city but in New England or Western New York." She then parenthetically adds, "Though conclusive evidence is of course lacking, it seems likely that their participation in the Society's activities was an assertion of the legitimacy of their own roles through a defensive attack on the implied godlessness of established families who did not live as Christians should."[91] Although Smith-Rosenberg, among others, likely would disagree with my contention that in comparison with the Chapman-led radicals these evangelical moral reformers were more cautious in regard to social change, she does note that the New York Female Moral Reform Society disassociated itself from the women's rights movement and "would not tolerate explicit attacks upon traditional family structure and orthodox Christianity."[92]

African Americans are another group of women abolitionists who have yet to be fully incorporated into the female abolition story. In my own work, for example, I have generally discounted the role of black women in the debates over the society's division because they do not appear to have been influential in the proceedings. During the controversies they served as mediators, not competitors, and appealed for continued cooperation. Ultimately, the majority of the society's African Americans supported the Chapman faction, though several black women, including two ministers' wives, joined the Massachusetts Female Emancipation Society. Shirley Yee's study agrees that black women abolitionists were not fully engaged in the controversies between the whites, but they ultimately favored the radicals because Garrison was "a true friend of the slave" and "consistently supported black community improvement as part of the abolitionist agenda."[93] However, some African Americans did support the evangelical faction, though preliminary research indicates that these "conservative" black women (their husbands, that is) supported the clericals not for religious reasons but because the New Organization was interested in political action.[94] This suggests that although black women often participated in white-sponsored activities it cannot be assumed that their motives and priorities mirrored those of their white sisters. In short, much work remains to be done on the varieties of the African-American experience, too.

When viewed from these different perspectives—feminist abolitionist, male abolitionist, African-American abolitionist, even moral reformer—the variety of individual beliefs and commitments to antislavery becomes quite clear. Yet the complexities of how regional, socioeconomic, religious, racial, and gender differences determined not only personal ideologies and actions but also how individual female activists related to each other, to male abolitionists, and to the general community still seem beyond our grasp. As a start, in the following chapter I will attempt to make some preliminary connections, by comparing how the differences among Boston Female Anti-Slavery Society members were manifested in their abolition fairs. Then, in the final chapters I will explore further how the socioeconomic status, religious background, and social commitments of the women in the society's factions translated into fundamentally different conceptions of women's roles and responsibilities in antebellum society.

The Boston Female
Anti-Slavery Society Fair

THE MOST IMPORTANT STAGE UPON WHICH THE POLITICAL, SOCIAL, AND
religious contradictions of the two factions were enacted was the Boston
Female Anti-Slavery Society fair. Held annually since 1834, the fair was
the major abolition fundraiser in New England and the most significant
event organized solely by women. Because of the divisions within the
movement and the consequent controversies in the Boston Female Anti-
Slavery Society, after 1838 women in the organization began to put on two
fairs: the radicals' fair in support of Garrison and the Massachusetts Anti-
Slavery Society; and the evangelicals' fair to raise money for Phelps and the
Massachusetts Abolition Society. The management, goals, merchandise,
and general ambience of these fairs provide tangible evidence of the different values and styles that separated the upper- and middle-class women
in the society, and these differences will be the subject of this chapter.

The battle of the fairs began in the spring of 1839 when, at the society's
quarterly meeting, Martha Ball presented a motion that $1,000 of the
earnings from the upcoming sale be contributed to the American Anti-
Slavery Society, with another $100 donated to both the Samaritan Asylum
(at that time run by the evangelicals) and the Balls' school for black girls.
Predictably, Maria Chapman countered with a resolution that the $1,000
be awarded to the Massachusetts Anti-Slavery Society, arguing that the

American Anti-Slavery Society was currently more concerned with putting down Garrison than with abolishing slavery. Responding to Chapman's accusations, Judith Shipley, wife of prosperous Baptist baker Simon, pointedly remarked that she wished that all who attended antislavery meetings had the "Christian spirit" evinced by the leaders of the national society, and when the vote was taken Ball's original motion passed. "We have lost all but our honor," Anne Weston lamented. "The society," her sister Deborah added, "has peeled in a body."[1]

Once the Boston Female Anti-Slavery Society had officially aligned itself with the New Organization clericals, radical women not only disassociated themselves from the fair but embarked upon a campaign to discredit it. With the aid of her sisters, Chapman hastily sent letters to female antislavery societies throughout New England informing them of the fair's current objects and urging "friends of impartial freedom" to boycott the sale. "Maria and I spent most of the day in directing protests, writing a little in them as circumstances seemed to direct," reported Anne Weston. "We have written to many people (women) & to all the female societies."[2] Next, Chapman gathered together her supporters, and calling themselves the "Women of the Mass. A.S.S." they announced that they would be holding a separate "Fair of Individuals" in the fall.[3] Reacting to Chapman's ploy, the Boston Female Anti-Slavery Society's officers issued a public disclaimer, which stated in part, "We wish it distinctly understood, that the Fair to be held in October is not connected with the Boston Female Anti-Slavery Society."[4]

Throughout the spring and summer of 1839, notices appeared in reform newspapers announcing the two fairs. In the *Liberator,* the advertisements were placed adjacent to one another, each trying to identify itself as the legitimate Boston Female Anti-Slavery Society annual fair. The organizers of the Fair of Individuals solicited support by alluding to their "several years of experience in this mode of raising funds." Maintaining that theirs was the official fair, the officers of the Boston Female Anti-Slavery Society urged women "favorable to the cause of the SLAVE and the ELEVATION OF THE COLORED POPULATION" to join in their efforts, carefully using typography to distinguish their reform goals from the women's rights and nonresistance ideologies that the opposing camp espoused. In June the *Liberator* took pity on its readers and spelled out the difference between the two:

> FAIRS. Our readers have no doubt observed that *two* fairs are to be held in
> Boston during the present year—one under the direction of a committee of

the Boston Female A.S. Society, and the other under the management of a
voluntary committee of women, who are members of the Massachusetts
Anti-Slavery Society, and who have been most actively engaged in the Fairs
of former years. . . . [Those] who sympathize with the new organization will
doubtless contribute to the Fair of the Boston Female A.S. Society; while
those who believe that the Massachusetts Society ought to be sustained in the
present crisis will lend their aid to the Fair which is to be held (under the
direction of Mrs. Chapman, Mrs. Child, and others) in October next.[5]

Over the next several years, even after the breakup of the Boston Female
Anti-Slavery Society in April 1840, women abolitionists in Boston continued to hold separate fairs to raise money for the male organization of
their choice. The differences in the nature, conduct, and objectives of
these fairs go to the very heart of what separated the factions in the Boston
Female Anti-Slavery Society and therefore warrant careful examination.

When the Boston Female Anti-Slavery Society board of officers decided
officially to assume control of the fair, Chapman and her sisters had
legitimate cause for complaint. During the fair's formative years, the Balls,
Parkers, and other evangelicals in the society had been reluctant to endorse
the sale as an official event. "Great objections were at first felt to adopting
the fair as a society measure," one report indicated, largely because of
"conscientious scruples on the part of the members." Indeed, "some considered it inconsistent with a Christian profession, and others were strongly
prejudiced against fairs by the manner in which they had seen them
conducted." Another unnamed member confessed that over the years the
women's society "had little or nothing to do with the fairs, but to take credit
of them." She, too, noted that many members had "religious scruples"
against such activity and that "the burden and the heat of the work"
routinely fell on a few individuals. A compromise between fair proponents
and detractors ultimately was reached whereby no money was taken from
the organization's treasury, so, as Caroline Weston put it, "no one's conscience was troubled."[6]

Before 1838, then, the fair was only nominally a project of the society.
In reality, it was the production of the Weston–Chapman clan, the South-
wicks, Lydia Maria Child, and Louisa Loring, as well as whatever family,
friends, and associates they could cajole into assisting. On a day-to-day
basis, Maria Weston Chapman ran the fair almost singlehandedly—high-
handedly, some complained.[7] Her imposing figure presided over nearly
every sale, a presence that moved James Russell Lowell to verse:

126

> There was Maria Chapman, too,
> With her swift eyes of clear steel-blue,
> The coiled-up mainspring of the fair
> Originating everywhere
> The expansive force, without a sound
> That whirls a hundred wheels around.[8]

Initially, the Boston Female Anti-Slavery Society fair was a modest enterprise, offering unpretentious goods made by local women's associations to be sold to other reformers. The first fairs were held in the Massachusetts Anti-Slavery Society's rooms. When in 1835 that became too dangerous, the sale was held in the Chauncy Place mansion of Sarah and Henry Chapman, Sr.[9] As the fair progressed, it expanded into larger, even more impressive quarters, and by 1849 the women were holding it in the celebrated Faneuil Hall.

Escalation in the size and scope of the fair reflected a sizable increase in earnings. The first sale held in 1834 earned $360; three years later it collected over $800. By the time of the society's split, the annual fundraiser was bringing in over $1,000. Proceeds from the earliest fairs went to the Massachusetts Anti-Slavery Society, allowing treasurer Henry G. Chapman to discharge accumulated debts. "The money was paid into Henry's hands this morning," Anne exulted after the 1836 fair netted $540. "Henry thinks the debts of the Mass. will now be paid all off."[10] Soon the society began to give money directly to Garrison—as much as $1,200 in some years—and later earnings were used to hire antislavery agents, subscribe to reform newspapers, and support other charitable programs.

An adroit entrepreneur, Chapman managed her fair as her merchant husband ran his ship chandlery business, using sophisticated advertising techniques and public relations campaigns to promote her sales. As Chapman herself indicated, her sale was in a good position to take "advantage of the city market for the benefit of the slave," and she wisely held the fair in late December to attract buyers of Christmas and New Year's presents. "Think of the cause," she entreated in one fair notice, "and for its sake reserve your gift-money till Christmas." Chapman also developed a scheme whereby persons could place orders for specific items in advance, thus using the fair as a clearinghouse that benefited the artisan, the buyer, and the slave. Although the sale had its origins in the "vanity fairs" popular among upper-class women's charities at the time, the ambitious Chapman saw her sale as more comparable to male-run enterprises. "If all the friends of the cause in Massachusetts thus united to secure the city market," she wrote in 1840, "there is no reason why this effort should not emulate the Mechanic's Fair in attraction, and productiveness."[11]

Chapman used her extensive connections in England and Europe to secure desirable merchandise, and many of her personal trips, as well as those of friends and family, were used to buy items for the event. Abby and Isaac Winslow's trip to the World Anti-Slavery Convention in London, for example, included a search for articles for the fair, as did the honeymoon of Ann Greene and Wendell Phillips. The gloom of Chapman's stay in Haiti as a last-ditch effort to treat her husband's tuberculosis was lightened by their discovery of exotic items to include in the sale. "We are quite active in picking up pretty things for the fair," wrote ailing Henry to Maria's sister Caroline. "The prettiest things at present are two medallions of Bayer & Petion—a present from the Abbe Roquefeuil."[12] In short, by the time of the fair controversy in 1839, the women's sale had developed into an ongoing, profitable, indeed international, enterprise.

Because of the divisions within the abolition movement, especially the stratification of the Boston Female Anti-Slavery Society along class and religious lines, the character of Chapman's fundraiser began to change, taking on political as well as economic overtones. For example, as a means of distinguishing her antislavery efforts from those of women like Martha and Lucy Ball, Chapman scorned the moral and religious restraints advocated by the evangelicals. Her sales offered "plenty of confectionary, jellies, meats, and gay dress." As she explained, restrictions against such indulgences merely demonstrated the "sectarian prejudice" and "narrow-minded intolerance" of her opponents. In Chapman's opinion, individuals who brought this merchandise to her fair "felt free to do so, knowing that they only were responsible and that no one who disapproved need purchase."[13]

Chapman also used her merchandise to turn the annual fundraiser into an upper-class affair. The socialite-turned-radical was relentless in her efforts to obtain goods that would appeal to wealthy Bostonians and procured epicurean delights like French jewelry, English china, and Greek vases to bring luxury and elegance to her sales. With its "varied and beautiful" collection of goods, the sale offered "Caps and *Fanchons* from the most fashionable *Megasins* of Paris," "Dresden China of the time of *Louis Quinze*," Chinese envelope boxes, Scotch shawls, silk and satin aprons, lace cuffs and collars, and so on.[14] In advertisements, Chapman dwelled upon the rarity and sumptuousness of these items. In one short circular she used the word "rich" five separate times, and in another she claimed that *"no* where could a more exquisite or reasonable selection be made than from the tables of the Massachusetts Anti-Slavery Society Fair." Likewise, the 1855 fair report described the sale as a "perfect museum" where one could purchase the "most recherché articles of taste and fancy from the old world."[15]

Chapman's importing efforts were so successful that the women's fair, to quote Harriet Beecher Stowe, became "decidedly the most fashionable shopping resort of the holidays."[16] Indeed, articles were so esteemed that Boston merchants would buy unsold merchandise to stock their own shelves. In a Christmas Eve note to her mother, Margaret Fuller gives a sense of the fair's appeal: "Every body is running to the Anti-Slavery fair, said to be full of beautiful things from England. I wish I could go and buy pretty new years gifts for you and those I love, but I must not so avoid temptation. I had myself a beautiful present from there yesterday."[17]

The decoration of the hall and the display of the merchandise were also calculated to impress upper-class patrons. For example, culture and taste were the themes of the exclusive "Soirée" Chapman organized in 1840. The Westons decorated Marlborough Hall with "all the luxury of all seasons . . . [with] no end of beautiful porcelain and silver, a wealth of candelabras & lamps which flushed on beautiful flowers and prints." A bust of Garrison stood in the center of the room, flanked by an English Warwick vase and a reproduction of a painting by eighteenth-century Venetian artist Giovanni Battista Tiepolo that evidenced "the highest style of art" and the "execution of a master."[18] Ever ready with the political barb, Chapman had selected Tiepolo's portrait of Saint Catherine of Siena, a Dominican visionary who was very influential in fourteenth-century ecclesiastical politics and Florentine public life. Christ is said to have offered Saint Catherine her choice of a crown of gold or a crown of thorns, and the painting adorning the fair was of the religious woman wearing her crown of thorns, symbolic, no doubt, of the choice wealthy women like Chapman had made.

Yet even Chapman's political statements communicated certain upper-class pretensions. The 1839 fair provides a good case in point. The radical arranged the donations from local societies on separate tables and draped banners bearing the town name, its motto, and original English coat of arms overhead. By displaying traditional armorial symbols, Chapman "commemorated," as she put it, New England's Puritan ancestry, particularly its legacy of "moral warfare with wrong and oppression."[19] Chapman also included the names of the town's founders on these banners, pointing out that many of the names were the same as those of women presiding over the tables (as in her own case). As she made clear in her report in the *Liberator*, these town founders are "*our* remote progenitors," individuals "who have been renown in song and story for their devotedness to freedom."[20] By evoking images that she felt were "fraught with old historical associations," Chapman linked abolitionism with New England's Puritan and revolutionary past to capitalize upon the status and respectability of the women involved.

Chapman and her sisters sought to associate their enterprise with the local aristocracy in other ways. The Westons usually appended twenty or more women's names to fair announcements, and they were particularly desirous to include those of prominent Bostonians on the list of sponsors. In 1840 Deborah was very pleased to report that the announcement for the Fair of Individuals would be signed by Louisa Loring, Eliza Cabot Follen, "and other respectable names . . . giving it the ladylike touches." Weston goes on to enumerate other women they hoped would sign, a list dominated by women from established families like Sargent, Sewell, and Shaw.[21]

Since fair organizers were anxious that members of the upper class patronize their sale, they scrutinized customers for evidence of success. In 1836, for example, they were overjoyed when "not a few of the wives and daughters of 'gentlemen of property and standing' were among the purchasers." Although "no body of special note" had come in the morning, later in the day the fair was visited by "Mrs. Lowell, Mrs. Chief Justice Shaw and some of that sort."[22] They were equally pleased with a fair they organized in Fitchburg in 1845, which had attracted "all the elite of Worcester County."[23]

In light of the fair's financial success and public impact, it is not surprising that Chapman, her sisters, and other longtime fair workers were furious when they discovered that the Parkers, Balls, and other Boston Female Anti-Slavery Society officers had suddenly "gotten over all their conscientious scruples" and usurped the fair.[24] Radicals felt completely justified in luring away customers to their own Fair of Individuals and sneered at the board's attempt to compete with their seasoned enterprises. "It is rumoured that *they say* they have made $800 but nobody believes it," reported Deborah to Anne of the "official" Boston Female Anti-Slavery Society sale in 1840. "Every thing was very shabby, & some one of us, Miss Peterson I believe, who went in said there was no one there hardly the first evening & that she asked one of the ladies how they were getting on & the answer was rather poorly, not as well as they had hoped." Mary Robbins, whose family traced its Massachusetts ancestry back to 1639, also commented upon the "paucity and nothingness of all she saw" and "execruted" the New Organization "for bringing the cause so low."[25]

In truth, the fair sponsored by the society's officers in 1839 and subsequent ones organized by the Massachusetts Female Emancipation Society after the Boston Female Anti-Slavery Society divided were poor reflections of those Maria Chapman had created. In their defense, though, religious and moral concerns, not the marketplace, dictated the manner and style of these middle-class fundraisers. Furthermore, evangelical women were not preoccupied with impressing Boston society with the respectability or social status of the abolition movement. Their dilemma was to reconcile the expectation that auxiliary female groups raise money for their male sponsors (with the specter of the huge monetary success of Chapman's sales) with their personal "scruples" against frivolous or, as in Chapman's case, worldly and materialistic enterprises.

The Balls, Parkers, Goulds, and other middle-class managers of the "official" Boston Female Anti-Slavery Society fair were not entrepreneurs, nor did they enjoy extensive ties to Boston's mercantile and commercial elite. Instead of working within established family and business networks in the way that Chapman and her associates could, they turned to local religious and reform leaders to help them promote their fundraisers. Clerical abolitionists were especially active in rallying support for the Boston Female Anti-Slavery Society fair, so much so that radicals came to believe that ministers were running the women's organization behind the scenes. The Westons even accused Amos Phelps and other abolition clergy of publishing editorials and announcements attributed to anonymous Boston Female Anti-Slavery Society members.[26]

Amos Phelps, in particular, used his influence among Boston evangelicals and his ties with the American Anti-Slavery Society to promote "official" Boston Female Anti-Slavery Society events. In a letter to James G. Birney, for example, the clergyman described the situation in Massachusetts as a war of extermination. "You *must not fail to come here on the last Monday evening of December* in compliance with the wishes of the ladies society," he urged. "Their object of course is to have a large meeting for you to address on that evening & take that opportunity to advertise the public of the fair." Phelps hoped to impress upon Birney the symbolic as well as the political importance of the sale. "It is very important not only for the sake of the money but for many other reasons that the fair should go off well," the clergyman emphasized. "We wish the regular December fair to be, and to *seem* to be, the people's; & with the proper effort we can make it so."[27] At the same time, Mary Parker also wrote to Birney, asking the American Anti-Slavery Society executive to endorse the fair with his presence. "May we not depend on you, sir?" she entreated. In 1843 Lucy Ball still looked to Phelps to serve as an advocate for the Massachusetts Female Emancipation Society fair. "We trust you will not forget to say something for us as you have the opportunity," she modestly asked.[28]

The fair announcements that evangelical women composed lacked the excessive commercial style that characterized those produced by the Unitarian elites. Whereas Chapman advertised her sales as an "unequalled opportunity for the selection of Christmas and New Years presents," the sales organized by the Balls and their colleagues offered items that "could not have been more choice either as to beauty, variety or purity of moral sentiment." Piano playing and simple refreshments were further inducements to the evangelicals' fairs, and organizers were sure that the American silk that they offered was "equal, or nearly so, to the Italian."[29]

Because middle-class activists in the Boston Female Anti-Slavery Society and later the Massachusetts Female Emancipation Society did not believe in inducing wealthy Bostonians to purchase luxuries and ornaments in the guise of aiding the abolition cause, their fair advertisements rarely dwelled upon the merchandise available at the sale. In truth, their fair notices were not advertisements at all but rather pieces of antislavery propaganda that appealed to women's religious sentiments and moral convictions. "Have we *no sympathies* to be awakened by the voice of grief, the wail of wo?" ran the 1839 fair notice signed by Mary Parker, Martha Ball, Lydia Gould, and others on the committee. "Will you, in view of these millions who wither under the blight of slavery, whose lamentations come to you on every breeze, whose united cry is, 'Help us, Christian, or we die!' Will you, we ask, in view of those perishing ones, sit down and quietly take your rest?"[30] Moreover, to appeal to middle-class women, evangelicals also emphasized domestic rather than materialistic themes. "Will any mother, sister or daughter leave that undone which she as a Christian is bound to perform?" asked this same advertisement. "We trust this will never be said of the women of Massachusetts, but that with *one* heart they will come up to the work of breaking every yoke."[31]

Middle-class female abolitionists were not interested in becoming importers or large retailers, and they purposely kept fair offerings manageable. For example, in 1840 Delia Gould, Maria Holland, Judith Shipley, and other Baptist abolitionists joined with the Boston Female Moral Reform Society in soliciting "fruit and cake" for a "sale of refreshments" to raise money for the Samaritan Asylum for Colored Indigent Children.[32] Merchandise solicited for the official Boston Female Anti-Slavery Society fair that year was only slightly more ambitious than the cakes and fruit available at the above-noted sale of refreshments. When asked to provide a list of articles they deemed "most saleable," the fair committee said anything would be suitable, "if neatly and properly made," but they preferred items such as aprons, capes, collars, handkerchiefs, hoods, shoes, hose, work bags, pin cushions, shell work, and toys. If ornamental or "fancy" articles were prepared, the board stipulated that they "should have upon them appropriate devices or mottoes."[33]

The religious and moral influences of the fair continued to be uppermost in the minds of evangelical reformers, and their homemade items were fitting evidence of the selflessness of their enterprise. Accordingly, sewing was "work for the slave," and as such they hoped that it would be rewarded with the "blessings" of God on "ourselves and those for whom we labor." Since they were engaged in God's work, when the 1838 fair raised over $1,000, organizers prayed, "Not unto us, not unto us, O Lord, but unto *thy* name, be all the glory."[34]

Because the evangelicals' fairs were of a modest, religious nature, they preferred to call their event a "sale" as opposed to the more frivolous-sounding "fair." The salesroom would be decorated in an earnest, even austere, manner. Missing were elaborate candelabras, silver vases, statutes, and paintings, as well as the draped banners bearing civil rights slogans. Instead, the salesroom in 1838, to give an example, was "tastefully ornamented with evergreens," which not only brought the country into the city but was said to have "presented a most interesting appearance, particularly when brilliantly illuminated in the evening." Furthermore, it was not the social standing or ancestry of the women overseeing the sales but, reportedly, their "bright eyes" that "won many a purchaser."[35]

Middle-class women thus endeavored to keep the fair sober and morally upright. A sale the Balls organized to assist the Seaman's Aid Society was typical of the kind of event deemed appropriate. At this "bazaar," there were "no grab-boxes, lotteries or raffles." As the circular announcing the sale explained:

If we cannot obtain funds without resorting to them, we shall cheerfully submit to failure. . . . In the absence of exciting and corrupting chance games,
the Bazaar will more than supply the place, in that eloquent and impressive
hall [Faneuil Hall], with sublime thoughts, and inspiring martial and vocal
music, will entertain and delight the visitors, both old and young. [36]

One of the main projects of women in the Massachusetts Female
Emancipation Society to benefit their 1841 fair was the production of the
Star of Emancipation. This small, unassuming paperbound giftbook was
undertaken as a direct competitor to Maria Chapman's annual miscellany,
the *Liberty Bell*, which the radical had begun publishing in 1839 as part of
her Fair of Individuals. Filled with poems, essays, and correspondence,
both the *Star of Emancipation* and the *Liberty Bell* hoped to reveal the
horrors of slavery in an attractive, salable format. Yet, despite similarities in
design and content, the competing volumes, like the fairs for which they
were produced, reveal striking differences between the two factions in the
Boston Female Anti-Slavery Society.

Emblazoned with a ringing bell and the inscription "Proclaim Liberty to
ALL the Inhabitants," the *Liberty Bell* represents Chapman's major editorial and literary output before 1860. Since prominence and celebrity
were central to Chapman's reform agenda, she used her influence, connections, and sheer boldness to procure original pieces from some of America's
premier literary and intellectual figures. As a result, the *Liberty Bell*
contains submissions by Ralph Waldo Emerson, Harriet Beecher Stowe,
James Russell Lowell, Margaret Fuller, Henry Wadsworth Longfellow,
Caroline Kirkland, and Bayard Taylor, as well as offerings by abolition
luminaries like William Lloyd Garrison, David and Lydia Maria Child,
Lucretia Mott, Theodore Parker, Wendell Phillips, and Edmund Quincy.

The upper-class activist proved fearless and unrelenting in her pursuit of
this type of contributor to her volumes. Typical of Chapman's approach
was a note penned to Charles Sumner regarding the 1842 edition. "May I
not depend on you for *the Cause's* sake, for a page or two for the Liberty
Bell?" she pressed, and in compliance with her wishes Sumner offered a
letter written to him by Samuel Gridley Howe that contained "a most
harrowing sketch of a scene which he [Howe] witnessed in a Southern
prison." Sumner indicated that Howe was in agreement that this missive
"should be published as a testimony against Slavery." [37]

Chapman also used the *Liberty Bell* to introduce Americans to prominent European writers and intellectuals, thereby connecting Boston activ-

ists to an international radical community. The cosmopolitanism of her miscellany is especially noteworthy in that at the time giftbooks, as a genre, were aggressively nationalistic, confusing parochialism with patriotism.[38] The majority of Chapman's foreign contributors were British and included Elizabeth Barrett Browning, Lady Byron, and Harriet Martineau, as well as the poet Bernard Barton, diplomat and linguist Sir John Bowring, and author-reformer Richard M. Milnes. Chapman also solicited material from notable Europeans of the stature of Alexis de Tocqueville and Victor Hugo, as well as French historians Jules Michelet and Jean Jacques Ampère, Swedish novelist Fredrika Bremer, Russian revolutionary Nikolai Turgenev, and Italian patriot Giuseppe Mazzini.

In contrast to Chapman's impressive material, the Massachusetts Female Emancipation Society's *Star of Emancipation* claimed "no great pretensions." As the evangelical women modestly explained, "We do not intend to vie with Virgil or Shakespeare." In their view, "If our 'Star' shines from the right point in the moral heavens, and with a certain light, though it be not one of the first magnitude, it serves the end at which we aim—the deliverance of the bound."[39]

The *Star of Emancipation* had an admittedly undistinguished group of contributors, though the women proudly included a piece of correspondence from the famous English abolitionist Thomas Clarkson. For the most part, however, New England clergymen and women charity workers, including some Massachusetts Female Emancipation Society members, composed the poems and essays that appeared in the small volume. Chapman, knowing that in many cases the contributor's name was as valuable as his or her message, almost always attributed authorship in the *Liberty Bell*. By contrast, articles in the *Star of Emancipation* often were anonymous.

Many of the topics and images that held emotional or ideological significance for middle-class women are present in the pages of their giftbook. Predictably, religious themes predominate, both as the source of antislavery sentiment and as a solution to slavery's misery. For example, a poem by an anonymous E.B. offers religion as balm to the slave.

> *Religion* gives the Captive scope,
> 'Mid galling chains to find his *hope*,
> And with oppression's iron rod
> May find sweet refuge in his God.[40]

Elsewhere, evangelicals' literary efforts dwell on nature and rural scenes—the "lovely-lit vale," the "odorous breeze," a tree's "branches waving free"—when expressing goodness, happiness, serenity, and, of course, liberty. In a poem "suggested by hearing of the death of Mary S. Parker," Martha Ball depicts heaven as a rural environment where "breezes soft fan the good and loved of earth," thereby conjoining religion with nature.[41]

Domestic images are also powerful devices in female evangelicals' anti-slavery literature, as a poem by C. L. North of Lowell entitled "Where Is the Captive's Home?" illustrates.

> *Where is my home?* the captive sighed,
> Where is that spot so dear?
> 'Tis not in all this land abroad
> My home—it is not here.
> I know this land is passing fair
> But 'tis not dear to me;
> While slavery's galling chain I wear
> My home it cannot be.[42]

In "The Refugee Mother in Canada," Sarah Dymond describes the flight of a female slave to prevent her child from being sold. Appealing to Queen Victoria, the author, in the voice of the slave, beseeches:

> Look on thy own young child, and list
> With patient ear to me:
> I am a mother too—my heart,
> like thine, with love o'erflows
> *Thou* know'st a mother's joys, but *I*
> only a mother's woes.[43]

One of the more touching articles in the *Star of Emancipation* is a tribute to Mary Parker. Typical of obituaries written at that time, the essay invokes many of the esteemed virtues of the middle-class, evangelical woman. "Her character was a rare compound of feeling and judgment," the author recalls, "of retiring delicacy and Christian faithfulness—of sweet humility, and heroic boldness in defending the cause of truth—of feminine reserve and unconquerable energy and perseverance." Parker's "crowning excellence," however, was her "consistent, devoted piety." Finally, the former Boston Female Anti-Slavery Society president's "patient endurance and perseverance in well-doing, under reproach and obloquy," was held up as a "precious legacy to all who are bearing the burden and heat of the day, in any portion of the field."[44]

The Massachusetts Female Emancipation Society produced only one edition of the *Star of Emancipation*, whereas Chapman published the *Liberty Bell* annually until 1857. Likewise, within a few years after the rupture in the Boston Female Anti-Slavery Society, evangelical women discontinued holding regular fairs or bazaars to raise money for their benevolent causes, as they shifted their efforts over to the Boston Female Moral Reform Society. Moral reformers rarely sponsored fairs; its leaders preferred direct appeals, dues, and journal subscriptions for funds. Later on, to earn money the moral reform society operated an employment agency, and their house of refuge for homeless, pregnant, or otherwise troubled women sold articles made by the home's inmates. The treasurer's report for 1858, for example, shows that the society collected $1,368 in dues and donations, $894 from journal subscriptions, $478 from the employment office, and $417 from work performed at the temporary home.[45] The more conservative Baptist Sewing and Social Circle, formed by Judith Shipley and other disgruntled Boston Female Anti-Slavery Society members, seldom engaged in direct fund raising of any sort. Instead, the Baptist women created articles to be donated directly to individuals in response to specific needs. The society did elect a treasurer each year, but it appears that no treasurer's report was ever produced.

The struggle for control of the Boston Female Anti-Slavery Society fair and its earnings reveals the tremendous importance of the annual fundraiser. For one thing, the fair was the society's most visible public enterprise, and it was the major event for women abolitionists throughout New England. Each year contributions poured in from local women's societies, giving modest organizations a sustaining purpose. "What a training are the fairs to the younger members of the cause," Maria Chapman once exclaimed. "How are the co-operative faculties educated and improved." Middle-class representative Abigail Ordway similarly enthused that these collective efforts toward the fair "invariably tend to promote industry and economy and also improve the intellect as well as to cultivate the benevolent and social feelings of the heart."[46]

Second, fair work like sewing and baking was conducted within customary arenas of female activity, providing a noncontroversial way in which women of all political persuasions could assist the cause. Similarly, in the guise of visiting, others collected items for the sale, as an 1836 letter by Anne Weston suggests. "I called upon Mrs. Shipley to warn her to attend the meeting of the fair committee at our house Saturday. Mrs. S. gave me a

137

very nice veil for the fair which was valued at 12 dollars. I then called upon Mrs. Sibley [another fair participant] who is a pretty looking little creature. Then called at the Rooms, but there was no news."[47] In these ways, the fair capitalized upon and politicized traditional female functions.

Third, unlike the typical vanity fairs put on by antebellum women to raise money for charity, Boston abolitionists used their sales to expound publicly their religious and political beliefs. Banners reading "Let the oppressed go free and break every yoke," "Freedom and truth—by these we conquer," and "Remember them that are in bonds as bound with them" publicized women's antislavery ideology. Smaller items such as bowls bearing the slogan "Sugar not made by slaves" and iron-handlers labeled "non-slave-holders" suggested ways in which women, even in the household, could comment upon, if not directly influence, social policy.

In practical terms, the fair was crucial to the operation of the abolition movement in New England. In fact, it has been estimated that the twenty-four Boston Female Anti-Slavery Society fairs alone raised over $65,000 for the cause.[48] As significant as this money was, the fair assumed a symbolic importance far beyond monetary rewards. The annual fundraiser brought abolitionists together for sociability and profit while creating a public image of respectability, prosperity, and, for a time, solidarity.[49] The sale abounded with symbols and slogans that recalled abolitionist triumphs and sacrifices, as in 1836 when the fair managers displayed a new "Anti-Slavery Rooms" sign to replace the one destroyed by the Garrison Mob, or in 1839 when tables were decorated with silver vases filled with bouquets of wood from the demolished Pennsylvania Hall. In short, the Boston Female Anti-Slavery Society fair was central to the economic and emotional sustenance of the abolition movement, and the struggle over its control consumed not just women in the organization but most abolitionists, male and female, throughout the region.

Maria Weston Chapman was exultant over the ultimate defeat of the evangelical women who had dared arrogate to themselves control over the fair. In Chapman's view, the Massachusetts Female Emancipation Society's discontinuation of the fair was a sure sign that other activists had utterly repudiated those "treacherous" abolitionists who had plotted to make the Boston Female Anti-Slavery Society a "mere appendage of a proslavery church."[50] Yet the Balls and other middle-class activists were not seeking success on Chapman's terms, and their withdrawal from fairs as a moneymaking venture was not an admission of defeat but a recognition that their interests and skills lay elsewhere. Moral and religious constraints kept middle-class sales modest and austere. Since the radical elites had transformed the nature and extent of female fund raising, middle-class reformers sought alternative sources of income. In the long run, the philosophy and style of both these factions would have far-reaching implications for nineteenth-century women.[51]

Models of Womanhood within the
Boston Female Anti-Slavery Society

As one of its first official acts, the Boston Female Anti-Slavery Society invited Lydia Maria Child, the esteemed author of *An Appeal in Favor of That Class of Americans Called Africans,* to join their group. Child hesitated at first. As she graciously communicated to President Charlotte Phelps, though she appreciated the society's recognition of her work, her "sympathies do not, and never have, moved freely in this project."[1] Later, Child confided to Lucretia Mott: "I never have entered very earnestly into the plan of female conventions and societies. They always seemed to me like half a pair of scissors." Maria Weston Chapman agreed: "We think that the best hopes of the sexes are in each other," she wrote in 1837, "and that the plan of separate sources of knowledge, and separate means of mental and moral improvement is likely to produce a characteristic difference fatal to the happiness and usefulness of both."[2]

Well before the "woman question" arose, some abolitionists worried about the wisdom of gender-segregated activities and were reluctant to become involved in the Boston Female Anti-Slavery Society. Yet a number of these women, despite their different denominational affiliations and socioeconomic backgrounds, were persuaded by the crime of slavery (and the early organizing efforts of men like Garrison and Child's husband David) that concerted action was necessary.

In aligning themselves with the evangelical-based Boston Female Anti-Slavery Society, white, upper-class Unitarians and Quakers quickly came up against custom and tradition that limited women's functions within religious associations. On a number of occasions, radicals submitted to cultural expectation either by disguising their agency or by undertaking certain actions independently and not as society representatives. Angelina and Sarah Grimké, for example, did not receive a salary from the American Anti-Slavery Society for the work they performed as abolition lecturers. In this way the men's organization could not be accused of employing women. Similarly, leaders of the Massachusetts Anti-Slavery Society often gathered at Maria Weston Chapman's home instead of at their offices so as to "have the benefit of the ladies' advice," as Anne Weston put it, without including women at official, policy-making meetings.[3] And though the Boston Female Anti-Slavery Society hired Amos Phelps as their agent in 1836, members let the public assume that the minister represented the Massachusetts Anti-Slavery Society instead, anticipating that Phelps would be "more favorably received."[4]

Increasingly, Boston Female Anti-Slavery Society elites, their social consciences being stronger than their regard for white middle-class cultural prescription, overstepped the boundaries of appropriate public behavior for females. Sarah Southwick, for example, told of the unusual presence of women at a public forum held in Faneuil Hall in December 1837. The forum had been organized by Boston leaders to consider the murder of Ohio abolitionist Elijah Lovejoy at the hands of a mob, and Southwick recalled that, although "women at that time were not in the habit of attending political gatherings of any kind," a "handful of them, thirteen in all, made the venture at this time and ranged themselves in the front seat of the right gallery as one enters the Hall. After that, Anti-Slavery women, certainly, always went when they wanted to."[5] Probably the significance of women attending this particular political meeting has been overdrawn, but Southwick's recollection suggests the extent to which they perceived themselves to be making important inroads for women's political rights.

Boston Female Anti-Slavery Society elites grew restive under the restraints imposed upon their activities by evangelical abolitionists—male and female—and the hypocrisy of hiding the prominent role that they played in the movement in New England. In dealing with their colleagues, they increasingly insisted that they be allowed to assume responsibility for their actions. For instance, in early 1838 the society sponsored a series of lectures by the Grimkés in the city's largest theater, the Odeon. During the planning, Anne Weston complained that "the brethren thought that the matter of the lectures was altogether in their hands, that they had to settle everything." Resentful of this cavalier interference, women "stepped in and informed them that we should *transact* this business and they, finding we were not to be guided by their superior wisdom, gave in."[6] On another occasion, Anne and Caroline Weston walked with Amos Phelps to the Anti-Slavery Rooms where a meeting of a committee of the Massachusetts Anti-Slavery Society was just getting underway. Upon being asked to join the discussion, Caroline jokingly commented that she "threw the whole burden of introducing women into the Committee upon Mr. Phelps." According to Anne, "This made a laugh, but it was a constrained one on the part of Mr. P. To say the truth, he is so sensitive on this subject that he can not laugh about it."[7]

By 1839 radical elites in the Boston Female Anti-Slavery Society would not be satisfied with less than an official role within male abolition societies, each person ready, as Anne Weston said, "to man or rather *woman* her point to the last."[8] In their view it was an "immoral custom" and an "unutterable wrong" to continue to disguise women's power within the antislavery movement. To limit women's participation to "that subservient capacity" of auxiliary had the effect of excluding them "except as beasts of burden." Henceforth, Chapman declared, women would no longer act "slavishly by permission, but freely by inward determination."[9]

Initially, white evangelical women were swept along with the elites' defense of women's rights within the antislavery movement. As Mrs. Low, wife of a local tailor, once exclaimed, she "could not see how any *woman* could sanction for a moment, a society which would put a plaster on her mouth, tie her feet, and leave her hands to be used as cat's paws." So, bravely, they joined with the Chapmanites in support of Sarah and Angelina Grimké against those who would deny them the opportunity to testify against slavery. "Mary Parker sent us word that the Boston women would stand by us if *every* body else forsook us," wrote Angelina Grimké after the publication of the "Pastoral Letter." Accordingly, Sarah Grimké addressed her *Letters on the Equality of the Sexes* to Congregationalist Mary Parker, as president and representative of the entire Boston Female Anti-Slavery Society.[10]

These *Letters*, especially Grimké's claim that males had misrepresented Scripture in asserting the inferiority of women, elicited much comment among women abolitionists and helped bring into focus both evangelicals' and elites' opinions regarding women's roles and responsibilities. Eventually, however, evangelicals rejected Grimké's advanced views on the equality of the sexes and reasserted the legitimacy of traditional biblical teachings. As one anonymous woman remarked in her critique of Grimké's work, "I want women to understand their rights before they quarrel for them, and I want also that they should believe and reverence the holy scriptures, even though they teach *submission*."[11]

In their writings on women's sphere, the evangelical middle class endorsed the patriarchal household and defended hierarchical family structure. "God designed that man should be our protector, the guardian of our peace, our happiness and our honor," they maintained. Moreover, according to the Bible, "Man is always considered as the head of the family and woman as the helper." Evangelicals wondered, "How could a well-disciplined family ever be expected to exist where both parents claimed the right to rule?" Marriage, then, required "concession and submission" on the part of women, and "the more cheerful and voluntary the submission, the happier the results."[12]

Middle-class women in the Boston Female Anti-Slavery Society believed that a well-regulated society, like a properly functioning family, was ordered around the natural distinctions between the sexes. "The idea that there is no difference in the moral and intellectual capacities of men and women," asserted one female reformer, is "utterly at variance with the whole tenor of scripture." Another anonymous woman explained that males and females had "their own peculiar stations . . . assigned by the Creator," and each sex must be prepared to "fulfill these immutable obligations." Directly addressing Grimké's claims for expanded freedom of action and opportunity for women, she added, "The wonderful adaptation of each [sex], is calculated to produce such perfect regularity and harmony, that when either swerves from its appropriate sphere, one of the beauties of creation is destroyed."[13]

In articulating their ideology regarding white women's roles, middle-class evangelicals relied on the biblical teachings of Paul, which reinforced the idea that women's primary sphere of action must be in the home. An anonymous contributor to the *Friend of Virtue* outlined women's requisite duties. "It is evident that the domestic duties belong appropriately to the sphere of *woman*," she wrote, "for 1st she is to sustain the relations of wife and mother; 2d, she is to regulate the affairs of her household; and 3rd, she is to exercise hospitality." Finally, "as circumstances and situation" allowed, a woman should "employ herself in some of those works of love and mercy, which are incumbent on our race in general."[14]

Middle-class women also felt that a girl should be specifically educated for "the station she is to fill." Any "talents or acquirements she may possess" must be regarded "as so many auxiliaries to be employed for the good of her household and the well being of her race." Evangelicals condemned "modern fashionable" women who, despite expensive educations, were unable "to darn a stocking or boil a potato or roast a bit of beef." Furthermore, "a good temper" and a "look of cheerfulness" were of higher value "than many more brilliant endowments."[15]

Middle-class women's progression from questioning women's circumscribed sphere of action to reaffirming women's primary responsibility in the home was reflected in the benevolent organizations they operated. The Boston Female Moral Reform Society is a good case in point. Initially, moral reformers were concerned about the plight of single, self-supporting women newly arrived in Boston. As discussed earlier, the society established a halfway house and an employment agency, as well as providing other social services, for independent women in the city. The society's journal, the *Friend of Virtue*, was filled with true-confession-type articles that exposed the dangers awaiting unsupervised, hence unprotected, women. It also ran forums on women's rights and other political issues of the day.

In 1839, however, a number of more liberal Boston Female Anti-Slavery Society members, including Thankful and Sarah Southwick, Mary Ann Johnson, and Abigail Ordway, seceded from the moral reform group to form the New England Golden Rule Association. According to Ordway, the Balls had "acted quite as bad" in the moral reform society as they had among the abolitionists.[16] After this division, the Balls' moral reform group increasingly avoided political issues such as women's rights to concentrate upon the maternal and domestic roles of women. By the mid 1850s the *Friend of Virtue* added regular features like "The Mother's Bureau" and "The Children's Fireside" to its columns. Finally, in the early 1860s editor Martha Ball changed the name of the journal to the *Home Guardian*, signaling the triumph of domesticity.

According to the evangelical middle class, then, white women's assigned station entailed submitting to male authority, limiting their sphere of action to the private world of home and family, denying personal talents or interests save those that impinged upon the household, and doing so cheerfully and willingly. As Martha Ball once wrote, "Marriage is to woman at once the happiest and the saddest event of her life."[17] However, evangelical women were not unaffected by the feminist stirrings of their colleagues, and feminist language and ideas frequently found their way into evangelicals' writings. Moreover, by developing what one activist termed an "enlightened scriptural" definition of womanhood, evangelicals modified some of the more oppressive strictures regarding woman's sphere.[18]

For one thing, evangelicals made it clear that they did not equate female domesticity with female inferiority. As one woman wrote, "Difference in character and condition does not necessarily imply inferiority." The duties of both sexes, agreed another, were "assigned by the Creator without superiority conferred on the one or degradation imposed on the other." This separate-but-equal philosophy enabled Congregational and Baptist women simultaneously to uphold the ideal of male authority and advocate a limited version of women's rights. These reformers sought to "elevate woman as a moral and intellectual being" as a way of fulfilling her domestic responsibilities, not to make "a farmer or politician of her." Thus the typical argument ran: "I am not so much for elevating woman *out* of her present sphere, as for elevating her *in it*."[19]

This redefinition of the patriarchal household also encouraged middle-class women to modify the more oppressive interpretations of the "divine law of female subjugation." In an angry editorial on Hubbard Winslow's *Woman as She Should Be* (1838), the *Friend of Virtue* dismissed the scriptural writings of Boston's Bowdoin Street Congregational Church minister as "grossly insulting." The reviewer took particular offense at Winslow's contention that the test of female excellence is found in the "consciousness" of her "inferiority to man." Such pronouncements, the woman protested, converted "the holy and pure institution of marriage into the relationship of master and servant." In short, the evangelical woman could "speak and think and act in her appropriate sphere" and should do so "in obedience to the commands of God rather than of man."[20]

Nowhere was this enhanced appreciation of white women's status within the home better revealed than in the heightened expectations accorded personal relationships. Religious strictures regarding male authority were deemphasized while the cooperative, companionate features of married life were accentuated. "God made *woman* and brought her to man," evangelicals explicated, because "it was not good for man to be alone" and his "happiness was not complete without her."[21] Moreover, strong emotional ties between husband and wife were considered imperative to the stability of the middle-class household, for a cheerful and competent wife helped her mate cope with the stress and insecurity of the urban workplace. In February 1839 the *Friend of Virtue* put forth this idealized bourgeois household scene.

The husband goes forth in the morning to his professional duties—he cannot foresee what trial he may encounter—what failure of hopes, of friendships, or of prospects may meet him before he returns to his home; but if he can anticipate that the beaming and hopeful smile, and the soothing attention will meet him there, he feels that his cross, whatever it may be, will be lightened, and that his domestic happiness is still secure.[22]

Woman's authority over her body, particularly reproduction, emerged as another important feature of the cooperative, companionate marriage. Moral reformers were extremists on the subject of sexual exploitation, and their writings reflected a growing assertiveness on the part of women against this often hidden form of male oppression. Men's "trampling" upon women's honor "with impunity" would be tolerated no longer, evangelicals announced, and they condemned "*covetous* men" whose lust threatened "all those hallowed joys which flow from domestic relations." Marriage must represent more than "mere sensual gratification," middle-class women maintained, and be a source of "mutual improvement, *spiritual* benefit, [and] social progress."[23]

Middle-class women recognized the universality of women's lives regardless of race, ethnicity, or socioeconomic status and considered women to be a distinct class, often arrayed against men. As one woman remarked in an open letter to Sarah Grimké, all "females must be daughters, wives, and mothers" with the same maternal and domestic duties to attend. This same sisterhood extended to morally and economically needy women as well. Prostitutes were referred to as "fallen sisters," and they were pitied as once "respectable and innocent girls from the country" who had been duped by the "treachery and depravity of man." Female slaves became "our colored sisters" who likewise were "so cruelly and unmercifully subjected to the brutal lusts and appetites" of southern men.[24]

Having elevated women's status and power within the home and promoted gender solidarity without, white evangelicals proceeded to use these ideals to encourage women's participation in the social and political movements of the day. These women believed they had an important role to play in urban public life precisely because of the unique sensibilities of their sex. "There is a distinction in the nature of woman's power and man's power in the promotion of the same great objects," argued the *Friend of Virtue*. The magazine urged every woman to make use of "those peculiarities" which comprised "the very elements of her strength" to better glorify God and benefit mankind.[25] As the women of the Massachusetts Female Emancipation Society declared:

If woman has nothing to do with politics, then she has nothing to do with the rising generation; then she has no duty to her husband—none to her neighbor—in fine, none to the world. . . . We cannot live without exerting a *direct* influence on the destiny of our country, and how important is it that we understand its policy and give our proportion of effort to increase its stability.[76]

As a result of this appreciation for women's political potential, many evangelical women joined their radical sisters in becoming members of the New England Anti-Slavery Society and the Massachusetts Anti-Slavery Society when these organizations admitted women for the first time.[27]

Regardless of their advocacy of women's duty to be socially aware and politically active and their initial interest in joining male societies, middle-class reformers were still loath to abandon their female-only societies or renounce their customary role in the movement. After the defection of many clerical abolitionists, middle-class women, for the most part, quit their memberships in the Garrison-controlled men's societies to affiliate with the evangelical New Organization. Ultimately, they preferred to organize their charities as they did their households, with each sex having important but separate roles to play. Evangelical women endorsed Lewis Tappan's assertions that "women have equal rights with men." As the New York evangelical explained: "They have a right to form societies of women only. Men have the same right."[28] Within their female-only organizations, women were able to retain control over their operations and thus maintain relative independence.

Boston Female Anti-Slavery Society Unitarians and Quakers were frustrated by the traditionalism of evangelical women and accused them of being both ignorant and servile in their continued deference to male authorities. A disgusted Maria Weston Chapman felt that Congregational and Baptist women like the Parkers and Balls had been efficient, even courageous, laborers for the cause "when they fancied the enterprise under the blessing and direction of a portion of the ministry." But, the Unitarian leader lamented, "no sooner did it appear that they must advance alone and self-sustained, than they turned to flight." Radical elites also disparaged the limited ambition of their middle-class colleagues. In a November 1839 *Liberator* article describing the society's activities under the direction of Mary Parker, Catherine Sullivan, and the Balls, the reporter, probably Maria Weston Chapman, could not refrain from noting: "The society which in former years established the right of slaves brought into the state, to their freedom, recorded as one of their most important efforts the transmission of a box of fancy articles to the Hon. Mr. Elmore."[29]

White upper-class women in the Boston Female Anti-Slavery Society resisted the social and personal constraints imposed upon them by the evangelicals' doctrine of separate spheres. As Chapman once declared, "We experience no inclination to contract our sphere of usefulness on the ground that its present enlargement will shock the prejudices of the world." So while the Boston Female Anti-Slavery Society board was organizing a "day of fasting, humiliation and prayer" to benefit the slaves, Chapman and associates aggressively pursued an increasingly political agenda.[30]

Angelina Grimké was perhaps the first female abolitionist to proclaim publicly this emerging philosophy regarding women's political and social rights. At the first women's antislavery convention, held just prior to the Grimkés' lecture tour of Massachusetts in 1837, Angelina announced from the podium: "The time has come for woman to move in that sphere which Providence has assigned her and no longer remain satisfied in the circumscribed limits with which corrupt custom and a perverted application of Scripture have encircled her."[31]

Unitarians and Quakers in the Boston Female Anti-Slavery Society were responsive to Grimké's call for a reinterpretation, indeed a feminist interpretation, of the Bible to create a more authentic sphere of action for women. As Maria Chapman wrote several months after Grimké's speech, "Scripture has generally been presented to woman through a distorted medium. She is fettered in body and in mind by commentators and translators and partial reasoners, but by revelation never. What is the sphere and duty of woman, it rests with each one for herself to interpret." Elite women thus refused to back away from women's equality in the antislavery movement. "When a man advises me to withdraw from a society or convention, or not to act there according to the dictates of my own judgment," Child asserted, "I am constrained to reply, 'Thou canst not touch the freedom of my soul. I deem that I have duties to perform here.' "[32]

White elites clearly discerned the ways in which social structures and cultural assumption combined to subjugate women. In an early issue of the *Friend of Virtue*, an anonymous contributor attempted to impress upon readers the extent to which tradition and society inhibited women. In "our own happy America," she bitterly observed,

> Man is permitted to treat [a woman] as he likes; he has by means of the press of which he has the control, by means of the pulpit which he exclusively

occupies, and by means of the duties which are required of woman, and which in most cases leave her little leisure to think of her own rights, or to write in their defense, created a public sentiment, that renders it disgraceful for a wife even to complain of her husband however she may be treated by him.[33]

In rejecting the white middle-class ideology of woman's sphere, upper-class abolitionists believed that the rights and duties of females and males were the same. "In all spiritual things, their functions are identical," argued Chapman in an 1837 circular to female antislavery societies in New England. "With respect to secondary pursuits—whether mercantile, mechanical, domestic or professional," she added, "the tools to whosoever can use them. All are alike bound to the free and strenuous exercise of such faculties as God has given them."[34]

Unitarians and Quakers scoffed at evangelicals' reiteration that women, by nature and predisposition, were different from men. As a leading proponent of women's rights within the abolition movement, Lydia Maria Child discussed this subject at length in her response to a *Friend of Virtue* article on the "female character." "In the Gospel there is no such sexual classification of virtues," Child argued. "*All* are instructed to be pure, meek, and gentle, yet strong and fearless in the discharge of Christian duty." Citing not Scripture but what she termed the "Book of Life," Child maintained that the source of gender-based distinctions and inequality could be found in American "laws, customs, popular preaching, current literature, and every-day conversations."[35] This controversy was not over "*woman's* rights," agreed Maria Chapman, but over "*person's* rights."[36]

Elites were skeptical of evangelicals' assurances that men and women could occupy different stations yet enjoy the same status and privileges. Despite evangelicals' modifications in the hierarchical family structure, upper-class activists associated the patriarchal household with continued female subjugation. Sarah Grimké voiced radicals' reservations in a response to evangelical reformers' assertion that "God *designed* that man should be our protector." This widespread and "pernicious" sentiment, declared Grimké, exalted man "into a deity" and degraded woman "into a being whose peace and happiness are dependent upon man." In Child's opinion as well, women gained little from time-honored "chivalry" and therefore should demand the "respect due [women] from representatives of a free and enlightened people."[37]

Although the society's elites were concerned with freedom and oppor-

tunity, they did not associate women's equality with economic independence. Preoccupied with abstract ideals, wealthy abolitionists fairly ignored
the plight of the urban working woman, save for individual distress that
came to their attention. "Friday Miss Grey called," wrote Anne Weston of
one such situation. "She wants to get a place as housekeeper or she will be
willing to sew. I promised her I would inquire all around among my
friends." Weston goes on to admit that she "pitied her very much, more
than I need to I suppose for where I have $1, I dare say she had $10, but
then she is more dependent on herself than I am. She has properly no
home, which is a sad thing."[38]

Upper-class activists disapproved of middle-class women like Abigail
Ordway and Lucy and Martha Ball who accepted wages for performing the
social work that leisured females handled voluntarily. In fact, elites once
opposed a measure that would have funded a female agent to manage the
day-to-day operations of the Boston Female Anti-Slavery Society. In voting
against the motion, they declared it was an "unnecessary expenditure"
since they had been "happy to perform" these tasks for the "love of the
cause alone." As Deborah Weston commented to sister Anne, "$252 a year
for an agent, that would be a very pretty income for Miss Ball, & I dont
doubt has been her object from the beginning."[39] Upper-class activists thus
were insensitive to some of their colleagues' financial needs and their
attempts to support themselves through reform-related employment.

Not surprisingly, then, evangelicals evinced more sensitivity than did
the elites to single and working women's situation. However, middle-class
activism in behalf of female laborers, including themselves, cannot be
construed as a particularly liberal feminist interpretation, for evangelicals'
primary concern was that working women adequately meet their maternal
and domestic duties. As an editorial in the *Friend of Virtue* made clear:
"Think not that we are about to vindicate the Rights of Women so called.
We do not intend to assert their right to vote or to go to Congress. We claim
for them what you grant your ox and your horse—a bare living."[40]

Because liberal abstractions concerning the inviolability of human rights
formed the basis of the elites' ideology, their public writings contained few
of the domestic images that permeated evangelicals' rhetoric. In private
documents as well, the domestic scenes portrayed by women like the Westons were less idealized and less stylized than those depicted by the Balls and
others of the middle class, openly displaying more ambivalence about
prescribed domestic roles. In a letter to her sister Deborah, Anne commented on her disappointment with Henry B. Stanton; "I doubt whether

he'll do for you," she concluded. Anne then proceeded to describe a marriage proposal she spurned. "Now I am to tell you a thing that will amuse
you and some what interest you," she began. Later in this missive, Anne
moves into a less flippant, more regretful frame of mind. "I have heard that
every body has one chance. I am fearful that this is mine."[41] As it turned
out, it was.

Children, as well, elicited not altogether joyous feelings among the
Westons. In December 1836 Anne received what she described as a "fearful
piece of news"—Maria was pregnant. Elsewhere, Anne wrote of her young
nephew: "We have been much tried with little Henry. He acts like sin; we
think it is because he is in boy's clothes."[42] Although a productive mother
herself, Maria Chapman had reservations about combining childrearing
and creative activity and expressed the opinion that intellectual achievement was not to be expected from women raising families and that superior
women should not marry at all.[43]

Whereas evangelicals believed that women should devote their energy
and talents to domestic work, the correspondence and diaries of the Westons and their friends contain very few references to homemaking per se. Of
course, most household items were available for purchase in Boston, and
Chapman and other upper-class abolitionists enjoyed the assistance of
female servants. Sarah Southwick, for example, recalled that during her
teenage years living on High Street the family had two servants: "one a
trusted colored woman, Phillis Salem, who lived with us twenty-five years;
the other a stupid Irish girl."[44] Similarly, descriptions of the Garrison Mob
mention the fact that during the evening Chapman courageously sent her
servants away to save them from becoming involved in an anticipated
second attack.

Regardless of middle-class criticisms about the domestic ineptitude of
"fashionable" women, those of the urban, white, upper class did continue
to sew, knit, and perform other handwork. "The thermometer stands at 22
degrees below zero," Deborah Weston mentioned in her diary on a winter's
day in 1835. "Have been trying all day to knit and to keep warm, but did not
succeed very well in either." Nonetheless, wealthy women generally employed a tailoress or upholstress to handle the more laborious and func-
tional sewing, thus freeing the females of the elite household to pursue
more creative, expressive work. In Weymouth, the Westons used the
services of a Mrs. White, as indicated in Deborah's diary entry: "Mrs.
White here to cut my gown." At other times, Weston mentions sewing
pillows, cuffs, pelisses, and other decorative pieces herself.[45]

Feminism and independence notwithstanding, the lives of wealthy women—as with their middle-class counterparts—continued to revolve around family and personal relationships. The correspondence among them is an admixture of abolition gossip and family news detailing the health, personal entanglements, and comings and goings of friends and relatives. The complex Weston–Chapman households seem to have had a rotating membership, as brothers, sisters, nieces, nephews, and in-laws moved between three homes in Boston, brother Henry's residence in Cambridge, and the family compound in Weymouth. Extended family relationships also meant that domestic and childrearing duties were shared among many individuals. Typical was Mother Weston's suggestion that she care for Maria's little Henry while the Chapmans take brother Warren into their household. There was similar cooperation in caring for the ill, as a letter from Caroline telling of the afternoons she devoted to nursing her dying brother-in-law illustrated.[46]

Perhaps one ramification of this extended network of family and social relationships among the upper class was a more elastic conception of gender roles than that of the evangelical middle class. As discussed at the outset of this chapter, radical elites were, for the most part, opposed to female-only organizations, considering them to be a holdover of corrupt and outdated custom. In fact, Chapman admitted that after the division of the Boston Female Anti-Slavery Society she would have preferred dropping the word "female" from the society's name and replacing it with a "choicer" one. But to make such an alteration at that point, she decided, would give "credence to the idea" that the women's society "had undergone some change in principle or condition."[47]

The challenge of the woman question forced white upper- and middle-class Boston Female Anti-Slavery Society members to confront their feelings regarding women's sphere of action and articulate an ideology that would explain their participation in the political world.[48] The evangelicals drew their ideology from Old Testament theology and traditional social arrangements. For the most part Congregationalists and Baptists, they upheld scriptural teachings regarding patriarchy and female submission and conceived of human society as divided into two discrete arenas of activity, the public male sphere and the private female sphere. As a result, they discouraged women's participation in many nondomestic activities, save those connected with church and charity. Within religious and benevolent organizations, evangelicals preferred the role of assistant rather than that of equal. Schooled in self-effacement and self-denial, they expected and accepted the age-old dominance of male household, religious, and political authorities.

Nonetheless, the ideas and language of early feminism subtly influenced evangelicals' thinking. Even Martha Ball once rather forcefully stated that "there is but little doubt that women of this country have it in their power (under God) to overthrow slavery," and she urged members of her sex to rise "in all the dignity in which God hath created them, to supplicate for their sisters in bonds."[49] In reconciling the ideology of separate spheres with expanding expectations of freedom and equality, evangelicals emphasized that women were men's spiritual and moral peers and therefore entitled to certain inalienable rights. Moreover, although women were admittedly different from men in biology and character, they were not inferior. In the eyes of God and society, middle-class women's domestic and maternal responsibilities were certainly as important as the political and economic roles assigned to men.

Ultimately, abstractions regarding human liberty and personal fulfillment proved incompatible with middle-class concerns for self-control and law and order. Still subject to the dark visions of Calvin, evangelical women sought to repress human nature, not release it. Accordingly, middle-class activists quickly converted discussions of women's rights to a litany of women's wrongs. "Do not get into a dispute" with Henry C. Wright over the woman question, Lucy Ball warned Amos Phelps in 1843, "or else we shall have to read the brethren a tract on *Women's Wrongs*." Evangelicals also preferred to dwell not upon women's rights but upon their responsibilities. As one moral reformer from New Hampshire explained, "In asserting and maintaining the *rights* of our sex, we will not forget or neglect our appropriate *duties*." She continued, "The more strongly these duties are enforced, the more definitely marked out, and strictly fulfilled, the better our *rights* will be understood and acknowledged."[50]

Finally, middle-class discussions of women's roles took place within a wider social context as middle-class women compared their life styles to those of other women in Boston. Evangelicals condemned the boisterous, hence immoral, behavior of girls in the city's slums and considered them to be traveling the road to dishonor, prostitution, and death. Middle-class activists were equally critical of what they considered the frivolous and self-indulgent existence of wealthy women and often judged them unfit to raise the next generation of Americans. In short, the development of the cultural and religious strictures composing the ideal type of woman's sphere was connected to the more general process of class formation in antebellum Boston and the emergence of an identifiable middle-class consciousness.

Wealthy women in the Boston Female Anti-Slavery Society also drew upon the cultural predispositions and prejudices of their class in formulating what they considered the rights and responsibilities of women in urban society. As socially committed Unitarians and Quakers, they rejected Old Testament lessons concerning sin, punishment, and submission to worldly authorities, arguing that the Bible had been misrepresented by self-seeking males in order to defend and perpetuate all forms of oppression. Each individual was accountable to God not man and therefore entitled to follow his or her personal, spiritual, and intellectual commission, regardless of strictures laid down by self-appointed rulers and judges. Anne Weston urged women not to let male criticism deter them from participation in liberation movements. "Will you allow these men who have been for years unmindful of their own most solemn duties to prescribe to you yours? Shall . . . they be esteemed by you as fit judges of the sphere you shall occupy?"[51]

Upper-class abolitionists found so-called woman's sphere one of the primary sources of continued female subjugation. According to Chapman, asking women to remain within such circumscribed limits (and, she might have added, to restrict women to tasks better done by servants) was "the most insulting" request "to human nature of all."[52] There were no differences between the sexes, wealthy radicals maintained, save for those created by improper socialization and education, and the time had come for women to assume their proper station as men's social and political equals. As Chapman once declared in connection with Abby Kelley, women would never attain their full potential until they "called no man master."[53]

Perhaps the ideological distinctions between middle-class women who believed in a separate female sphere of activity and upper-class women who sought political and social equality are best captured in the following two quotations. The first, which appeared as a filler in an 1838 issue of the *Friend of Virtue*, was taken from the writings of the Old Testament king and prophet, Solomon: "He that ruleth his own spirit is better than he that ruleth a city." The other, used by Maria Weston Chapman in her disputed 1837 Boston Female Anti-Slavery Society annual report, was drawn from a contemporary, English romantic Thomas Carlyle: "Happy is he who, when a symbol loses its significancy, knows how to substitute another in its place."[54]

The passage from Solomon suggests the extent to which the middle-class construction of separate spheres was built upon female self-abnegation and self-denial, a kind of martyrdom to the needs of home and family. This middle-class preoccupation with self-limitation raises some question as to the liberating potential of its model of womanhood. Though some historians have suggested that the creation of a separate female sphere generated the self-respect, independence, and sex solidarity that were prerequisite to the formulation of a feminist ideology,[55] it appears that the separate-spheres ideology was essentially conservative, recasting, while reaffirming, biblical teachings and society's assumptions regarding women. As Lori Ginzberg has observed, although "the ideology of female benevolence and of a shared female sensibility informed the earliest critiques of men's dominance over women," it also "always sustained the opposite view, one that emphasized the continuance of a social hierarchy based on women's subordination to men."[56] Nancy Hewitt offers a similar critique of the evangelicals' beliefs which, in her view, represented "a self-imposed detour from the feminist path" that involved an "internalization of the tenets of true womanhood . . . combined with the ritual humiliation before God demanded in the conversion experience."[57]

Yet this new middle-class ideology of separate spheres did include a compensatory component wherein women believed that they derived status and influence through the faithful fulfillment of domestic and nurturing roles. Some historians have attributed this liberalization of the patriarchal family to socioeconomic changes and uncertainties that undermined men's traditional authority and increased the significance of women's position in the home.[58] Others have felt that by elevating the female sphere in opposition to the dominant male one, women were able to modify patriarchy without threatening the established organization of the household.[59]

I would add here that middle-class women also formulated the model of separate spheres within the context of their debates with elite women at that time. Thus evangelical women responded to the growing demand among upper-class women for equal rights by incorporating some of the radicals' feminist ideas into their own model of womanhood. However, by refusing to adopt fully the liberal model articulated by their upper-class sisters, middle-class women asserted their right to create an ideology more consistent with their class values and expectations.[60] In doing this, they did indeed seek to rule their "own spirit," to return to Solomon, not only by rejecting some of the more repressive aspects of male domination but also by challenging the dictates of that class of women who, by association, "ruleth a city."

Cultured, cosmopolitan, and irreverent, upper-class women sought to break the bonds of custom and religion and release repressed female potential. Like Carlyle's, theirs was an ideology of liberation and personal fulfillment, as they called for the free expression of women's ideas and personalities regardless of tradition or cultural dictates concerning appropriate feminine decorum. Also as with Carlyle, whose work on great men appeared about this same time, the message of upper-class activists was geared toward New England's cultural and intellectual elite and largely ignored the concerns of lower- and middle-class women.[61]

Boston's early feminists were not drawn from groups outside the socioeconomic mainstream, as historians have found elsewhere.[62] In Boston, upper-class women, with their influential families and familiarity with the local power structure, were the ones demanding equal rights for themselves. Moreover, their feminism was not simply a natural outgrowth of their antislavery rhetoric and experiences[63] but represented an amalgam of religious, political, and philosophical ideals of which antislavery was just a part. During the antislavery schisms, the feminist component of this ideology served as a corrective to the model of separate spheres espoused by their middle-class associates. Indeed, the more middle-class evangelicals reiterated their scriptural beliefs regarding women's predetermined character and roles, the more vehement upper-class women became in advocating individualism and personal freedom.

In sum, the debates within the Boston Female Anti-Slavery Society revealed two models of womanhood—one based upon women's difference from men, the other on women's equality with men. These models appear to have emerged almost simultaneously in response both to socioeconomic change and the ensuing dialog among women and men about this change. Finally, in establishing opposing models of womanhood, Boston's upper- and middle-class female abolitionists expressed fundamentally different beliefs about their personal identities and their appropriate place in contemporary urban society. Individuals working within each of these models found a temporary haven in abolitionism, because the movement's ideology encompassed both a commitment to personal freedom and a concern for family life. But once these activists were forced to examine their positions relative to women's roles in the movement, their ideological differences became irreconcilable.

CHAPTER 8

Conclusion

THE 1830S IN BOSTON WAS A PERIOD OF ENORMOUS SOCIAL, ECONOMIC, AND demographic change, a time of great energy, excitement, and concern. During the decade, the city's population increased more than 50 percent, as men and women, particularly those between the ages of twenty and forty, arrived from rural New England and upstate New York to seek employment in the commercial center. Urban development and redevelopment transformed the city's physical contours and appearance, and the construction of bridges, canals, turnpikes, and railroads more efficiently connected Boston to its agricultural and manufacturing hinterland, reinforcing and expanding the city's position as the financial capital of the region.

Boston's preindustrial elites, individuals who had earned their wealth through mercantile trade, designed and directed much of the city's commercial growth and civic expansion as they adjusted to and profited from the industrialization of the region's economy. In fact, by the end of the decade, Brahmin merchants, bankers, and manufacturers owned over half of the state's resources, including mills, railroads, and real estate developments, as well as the major banks and insurance companies. The upper class also continued to occupy prestigious positions in the city's cultural,

157

educational, and religious institutions and retained a hold over most of the important local, state, and national political seats.

Despite the enduring economic and political dominance of Boston's preindustrial aristocracy, the advent of commercial capitalism precipitated a realignment of the city's social composition. During the 1820s and 1830s, skilled and artisanal segments of the labor force were displaced as unskilled and day laborers at one end of the spectrum and upwardly mobile clerks, businessmen, and professionals at the other found employment in the urban workforce. In the late 1820s and 1830s, these emerging socio-economic groups coalesced into viable political entities and began to challenge the assumed authority of the city's traditional elites. The middle group channeled its social and political impulses into myriad religious, charitable, and political organizations, giving voice to new collective values and goals that expressed their dissatisfaction with the sociopolitical status quo. In what seemed to be scenes of commotion and riot, the lower classes, too, exhibited behaviors and cultural orientations that often were in contradistinction to those promoted by the "respectable" population though, perhaps, more in keeping with life in the urban slum.

Women, of course, also participated in this teeming political, social, and economic world of 1830s Boston. As part of the massive rural-to-urban migration, young single women converged on the city to find work as domestics, seamstresses, boardinghouse keepers, social workers, teachers, and prostitutes. These rural girls represented a new social category: independent, wage-earning women who were able to establish households and life styles that were freer from the traditional constraints of custom and family. To cope with this unprecedented freedom—but also insecurity and relative powerlessness—some women threw themselves into the raucous street life of the urban lower class. Others, mostly the more prosperous, leisured women, established a vital community life for themselves within the city's burgeoning churches and charitable organizations. Indeed, during the antebellum period, women constituted nearly 70 percent of the converts to local evangelical churches, and the number of female charities in Boston nearly tripled. Women's church affiliation and benevolent activities corresponded closely with their socioeconomic background and status, and through their associational commitments they helped define women's images and roles in the emerging class-structured social order.

The history of the Boston Female Anti-Slavery Society is illustrative of this social climate in 1830s Boston and suggests the ways in which women reexamined and redefined their images and roles in urban society. Living and working within a community where traditional lines of social organization and control were becoming blurred, women abolitionists pushed for a more prominent female role in urban public life. At first, the society seemed to follow the models of female activism established by the previous generation of charity workers, since their initial projects involved educating needy children, organizing sewing societies, and hosting bazaars, activities typical of female charities at that time. Yet some society members expanded these socially acceptable women's activities to a national, indeed international, scale, helping to create a new female political style.[1] This political style transformed customary female tasks into politically significant acts and revealed the extent to which established women's networks could be mobilized for common ends.

This portion of Boston's female abolitionists also incorporated traditionally male forms of political action into this new female political style. They attended political rallies, organized conventions, petitioned, gave lectures, engaged in public debates, and even initiated court proceedings. Antislavery women proved so successful in imitating male political styles, and establishing women's right to do so, that they eventually demanded acceptance as equals into male organizations, and by 1845 women were serving as officers, editors, and lecturers at all levels of the abolition and other social movements. As historians of American women have amply demonstrated, future women activists built upon the political precedents set by female abolition groups like the Boston Female Anti-Slavery Society as they pursued women's rights and other reforms later in the century.[2]

The enterprises of the Boston Female Anti-Slavery Society had economic as well as political consequences. Projects like the fair, sales of edited volumes, and the management of dues and donations provided women abolitionists with invaluable entrepreneurial and commercial experience, while the monetary success of these activities gave them an unexpected source of power, at least within reform circles. At first, the women's group automatically donated its earnings to the "parent" male society, but as profits increased members were emboldened to choose which organization or organizations their funds would support. Because of the controversies within the movement, the society also began to designate exactly how its funds should be spent.

Other women's groups concurred with these views concerning female-generated funds. As one member of the New England Female Moral Reform Society asserted in 1838:

Why treat women as if they had no part whatsoever to perform, as if their power and influence must be delegated wholly to men, as if they must exercise no judgment in regard to the disposal of their means, save that they may be permitted to choose into whose hands to deposit their earnings? I believe that when young ladies form sewing circles for the purpose of earning money, they may appropriate those earnings to purposes in which they are more immediately interested.[3]

Women's economic independence, especially the right to control their own resources, would become a central component in the extension of rights to women in the last half of the nineteenth century and thus represents another area in which Boston's female abolitionists confronted prevailing attitudes and customs.[4]

As important as these political and economic consequences were, perhaps the society's most compelling legacy was cultural. As Boston's women abolitionists confronted the controversies that their activities engendered, a dialog among them ensued that clarified their personal beliefs regarding women's rights and responsibilities. After several years of disagreement and debate, two broadly based coalitions emerged—one consisting of women drawn from Boston's established aristocracy, the other composed of women associated with the city's new middle class—each with its own internally consistent explanation of white women's roles in urban society.

Elites envisioned women assuming an equal role in society and politics, working side by side with upper-class men. As the wives, sisters, and daughters of Boston merchants, lawyers, and entrepreneurs and as members of the city's most influential Unitarian, Episcopalian, and, to a lesser extent, Congregational churches, they were well located within the city's traditional authority structure and were accustomed to male definitions and uses of power. It was, by and large, these upper-class women who petitioned Congress, filed lawsuits, published political tracts, and spoke at public rallies, thus adopting male political methods with which they were already quite familiar. At the same time, they politicized women's sphere, using customary upper-class female activities like parties and visiting to advance their reform agenda. Ultimately, they demanded women's full admission into male-controlled organizations and programs, seeing this as a prelude to women gaining complete, unimpeded access to public life.

Although elite women considered Boston's present governmental system corrupt and used nonresistance as a generalized critique of the political status quo, they continued to operate within the hegemonic assumptions of the white, male ruling class.[5] Not only did they adapt male political styles to their own ends, they also continued to direct their political message toward individuals in positions of authority and others among the upper class. They located women's oppression within outdated customs of church and state and reserved some of their harshest criticism for the most visible representatives of these institutions, ministers and politicians. In short, wealthy white abolitionists defined women's equality in republican terms, stressing equal opportunity and self-determination as their primary goals. Karen Offen has termed this approach "individualist feminism,"[6] a political philosophy that seeks to advance women's rights in terms of male political norms. It was thus as republicans that Boston's wealthy women joined the abolition movement in 1833, and it was as republicans, too, that they turned their attention to women's rights after 1837.

Boston's upper-class, white female abolitionists were less interested in women's biological differences from men than in their intellectual and spiritual equality with men, and they argued that women's rights should be based upon liberal ideals regarding human potential and freedom, not upon an elevation or revaluation of established gender roles. They did not consider women as a distinctive political or social category, and they increasingly opposed sex-segregated activities. Rarely did these elite women use female roles or stereotypes to justify their activities or demands, and they expressed only minimal interest in specifically female issues or concerns, particularly those of the working class. Finally, there was little elasticity in their model of womanhood, and they refused to incorporate or even countenance components that might be more relevant to the middle and lower classes. As a result, their women's rights agenda had limited appeal beyond those individuals experienced with and acquiescent to traditional definitions of status and power.

Initially, white middle-class women in the Boston Female Anti-Slavery Society were supportive of the elites' innovative political style and intrigued by their early feminist statements. However, once middle-class women began to have reservations concerning the elites' projects and public behavior, they had difficulty communicating their concerns since they were more accustomed to behind-the-scenes maneuvering than aggressive politicking or open debate. Moreover, upper-class women responded to the reticence expressed by their associates with the presumptions and accustomed authority of their class and simply disregarded middle-class protests and demands. Yet it was during their struggles with upper-class Boston Female Anti-Slavery Society members that middle-class women developed their own model of white womanhood, a model that rejected male (and upper-class) definitions of politics and power and substituted female priorities for status and fulfillment.

Primarily evangelical Congregationalists and Baptists, white middle-class abolitionists articulated what they described as an "enlightened scriptural" definition of women's roles in urban society. Claiming that women's rights resided within the family rather than within politics or commerce, they argued that women should expect a reasonably companionate marriage, should not be subjected to undue sexual demands, should be able to nurture children to their fullest potential, and should have the opportunity to work toward the moral and spiritual betterment of humankind. Middle-class activists also claimed for women access to a limited number of suitable occupations, not for material gain or personal advancement but to earn a living wage so as not to be victimized by men.[7]

In delineating their model of womanhood, middle-class abolitionists also reinterpreted the meaning and uses of gender segregation, transforming it from a form of female subordination to a source of autonomy and political power.[8] Whereas women activists customarily assumed a supportive, nonpublic role within male charitable organizations, within female-only societies they were able to define their own issues, develop their own programs, and control the dispensation of their energy and funds. Thus the elites' plan to abandon sex segregation was unthinkable, for it meant losing a source of independent action rather than being a step toward autonomy and freedom.

Once freed from the domination of both males and upper-class females, middle-class women, upon leaving the Boston Female Anti-Slavery Society, increasingly committed themselves to what they considered to be their causes, women's causes: the orphan, the destitute minister, the prostitute, and so forth. Invoking their model of womanhood, they also felt justified in battling what they saw as crimes against women—enslavement and rape, seduction and adultery, and abandonment and abuse—all of which limited women's ability to fulfill prescribed roles. It was as women, then, that they had reached out to their enslaved African sisters, and it was as mothers that they had demanded that black females be restored to their rightful position at the center of their families.

Excluded by reason of class and gender from Boston's sociopolitical hierarchy, white middle-class women articulated a value system based not upon power, privilege, and personal success but upon morality, piety, and domesticity.[9] They sought virtue not wealth, pleasure in self-control rather than in extravagance or self-indulgence. They hoped to secure status and respectability through upright Christian deportment, not through individual creativity or accomplishment. Middle-class women did not find their exclusion from public life or intellectual endeavor necessarily oppressive or demeaning, since they believed that women's roles and capabilities were entirely different from those of men. Although they acquiesced in the patriarchal organization of society and politics, believing that the separation of the sexes and the fulfillment of prescribed gender roles were the natural order of things, they considered their responsibilities to be different from, not inferior to, men's.

These middle-class abolitionists can be compared to contemporary "cultural feminists," who advocate an apolitical concept of gender that assumes the existence of an identifiable female counterculture. "Far from denying the importance of biological differences, or seeing in them the cause of women's oppression," Lisa Tuttle has written, "cultural feminists tend to glorify the differences between the sexes, to imply that they are unchangeable."[10] As Linda Alcoff explains, "Cultural feminism is the ideology of a female nature or female essence reappropriated by feminists themselves in an effort to revalidate undervalued female attributes."[11] As cultural feminists, then, evangelical abolitionists believed that there did indeed exist a distinctive, immutable female consciousness, and they promoted the idea that the essential components of femininity had value in their own right. Their model of womanhood did not challenge accepted gender definitions and distinctions but sought to reevaluate the meanings of them to raise women's status in American society.

Gender segregation was central to this model, for it freed women from male domination and allowed them to operate within a cultural milieu of their own making. The benefits that bourgeois women derived from these female-only associations and activities have been amply documented. As Karen Blair concludes in her study of the women's club movement, female societies

> provided a meeting place for women, allowing them to know each other, to develop pride in their strengths, to grow sensitive to sexism, and to become aware of the possibilities for abolishing inequities through Domestic Feminism. In addition, club life taught women the speaking and organizing skills which they later applied to civic reform. Finally, clubs enabled women to become so closely associated with culture that they expropriated the previously male world of literature and the arts as their own, feeling they possessed a special humanistic sensitivity which provided an alternative to the acquisitive and competitive goals of men in an industrializing America.[12]

Ultimately, this white middle-class model of womanhood had limited potential as a vehicle for social change or the advancement of women's rights. For one thing, despite the fact that middle-class activists hoped to maintain their independence by sustaining female-only societies and woman-centered projects, they still felt obliged to seek male direction and legitimation. More importantly, although they attested to women's important social and familial functions and waxed eloquent about women's unique sensibilities, their rhetoric and imagery continued to dwell upon female meekness, subordination, and self-abnegation, urging upon women the "joys" of restraint, forbearance, and self-denial. Middle-class activists were inordinately preoccupied with controlling human desire and appetite, particularly women's, which had the effect of suppressing female hunger for autonomy, self-expression, and recognized achievement—essential ingredients in any human rights program.[13] In the end, their model of womanhood reinvoked and sustained images and values that had the effect of accommodating women to their limited status in American society. Although this reevaluation of women's character and social roles may have provided women with a "therapeutic self-affirmation," to quote Linda Alcoff, it failed to challenge the limiting stereotypes that had created them in the first place.[14]

The emergence of these two models of womanhood within the brief history of the Boston Female Anti-Slavery Society did not take place in a social vacuum. That women with a common conceptualization of gender roles also shared a similar socioeconomic and religious background suggests the extent to which ideology is socially constructed. Moreover, the dialog between these upper- and middle-class groups helped determine the shape their different models would take and, perhaps, made them more inflexible than they otherwise might have been. Unfortunately, the bitterness and intolerance out of which these ideologies emerged helped create an unnecessarily rigid dichotomy between the belief in gender equality and the assumption of gender difference.[15] This dichotomy plagued the women's movement throughout the nineteenth century, and although the women who inherited and perpetuated these two models united briefly in 1914 for the final push for suffrage, the coalition disintegrated with the passage of the Nineteenth Amendment. This inability to incorporate different ideologies into a universal model of feminism continues today, even among feminist scholars and theorists,[16] a testimony to the limits of women's solidarity based upon gender alone.

Notes

Introduction

1. *Liberator*, 5 September 1835.

2. Boston Female Anti-Slavery Society, *Report of the Boston Female Anti-Slavery Society; with a Concise Statement of Events, Previous and Subsequent to the Annual Meeting of 1835* (Boston: Published by the Society, 1836), 34.

3. Harriet Martineau, *Harriet Martineau's Autobiography*, ed. Maria Weston Chapman (Boston: James R. Osgood, 1877), 348.

4. Ibid., 349.

5. Ibid., 352–53, 350.

6. Martineau's other writings about abolitionists include *Retrospect of Western Travel*, 2 vols. (1838; New York: Greenwood Press, 1969), and *The Martyr Age of the United States* (1839; New York: Arno Press, 1969).

7. Debra Gold Hansen, "Right and Wrong in Abolitionism: The Crisis of Authority in the Boston Female Anti-Slavery Society, 1833–1840" (Master's thesis, California State University, Fullerton, 1979), and Debra Gold Hansen, "The Anti-Slavery Conventions of American Women, 1837–1839: An Index and Bibliography" (Master's thesis, University of California, Los Angeles, 1983).

8. Some of the primary examples are Gilbert H. Barnes, *The Antislavery Impulse, 1830–1844* (1933; New York: Peter Smith, 1973); Louis Filler, *The Crusade against Slavery, 1830–1860* (New York: Harper and Row, 1960); Dwight L. Dumond, *Antislavery: The Crusade for Freedom in America* (Ann Arbor: University of Michigan Press, 1961); Merton Dillon, *The Abolitionists: The Growth of a Dissenting Minority* (De Kalb: Northern Illinois University Press, 1974); James B. Stewart, *Holy Warriors: The*

Abolitionists and American Slavery (New York: Hill and Wang, 1976); and Richard Sewell, *Ballots for Freedom: Antislavery Politics in the United States* (New York: Oxford University Press, 1976).

9. Lawrence Friedman, "Historical Topics Sometimes Run Dry: The State of Abolitionist Studies," *Historian* 43 (February 1981): 177–94. Other extremely useful historiographical surveys of antislavery literature include Merton L. Dillon, "The Abolitionists: A Decade of Historiography, 1959–1969," *Journal of Southern History* 35 (November 1969): 500–522; Lewis Perry, "Psychology and the Abolitionists: Reflections on Martin Duberman and the Neoabolitionism of the 1960s," *Reviews in American History* 2 (September 1974): 309–22; Ronald Walters, "The Boundaries of Abolitionism," in Lewis Perry and Michael Fellman, eds., *Antislavery Reconsidered: New Perspectives on the Abolitionists* (Baton Rouge: Louisiana State University Press, 1979), 3–23.

10. See, for example, Perry and Fellman, *Antislavery Reconsidered*; Lawrence Friedman, *Gregarious Saints: Self and Community in American Abolitionism, 1830–1870* (New York: Cambridge University Press, 1982); Edward Magdol, *The Antislavery Rank and File: A Social Profile of the Abolitionists' Constituency* (Westport, Conn.: Greenwood Press, 1986); and Gerald Sorin, *The New York Abolitionists: A Case Study in Political Radicalism* (Westport, Conn.: Greenwood Press, 1971).

11. Alma Lutz, *Crusade for Freedom: Women of the Antislavery Movement* (Boston: Beacon Press, 1968); Blanche Glassman Hersh, *The Slavery of Sex: Feminist-Abolitionists in America* (Urbana: University of Illinois Press, 1978); Jean Fagan Yellin, *Women and Sisters: The Antislavery Feminists in American Culture* (New Haven: Yale University Press, 1989); and Shirley Yee, *Black Women Abolitionists: A Study in Activism, 1828–1860* (Knoxville: University of Tennessee Press, 1992). Jean Fagan Yellin and John C. Van Horne, eds., *An Untrodden Path: Antislavery and Women's Political Culture* (Ithaca: Cornell University Press, forthcoming), promises to make a significant contribution to female abolition historiography.

12. Ellen C. Du Bois, *Feminism and Suffrage: The Emergence of an Independent Women's Movement in America, 1848–1869* (Ithaca: Cornell University Press, 1978); Keith E. Melder, *Beginnings of Sisterhood: The American Women's Rights Movement, 1800–1850* (New York: Schocken Books, 1977), and "The Beginnings of the Women's Rights Movement in the United States, 1800–1840" (Ph.D. diss., Yale University, 1964); Hersh, *Slavery of Sex*; Gerda Lerner, *The Grimké Sisters from South Carolina: Rebels against Slavery* (Boston: Houghton Mifflin, 1967); and Sara Evans, *Personal Politics: The Roots of Women's Liberation in the Civil Rights Movement and the New Left* (New York: Alfred A. Knopf, 1979).

13. For a useful overview of this period of scholarship, see articles by Gerda Lerner, "New Approaches to the Study of Women in American History," *Journal of Social History* 3 (1969–70): 53–62, and "Placing Women in History: Definitions and Challenges," *Feminist Studies* 3 (Fall 1975): 5–14.

14. Hersh, *Slavery of Sex*, 74.

15. Yellin, *Women and Sisters*, 26.

16. For more on this historiographical debate, see Carroll Smith-Rosenberg, "The New Woman and the New History," *Feminist Studies* 3 (Fall 1975): 185–98; Leila J. Rupp, "Reflections on Twentieth-Century American Women's History," *Reviews in*

American History (June 1981): 275–84; Gerda Lerner, "Priorities and Challenges in Women's History Research," *Perspectives* 26 (April 1988): 17–20; and, more generally, Joan W. Scott, "Women in History: The Modern Period," *Past and Present* (November 1983): 141–57.

17. Nancy Cott, *The Bonds of Womanhood: Woman's Sphere in New England, 1780–1835* (New Haven: Yale University Press, 1977); Carroll Smith-Rosenberg, "The Female World of Love and Ritual: Relations between Women in Nineteenth-Century America," in *Disorderly Conduct: Visions of Gender in Victorian America* (New York: Oxford University Press, 1985), 53–76; and Carl N. Degler, *At Odds: Women and the Family in America from the Revolution to the Present* (New York: Oxford University Press, 1980). For a good overview, see Linda Kerber, "Separate Spheres, Female Worlds, Woman's Place: The Rhetoric of Women's History," *Journal of American History* 75 (June 1988): 9–39.

18. Linda Alcoff, "Cultural Feminism versus Poststructuralism: The Identity Crisis in Feminist Theory," *Signs* 13 (Spring 1988): 433.

19. Mary P. Ryan, *Cradle of the Middle Class: The Family in Oneida County, New York, 1790–1865* (New York: Cambridge University Press, 1981); Nancy A. Hewitt, *Women's Activism and Social Change: Rochester, New York, 1822–1872* (Ithaca: Cornell University Press, 1984); Barbara Epstein, *The Politics of Domesticity: Women, Evangelism, and Temperance in Nineteenth-Century America* (Middletown, Conn.: Wesleyan University Press, 1981); and Carroll Smith-Rosenberg, "Bourgeois Discourse in the Age of Jackson: An Introduction," in *Disorderly Conduct*, 79–89.

20. Christine Stansell, *City of Women: Sex and Class in New York, 1789–1860* (New York: Alfred A. Knopf, 1986), xii.

21. See Lori D. Ginzberg, *Women and the Work of Benevolence: Morality, Politics, and Class in the Nineteenth-Century United States* (New Haven: Yale University Press, 1990), and "Moral Suasion Is Moral Balderdash: Women, Politics, and Social Activism in the 1850s," *Journal of American History* 73 (December 1986): 601–22; Anne M. Boylan, "Women in Groups: An Analysis of Women's Benevolent Organizations in New York and Boston, 1797–1840," *Journal of American History* 71 (December 1984): 497–515, and "Timid Girls, Venerable Widows, and Dignified Matrons: Life Cycle Patterns among Organized Women in New York and Boston, 1797–1840," *American Quarterly* 38 (Winter 1986): 779–97.

22. For helpful discussions of gender as an analytical tool, see Diana Fuss, *Essentially Speaking: Feminism, Nature, and Difference* (New York: Routledge, 1989), 2–3, and Joan W. Scott, "Gender: A Useful Category of Historical Analysis," *American Historical Review* 91 (December 1986): 1053–75.

23. Catharine Beecher was the leading spokesperson for the elevation of female status through domesticity and childrearing. See Kathryn Kish Sklar, *Catharine Beecher: A Study in American Domesticity* (New York: W. W. Norton, 1976).

1. The Boston Female Anti-Slavery Society

1. For example, Phelps carefully instructed the new president upon the etiquette of public correspondence: "In regard to the letter from the Boston Ladies A.S.S., I think I would write a private note to Miss Grew, acknowledging the receipt of her letter etc.,

expressing y[ou]r thanks, your congratulations that they have thrown open the door of t[he] society to persons of every color, & urging them on to new & nobler efforts. I would also in a brief note acknowledge the receipt etc. in the ~~Liberator~~ Boston Recorder (try them) or Liberator" (strikeout his). Amos A. Phelps to Charlotte Phelps, 6 May 1834, Boston Public Library, Department of Rare Books and Manuscripts (hereafter cited as BPL). See also Charlotte Phelps to Amos A. Phelps, 29 August 1835, BPL.

2. Boston Female Anti-Slavery Society, "Preamble and Constitution," April 1834, BPL. In contrast, the constitution of the Providence Female Anti-Slavery Society renounced slave-labor products, adopted the controversial *Liberator* as its official organ, and promised to work by all means "agreeable with law and gospel to effect the abolition of slavery." See *Liberator*, 14 July 1832.

3. *Liberator*, 30 November 1840.

4. Ibid., 25 July 1835.

5. Susan Paul to the Editor of the *Liberator*, 1 April 1834, BPL.

6. *Liberator*, 3 January 1835.

7. *The Boston Mob of "Gentlemen of Property and Standing." Proceedings of the Anti-Slavery Meeting . . . on the Twentieth Anniversary of the Mob of October 21, 1835* (Boston: R. F. Wallcut, 1855), 10.

8. The American Union was a short-lived coalition of Congregational ministers and American Colonization Society members.

9. Deborah Weston, Diary, 30 June 1835, 30 May 1835, BPL. "Mr. Gurley" refers to Ralph Randolph Gurley, secretary of the American Colonization Society. "Mr. May" is Samuel J. May, brother of Boston Female Anti-Slavery Society member Abby Alcott.

10. Quoted in *Liberator*, 1 August 1835.

11. For articles in defense of women abolitionists, see ibid., 1 August 1835.

12. Anne Warren Weston to Mary Weston, 27 October 1835, BPL.

13. Ibid.

14. Deborah Weston to Mother, 5 June 1836, BPL. Zebedee Cook was a prominent Boston insurance broker.

15. Quotes taken from *Liberator*, 20 February 1836, 13 February 1836, 25 February 1837.

16. Boston Female Anti-Slavery Society, *Right and Wrong in Boston in 1836: Annual Report of the Boston Female Anti-Slavery Society . . .* (Boston: Published by the Society, 1836), 7.

17. *Liberator*, 20 August 1836.

18. Lydia Maria Child to Esther Carpenter, 4 September 1836, *Lydia Maria Child: Selected Letters, 1817–1880*, ed. Milton Meltzer and Patricia Holland (Amherst: University of Massachusetts Press, 1982), 53.

19. *Liberator*, 8 October 1836. For more information on the legal cases, see Boston Female Anti-Slavery Society, *Right and Wrong in Boston, 1836*, 40–72; Leonard Levy, "The 'Abolition Riot': Boston's First Slave Rescue," *New England Quarterly* 25 (March 1952): 85–92; and Thomas Aves, *Case of the Slave-Child Med* (Boston: I. Knapp, 1836).

20. Boston Female Anti-Slavery Society, *Right and Wrong in Boston, 1836*, 69. See also Boston Female Anti-Slavery Society, "Treasurer's Report," 1836, BPL.

21. Quoted in *Liberator*, 15 October 1836.

22. "To the Women of Massachusetts," reprinted in Boston Female Anti-Slavery Society, *Right and Wrong in Boston, 1836*, 30. Petitioning proved so enormously successful that in early 1836 Congress passed the Pinckney Gag, which automatically tabled antislavery petitions. Despite this congressional action, or inaction, petitioning continued to expand. As a result, the federal government extended the gag, in various forms, until it became a standing rule in 1840, thus linking the abolition movement even more closely with issues of human rights and free speech.

23. For petitioning figures, see *Liberator*, 28 April 1837. Gerda Lerner has found that Massachusetts women were the most prolific petitioners; see "The Political Activities of Antislavery Women," in *The Majority Finds Its Past: Placing Women in History* (New York: Oxford University Press, 1979), 112–28.

24. Sarah M. Grimké to Anne Warren Weston, 7 April 1837, in Larry Ceplair, ed., *The Public Years of Sarah and Angelina Grimké: Selected Writings, 1835–1839* (New York: Columbia University Press, 1989), 128.

25. Anne Warren Weston to Deborah Weston, 18 April 1837, BPL.

26. *Liberator*, 2 June 1837. Lydia Maria Child explained her indecision to Lucretia Mott: "I attended the first convention because I was urged by friends, and I feared I might fail in my duty if I obstinately refused"; Lydia Maria Child to Lucretia Mott, 5 March 1839, in *Lydia Maria Child: Selected Letters*, 107.

27. Anti-Slavery Convention of American Women, *Proceedings of the Anti-Slavery Convention of American Women, Held in the City of New York . . . 1837* (New York: William S. Dorr, 1837), 13.

28. Four official documents were approved by the convention: "Appeal to the Women of the *Nominally* Free States"; "Address to Free Colored Americans"; "Letter to the Women of Great Britain"; and "Circular to the Female Anti-Slavery Societies in the United States."

29. Reprinted in *Liberator*, 24 January 1837.

30. Articles published in Boston newspapers reprinted in Boston Female Anti-Slavery Society, *Right and Wrong in Boston, 1836*, 35–37, 60–61.

31. "Address to the Anti-Slavery Societies," *Proceedings of the Second Anti-Slavery Convention of American Women . . .*, reprinted in Pennsylvania Hall Association, *The History of Pennsylvania Hall, Which Was Destroyed by a Mob on the 17th of May 1838* (1838; New York: Negro Universities Press, 1969), 132.

32. Ibid.; *Liberator*, 11 February 1837.

33. Angelina Grimké to Theodore Weld, 18 May 1837, in Angelina Grimké and Sarah Grimké, *The Letters of Theodore Weld, Angelina Grimké Weld, and Sarah Grimké, 1822–1844*, ed. Gilbert H. Barnes and Dwight L. Dumond (1934; Gloucester: Peter Smith, 1965), 1:388 (hereafter cited as *Weld–Grimké Letters*).

34. Boston Female Anti-Slavery Society, *Right and Wrong in Boston, 1836*, 27.

35. Anne Warren Weston to Deborah Weston, 19 November 1836, BPL. Suzanne Lebsock, in *The Free Women of Petersburg: Status and Culture in a Southern Town, 1784–1860* (New York: W. W. Norton, 1984), 230–31, notes that identifying a woman as "Mrs. John Doe" did not become common until the 1840s and 1850s. She interprets this as part of a series of new rituals of female deference in emerging bourgeois society.

36. Anne Warren Weston to Deborah Weston, 19 November 1836, BPL.

37. For more details of the Grimkés' Massachusetts lecture tour, especially its role in

the early feminist movement, see Keith Melder, "Forerunners of Freedom: The Grimké Sisters in Massachusetts, 1837–1838," *Essex Institute Historical Collections* 103 (3, 1967): 223–49; Gerda Lerner, *The Grimké Sisters from South Carolina: Rebels against Slavery* (Boston: Houghton Mifflin, 1967); and Ceplair, *Public Years of Sarah and Angelina Grimké*. The Grimkés were not the first female public speakers in Massachusetts. African American Maria Stewart lectured to male and female audiences in the early 1830s; see Dorothy Sterling, ed., *We Are Your Sisters: Black Women in the Nineteenth Century* (New York: W. W. Norton, 1984), 153–59.

38. "To Female Anti-Slavery Societies throughout New England," 7 June 1837, as reprinted in Boston Female Anti-Slavery Society, *Right and Wrong in Boston: Annual Report of the Boston Female Anti-Slavery Society . . . in 1837* (Boston: Isaac Knapp, 1837), 42–43.

39. Sarah Grimké, *Letters on the Equality of the Sexes and Other Essays* (1838; New Haven: Yale University Press, 1988), 32, 35.

40. Angelina Grimké to Theodore Weld, as quoted in Alma Lutz, *Crusade for Freedom: Women of the Antislavery Movement* (Boston: Beacon Press, 1968), 105–6.

41. See *Liberator*, 11 August 1837, 18 August 1837, 1 September 1837.

42. Ibid., 18 August 1837.

43. For quotes, see Gamaliel Bailey to James G. Birney, 14 October 1837, in James G. Birney, *The Letters of James G. Birney, 1831–1875*, ed. Dwight L. Dumond (1938; Gloucester: Peter Smith, 1966), 1:428; William Lloyd Garrison to George Benson, 23 September 1837, in William Lloyd Garrison, *The Letters of William Lloyd Garrison*, ed. Walter Merrill and Louis Ruchames (Cambridge, Mass.: Belknap Press, 1971), 2:306; and James G. Birney to Lewis Tappan, 14 September 1837, *Letters of James G. Birney*, 1:424–25.

44. Angelina Grimké and Sarah Grimké to Henry C. Wright, 27 August 1837, *Weld–Grimké Letters*, 439.

45. Boston Female Anti-Slavery Society, *Right and Wrong in Boston*, 1837, 23–24, 71–72; Anne Warren Weston to Deborah Weston, 17 October 1837, BPL.

46. Boston Female Anti-Slavery Society, "Meeting Minutes," 1837, BPL.

47. Ibid.; Boston Female Anti-Slavery Society, *Right and Wrong in Boston*, 1837, 3.

48. Maria Weston Chapman to Mary Parker, 17 November 1837, BPL.

49. Boston Female Anti-Slavery Society, "Meeting Minutes," 1837, BPL.

50. See *Liberator*, 3 May 1839, 1 November 1839. See also Lawrence Friedman, *Gregarious Saints: Self and Community in American Abolitionism, 1830–1870* (New York: Cambridge University Press, 1982). Friedman divided abolitionists into three distinct groups: the radical Garrisonians of Boston, church-centered abolitionists revolving around the Tappans and Theodore Weld, and the politically oriented abolitionists in the West.

51. Deborah Weston to Anne Weston, 21 July 1838, BPL.

52. For quotes, see Anne Warren Weston to Deborah Weston, 8 March 1839, BPL; Martha V. Ball to Maria Weston Chapman, 13 March 1839, BPL; and Caroline Weston to Deborah Weston, 3 March [1839], BPL.

53. More information on this issue can be found in Anne Warren Weston to Deborah Weston, 11 July 1839, BPL, and *Liberator*, 15 March 1839. For details on abolitionists' fight against antimiscegenation laws, see Louis Ruchames, "Race, Mar-

riage, and Abolition in Massachusetts," *Journal of Negro History* 40 (July 1955): 250–73.

54. *Liberator*, 18 January 1839.

55. Ibid., 19 April 1839. Lucia Weston, in a letter to Deborah Weston, 28 April 1839, BPL, identifies Maria Weston Chapman as author of this article.

56. Discussion of these last meetings can be found in an undated *Liberator*, Extra [April 1840].

57. Ibid.

58. Ibid.

59. Thankful Southwick, Maria Weston Chapman, and Lydia Maria Child to Sarah Pugh and the Philadelphia Female Anti-Slavery Society, 14 January 1840, BPL. See also communication from Lydia Maria Child in *Liberator*, 3 April 1840.

60. *Abolitionist*, 14 May 1840. See also Massachusetts Abolition Society, *The True History of the Late Division in the Anti-Slavery Societies . . .* (Boston: David Ela, 1841), 40.

2. Boston in 1835

1. Quotes taken from "The Art of Packing," *New England Magazine* 8 (March 1835): 209; Frank Forbes, "The Old Boston Water Front, 1840–1850," in William S. Rossiter, ed., *Days and Ways in Old Boston* (Boston: R. H. Stearns, 1915), 45. Other contemporary descriptions of Boston include Abel Bowen, *Bowen's Picture of Boston . . .*, 3rd ed. (Boston: Otis, Broaders, 1838); J. R. Dix, *Local Loiterings and Visits in the Vicinity of Boston* (Boston: Redding, 1845); Edwin M. Bacon, *Rambles around Old Boston* (Boston: Little, Brown, 1921); J. Hancock, *The Merchant's and Trader's Guide and Stranger's Memorandum Book . . .* (Boston: J. Hancock, 1836); *The Stranger's Guide; or, Information about Boston and Vicinity* (Boston: J. B. Hall, 1844); C. H. Snow, *A Geography of Boston . . .* (Boston: Carter and Hendee, 1830); Isaac Smith Homans, *Sketches of Boston, Past and Present . . .* (Boston: Phillips, Sampson, 1851); *Boston Directory . . . 1835* (Boston: Charles Stimpson, 1835); E. H. Derby, *Boston: A Commercial Metropolis in 1850* (Boston: Redding, 1850); and *Old Boston Town, Early in This Century, by an 1801-er* (Boston: George F. Nesbitt, 1880).

2. Forbes, "Old Boston Water Front," 51. For another fine description of Boston's piers, see Aaron Sargent, "Recollections of Boston Merchants in the Eighteen-Forties," *Proceedings of the Bostonian Society*, 1904, 25–37.

3. Bowen, *Picture of Boston*, 206; see also "Temperance Dinner at the Marlboro' Hotel," *Liberator*, 30 June 1837.

4. Bowen, *Picture of Boston*, 61; see also *A New Guide to the Massachusetts State House* (Boston: John Hancock Mutual Life Insurance, 1964).

5. Sargent, "Boston Merchants," 26.

6. Hancock, *Merchant's and Trader's Guide*, 121; Sargent, "Boston Merchants," 26–27.

7. Lisa Beth Lubow, "Artisans in Transition: Early Capitalist Development and the Carpenters of Boston, 1787–1837" (Ph.D. diss., University of California, Los Angeles, 1987), 45–53; and David Ward, "The Industrial Revolution and the Emergence of Boston's Central Business District," *Economic Geography* 42 (April 1966): 152–71.

Lubow indicates that Harrison Gray Otis's 1832 tax assessment included sixty-nine lots, eight houses, thirteen stores, two yards, and one wharf, amounting to $147,000 in real estate assets (p. 72).

8. Figures taken from *Liberator,* 14 February 1835; William H. Pease and Jane H. Pease, "Parental Dilemmas: Education, Property, and Patrician Persistence in Jacksonian Boston," *New England Quarterly* 53 (June 1980): 149. Frederic Cople Jaher determined from Boston tax records that 75.8 percent of Boston's wealthy in 1835 (those owning assets over $100,000) remained so in 1860; see "Nineteenth-Century Elites in Boston and New York," *Journal of Social History* 6 (Fall 1972): 47.

9. Forbes, "Old Boston Water Front," 57; Sargent, "Boston Merchants," 27–28; see also "The Reading Room and Marine Diary in the Exchange Coffee House, 1810," *Bostonian Society Publications* 8 (1911): 123–31.

10. Quotes from Roland N. Stromberg, "Boston in the 1820s and 1830s," *History Today* 11 (September 1961): 591; Bowen, *Picture of Boston,* 66; and Ward, "Industrial Revolution and Boston's Business District," 153. For more on the modernization of Boston, see William H. Pease and Jane H. Pease, *The Web of Progress: Private Values and Public Styles in Boston and Charleston, 1828–1843* (New York: Oxford University Press, 1985); and Roger Lane, *Policing the City: Boston, 1822–1885* (Cambridge, Mass.: Harvard University Press, 1967).

11. Jaher, "Nineteenth-Century Elites"; and Ronald Formisano, *The Transformation of Political Culture: Massachusetts Parties, 1790s–1840s* (New York: Oxford University Press, 1983). For more on the politics of the Boston upper class, see Ronald Formisano and Constance Burns, *Boston, 1700–1980: The Evolution of Urban Politics* (Westport, Conn.: Greenwood Press, 1984); Robert Rich, "'A Wilderness of Whigs': The Wealthy Men of Boston," *Journal of Social History* 4 (Spring 1971): 263–76; Paul Goodman, "Ethic and Enterprise: The Values of a Boston Elite, 1800–1860," *American Quarterly* 18 (Fall 1966): 437–51; and Edward Pessen, "Did Fortunes Rise and Fall Mercurially in Antebellum America? The Tale of Two Cities: Boston and New York," *Journal of Social History* 4 (Spring 1971): 339–57.

12. For statistics, see Anne C. Rose, "Social Sources of Denominationalism Reconsidered: Post-Revolutionary Boston as a Case Study," *American Quarterly* 38 (Summer 1986): 248. In *The Forging of an Aristocracy: Harvard and the Boston Upper Class, 1800–1870* (Middletown, Conn.: Wesleyan University Press, 1980), 7–8, Ronald Story provides similar statistical evidence.

13. Quoted in Daniel Walker Howe, *The Unitarian Conscience: Harvard Moral Philosophy, 1805–1861* (Cambridge, Mass.: Harvard University Press, 1970), 8.

14. Howe (ibid.) describes Unitarians as practicing a "liberal Christianity," which revolved around ritual, rationality, and an enlightened optimism regarding human potential. For more on antebellum theologies, see George M. Marsden, *Religion and American Culture* (San Diego: Harcourt Brace Jovanovich, 1990), 45–93.

15. Quotes from Bacon, *Rambles around Old Boston,* 118; Snow, *Geography of Boston,* 64; and Henry F. Bond, "Old Summer Street, Boston," *New England Magazine* 19 (November 1898): 334. E. C. Wines, *A Trip to Boston, in a Series of Letters to the Editor of the "United States Gazette"* (Boston: Charles C. Little and James Brown, 1838), 207–8. For descriptions of the development of Boston neighborhoods, see Michael P. Conzen and George K. Lewis, *Boston: A Geographical Portrait* (Cam-

bridge, Mass.: Ballinger, 1976); [Edwin M. Bacon], *Washington Street, Old and New* (Boston: Macullar Parker, 1913); Leona Rostenberg, "Number Thirteen West Street," *Book Collector's Packet*, September 1945, 7–9; Lemuel Shattuck, *Report to the Committee of the City Council Appointed to Obtain the Census of Boston for the Year 1845* . . . (Boston: John H. Eastburn, 1846); and Lubow, "Artisans in Transition," 85–92.

16. Figures taken from Peter R. Knights, *The Plain People of Boston, 1830–1860: A Study in City Growth* (New York: Oxford University Press, 1971), 84.

17. For a good overview of Boston's incorporation, see Formisano and Burns, *Boston, 1700–1980*; Robert A. McCaughey, "From Town to City: Boston in the 1820s," *Political Science Quarterly* 88 (June 1973): 191–213; and Charles P. Huse, *The Financial History of Boston, from May 1, 1822, to January 31, 1909* (Cambridge, Mass.: Harvard University Press, 1916), chap. 2.

18. See Mary P. Ryan, *Cradle of the Middle Class: The Family in Oneida County, New York, 1790–1865* (New York: Cambridge University Press, 1981), and Paul Johnson, *A Shopkeeper's Millennium: Society and Revivals in Rochester, New York, 1815–1837* (New York: Hill and Wang, 1978).

19. Clarendon Street Baptist Church, *A Brief History of the Clarendon Street Baptist Church* . . . (Boston: Gould and Lincoln, 1872), 67–68.

20. Bowdoin Street Congregational Church, *The Articles of Faith and Covenant of the Bowdoin Street Church, Boston* . . . (Boston: Perkins and Marvin, 1837); and Franklin Street Congregational Church, *Origin and Formation of the Franklin Street Church in Boston* . . . (Boston: Light and Stearns, 1836).

21. Rose, "Social Sources of Denominationalism," 251–52; and Marsden, *Religion and American Culture*, 47–64. For a firsthand account of evangelicalism in Boston, see Martin Moore, *Boston Revival, 1842: A Brief History of the Evangelical Churches of Boston* (Boston: John Putnam, 1842).

22. Knights, *Plain People of Boston*, 120.

23. Lubow, "Artisans in Transition," 108–9.

24. Gary Nash, *The Urban Crucible: Social Change, Political Consciousness, and the Origins of the American Revolution* (Cambridge, Mass.: Harvard University Press, 1979).

25. James A. Henretta, "Economic Development and Social Structure in Colonial Boston," *William and Mary Quarterly* 22 (January 1965): 85. See also Allan Kulikoff, "The Progress of Inequality in Revolutionary Boston," *William and Mary Quarterly* 28 (July 1971): 375–412.

26. Quote from "Art of Packing," 211. See also Nathan Kantrowitz, "Racial and Ethnic Residential Segregation in Boston, 1830–1970," *Annals of the American Academy of Political and Social Science* 441 (January 1979): 41–54, and Peter R. Knights and Leo F. Schnore, "Residence and Social Structure: Boston in the Antebellum Period," in Stephan Thernstrom and Richard Sennett, eds., *Nineteenth-Century Cities: Essays in the New Urban History* (New Haven: Yale University Press, 1969).

27. James O. Horton and Lois E. Horton, *Black Bostonians: Family Life and Community Struggle in the Antebellum North* (New York: Holmes and Meier, 1979); and George A. Levesque, "Black Boston: Negro Life in Garrison's Boston, 1800–1860" (Ph.D. diss., State University of New York, Binghampton, 1976).

28. *Old Boston Town*, 29.

29. "Mobs," *New England Magazine* 7 (December 1834): 473.

30. The South Boston arsonists were identified as Stephen Russell, a housewright, and Simeon Crockett, occupation unknown; see report in *Liberator*, 31 October 1835. For more on Boston's mobs, see Theodore M. Hammett, "Two Mobs of Jacksonian Boston: Ideology and Interest," *Journal of American History* 62 (March 1976): 845–68, and Wilfred J. Bisson, "Some Conditions for Collective Violence: The Charlestown Convent Riot of 1834" (Ph.D. diss., Michigan State University, 1974).

31. Hammett, "Two Mobs"; E. P. Thompson, "The Moral Economy of the English Crowd in the Eighteenth Century," *Past and Present* 50 (February 1971): 76–136.

32. James Walker, *Memoir of Josiah Quincy* (Cambridge, Mass.: John Wilson and Son, 1867), 37.

33. Josiah Quincy, *A Municipal History of the Town and City of Boston during Two Centuries* . . . (Boston: Charles C. Little and James Brown, 1852), 102.

34. For further explanation, see Eric C. Schneider, "In the Web of Class: Youth, Class, and Culture in Boston, 1840–1940" (Ph.D. diss., Boston University, 1980).

35. Quincy, *Municipal History*, 104.

36. For views of the early-nineteenth-century Boston Common, see Joseph Edgar Chamberlin, "Winter on Boston Common," *New England Magazine* 11 (December 1894): 425–37; Bowen, *Picture of Boston*, 17–18; Dix, *Local Loiterings*, 61–67; Abbie Farwell Brown, "Notable Trees about Boston," *New England Magazine* 22 (July 1900): 508–10.

37. Dix, *Local Loiterings*, 65–66.

38. Knights, *Plain People of Boston*, 35, 60.

39. Anne Rose argues that, in response to the Second Great Awakening among Congregationalists and Baptists, Unitarians developed an evangelical movement of their own that combined personal piety with reform activity and served as an "antidote to the problems that came with socioeconomic change"; see *Transcendentalism as a Social Movement, 1830–1850* (New Haven: Yale University Press, 1981), 2–3.

40. Quotes from Sargent, "Boston Merchants," 37; Brown, "Notable Trees about Boston," 510; *Old Boston Town*, 41.

3. Women of Antebellum Boston

1. Ednah Cheney, "The Women of Boston," in Justin Winsor, ed., *The Memorial History of Boston* . . . (Boston: James R. Osgood, 1883), 4:331.

2. Some interesting examples are Claudia Goldin, "The Economic Status of Women in the Early Republic: Quantitative Evidence," *Journal of Interdisciplinary History* 16 (Winter 1986): 375–405; Christine Stansell, "Women, Children, and the Uses of the Streets: Class and Gender Conflict in New York City, 1850–1860," *Feminist Studies* 8 (Summer 1982): 309–35; and Suzanne Lebsock, *The Free Women of Petersburg: Status and Culture in a Southern Town, 1784–1860* (New York: W. W. Norton, 1984).

3. Harriet Martineau, *Retrospect of Western Travel* (1838; New York: Greenwood Press, 1969), 3:48–51.

4. Gayle Graham Yates, *Harriet Martineau on Women* (New Brunswick, N.J.: Rutgers University Press, 1985), 62–63, 129.

5. As quoted in Kathryn Kish Sklar, *Catharine Beecher: A Study in American Domesticity* (New York: W. W. Norton, 1976), 156–57.

6. Louise Tilly and Joan Scott, in *Women, Work, and Family* (New York: Holt, Rinehart and Winston, 1978), were among the first to observe the persistence of women's roles within the working-class family in industrializing England. Thomas Dublin, *Women at Work: The Transformation of Work and Community in Lowell, Massachusetts, 1826–1860* (New York: Columbia University Press, 1979), 35–36, argues that American factory girls, unlike their English counterparts, gained personal and economic independence through wage work and did not automatically send their earnings home.

7. Mary P. Ryan, *Womanhood in America: From Colonial Times to the Present*, 3rd ed. (New York: Franklin Watts, 1983), 113; Gerda Lerner, "The Lady and the Mill Girl: Changes in the Status of Women in the Age of Jackson," *MidContinent American Studies Journal* 10 (Spring 1969): 5–15, as discussed in Goldin, "Economic Status of Women," 375. For more on this line of argument, see Ann Douglas, *The Feminization of American Culture* (New York: Alfred A. Knopf, 1978), and Barbara Harris, *Beyond Her Sphere: Women and the Professions in American History* (Westport, Conn.: Greenwood Press, 1978).

8. Though now more than twenty-five years old, Barbara Welter's description of true womanhood remains standard; see "The Cult of True Womanhood, 1820–1860," *American Quarterly* 18 (Summer 1966): 151–74.

9. See Nancy F. Cott, *The Bonds of Womanhood: Woman's Sphere in New England, 1780–1835* (New Haven: Yale University Press, 1977); Carroll Smith-Rosenberg, "The Female World of Love and Ritual: Relations between Women in Nineteenth-Century America," in *Disorderly Conduct: Visions of Gender in Victorian America* (New York: Oxford University Press, 1985), 53–76; and Carl N. Degler, *At Odds: Women and the Family in America from the Revolution to the Present* (New York: Oxford University Press, 1980).

10. Obituary of Eliza Ripley of Jaffrey, New Hampshire, in *Home Guardian* 37 (March 1875): 136. For more information, see Lee Chambers-Schiller, *Liberty, a Better Husband: Single Women in America, the Generations of 1780–1840* (New Haven: Yale University Press, 1984).

11. Carroll Smith-Rosenberg, "The Cross and the Pedestal," in *Disorderly Conduct*, 130. See also Blanche Glassman Hersh, *The Slavery of Sex: Feminist-Abolitionists in America* (Urbana: University of Illinois Press, 1978); Ellen C. Du Bois, *Feminism and Suffrage: The Emergence of an Independent Women's Movement in America, 1848–1869* (Ithaca: Cornell University Press, 1978); and Keith E. Melder, *Beginnings of Sisterhood: The American Woman's Rights Movement, 1800–1850* (New York: Schocken Books, 1977). Others discount the impact of the women's rights movement, arguing that by continuing to use the language and symbols of domesticity reformers in effect strengthened the very ideology that oppressed them and failed to address the primary sources of women's oppression—the home and family. See, for example, William L. O'Neill, *Everyone Was Brave: A History of Feminism in America* (Chicago: Quad-

rangle/New York Times, 1969), and Degler, *At Odds*. Suzanne Lebsock, in *Free Women of Petersburg*, adds a new dimension to the debate by suggesting that southern women's situation improved during the nineteenth century without an organized feminist movement.

12. Two of many examples are Mary P. Ryan, *Cradle of the Middle Class: The Family in Oneida County, New York, 1790–1865* (New York: Cambridge University Press, 1981), and Christine Stansell, *City of Women: Sex and Class in New York, 1789–1860* (New York: Alfred A. Knopf, 1986).

13. Nancy A. Hewitt, *Women's Activism and Social Change: Rochester, New York, 1822–1872* (Ithaca: Cornell University Press, 1984), and Lori D. Ginzberg, *Women and the Work of Benevolence: Morality, Politics, and Class in the Nineteenth-Century United States* (New Haven: Yale University Press, 1990).

14. Goldin, "Economic Status of Women"; Lebsock, *Free Women of Petersburg*; Stansell, *City of Women*; and Jacqueline Jones, *Labor of Love, Labor of Sorrow: Black Women, Work, and the Family from Slavery to the Present* (New York: Vintage Books, 1985).

15.

	Ages	1830	1840
Boston white males	20–30	7,729	15,612
	30–40	4,132	9,404
All white males in Boston		28,171	47,844
All white males in Mass.		298,000	365,000
Boston white females	20–30	7,958	11,242
	30–40	4,661	6,566
All white females in Boston		31,316	43,112
All white females in Mass.		312,000	372,000

Statistics from U.S., Bureau of the Census, *Historical Statistics of the United States: Colonial Times to 1970* (Washington, D.C.: Government Printing Office, 1975), vol. 1; U.S., Department of State, *Aggregate Amount of Each Description of Persons . . . According to the Census of 1840* (Washington, D.C.: Blair and Rives, 1841); and U.S., Department of State, *Enumeration of the Inhabitants of the United States: 1830* (Washington, D.C.: Duff Green, 1832).

16. U.S., Department of State, *Aggregate Amount of the Census of 1840*.

17. Thomas Dublin, "Women Workers and the Study of Social Mobility," *Journal of Interdisciplinary History* 9 (Spring 1979): 654.

18. Gary Nash, "The Failure of Female Factory Labor in Colonial Boston," in *Race, Class, and Politics: Essays on American Colonial and Revolutionary Society* (Urbana: University of Illinois Press, 1986), 120. Nash studied the city's early efforts to cope with indigent, widowed females. In the 1740s Boston merchants established a textile factory in hopes of providing paid employment for poor women and children as an alternative to outright charity. The factory failed for want of female workers, and Nash concludes that its rapid demise was due primarily to the incompatibility of factory schedules with women's customary work habits. Despite this ready factory employ-

ment, late-eighteenth-century widows preferred sewing and spinning in their own homes, employment that allowed them also to meet domestic responsibilities.

19. Lee Chambers-Schiller, "The Single Woman Reformer: Conflicts between Family and Vocation, 1830–1860," *Frontiers* 3 (3, 1978): 43.

20. Lemuel Shattuck, *Report to the Committee of the City Council Appointed to Obtain the Census of Boston for the Year 1845* . . . (Boston: John H. Eastburn, 1846), 43.

21. Anne Warren Weston to Deborah Weston, 31 January 1839, as quoted in Margaret Munsterberg, "The Weston Sisters and the 'Boston Controversy,'" *Boston Public Library Quarterly* 10 (January 1958): 43.

22. *Old Boston Town* (New York: George F. Nesbitt, 1880), 34. Salaries listed in *Liberator*, 21 May 1836. Carol S. Lasser, in "A 'Pleasingly Oppressive Burden': The Transformation of Domestic Service and Female Charity in Salem, 1800–1840," *Essex Institute Historical Collections* 116 (April 1980): 156–75, discusses the "transformation" in the "social relations of domestic service," which turned traditional household help into wage labor.

23. See Christine Stansell, "Origins of the Sweatshop: Women and Early Industrialization in New York City," in Michael Frisch and Daniel Walkowitz, eds., *Working-Class America: Essays on Labor, Community, and American Society* (Urbana: University of Illinois Press, 1983), 78–103.

24. *Friend of Virtue* 2 (1 July 1839): 198.

25. See Dublin, "Women Workers and Social Mobility."

26. Isaac Smith Homans, *Sketches of Boston, Past and Present* . . . (Boston: Phillips, Sampson, 1851), 203; Keith E. Melder, "Woman's High Calling: The Teaching Profession in America, 1830–1860," *American Studies* 13 (2, 1972): 22.

27. Melder, "Woman's High Calling."

28. Richard M. Bernard and Maris A. Vinovskis, in "The Female School Teacher in Ante-bellum Massachusetts," *Journal of Social History* 10 (March 1977): 332–45, find that female teachers earned 60 percent less than their male counterparts, and their earning potential, compared to males, declined during the antebellum period. For a firsthand account of the nineteenth-century stereotype of the female teacher with her "pure and spotless . . . virgin soul," see James R. Gilmore, "Recollections of a New England School Mistress," *New England Magazine* 28 (July 1898): 566–76.

29. *Liberator*, 25 June 1847. Carroll Smith-Rosenberg, "The Abortion Movement and the AMA, 1850–1880," in *Disorderly Conduct*, 228–32, discusses the exclusion of women from higher-status positions in the medical profession. See also Goldin, "Economic Status of Women," 403–4.

30. For salary figures, see *Liberator*, 16 May 1835. Clerical work did not open up for Boston women until the 1870s. See Carol Srole, "'A Position that God Has Not Particularly Assigned to Men': The Feminization of Clerical Work, Boston, 1860–1915" (Ph.D. diss., University of California, Los Angeles, 1984).

31. Goldin, "Economic Status of Women," 378; Lebsock, *Free Women of Petersburg*, 151.

32. J. Hancock, *The Merchant's and Trader's Guide and Stranger's Memorandum Book for the Year of Our Lord, 1836* . . . (Boston: J. Hancock, 1836).

33. Cheney, "Women of Boston," 342.

34. James O. Horton, "Freedom's Yoke: Gender Conventions among Antebellum Free Blacks," *Feminist Studies* 12 (Spring 1986): 60–62. See also Jones, *Labor of Love*, 74–75, and Lebsock, *Free Women of Petersburg*, 185.

35. Black women in the 1835 city directory included twelve widows and fourteen others with no occupation listed; see *Boston Directory . . . 1835* (Boston: Charles Stimpson, 1835).

36. Quoted in Chambers-Schiller, "Single Woman Reformer," 43.

37. See Lebsock, *Free Women of Petersburg*, 176–81.

38. Caroline Weston, Diary, 17 September 1835, BPL.

39. Degler, *At Odds*, 144–51. For a fascinating and important reinterpretation of Victorian romantic life, see Karen Lystra, *Searching the Heart: Women, Men, and Romantic Love in Nineteenth-Century America* (New York: Oxford University Press, 1989).

40. See Karen Halttunen, *Confidence Men and Painted Women: A Study of Middle-Class Culture in America, 1830–1870* (New Haven: Yale University Press, 1982), for an interesting look at the "ritualization" of socializing. These social gatherings were not strictly female but regularly included males as well. George Emerson's reminiscences of his days as a Harvard professor contain several accounts of socializing among Harvard elites, and he recalled that the Sunday evenings spent with educated men and women at Harvard president John Kirkland's home were "far the most pleasant and really the most brilliant parties I have ever attended." George B. Emerson, "Schools as They Should Be: Reminiscences of an Old Teacher," *American Journal of Education* 28 (1878): 263.

41. Quoted in Aileen Kraditor, ed., *Up from the Pedestal: Selected Writings in the History of American Feminism* (New York: Quadrangle, 1968), 48.

42. For example, three of fourteen females admitted into the Federal Street Baptist Church in 1827 joined with a male of the same surname. In 1836 only two of thirty-one women entered the church with a male of the same surname. See Clarendon Street Baptist Church, *A Brief History of the Clarendon Street Baptist Church . . .* (Boston: Gould and Lincoln, 1872), 53, 69–70.

43. Cheney, "Women of Boston," 350.

44. Shattuck, *Census of Boston, 1845*, 100–6; see also Samuel Elkins Eliot, *An Article on Public and Private Charities in Boston* (Cambridge, Mass.: Metcalf, 1845); and Abel Bowen, *Bowen's Picture of Boston . . .*, 3rd ed. (Boston: Otis, Broaders, 1838), 44–59.

45. "Philanthropy of the Present Age," *New England Magazine* 6 (January 1834): 55.

46. See Peter Dobkin Hall's "Family Structure and Class Consolidation among the Boston Brahmins" (Ph.D. diss., State University of New York, Stony Brook, 1973), and "The Model of Boston Charity: A Theory of Charitable Benevolence and Class Development," *Science and Society* 38 (Winter 1974/75): 464–77.

47. Boston Female Society for Missionary Purposes, *Constitution* (Boston: Nathaniel Willis, 1816), 3.

48. *Report of the Committee of Delegates from the Benevolent Societies of Boston* (Boston: Tuttle and Weeks, 1834).

49. For more on this topic, see Leonard Sweet, *The Minister's Wife: Her Role in*

Nineteenth-Century American Evangelism (Philadelphia: Temple University Press, 1983).

50. Boston Society for the Care of Girls, *One Hundred Years of Work with Girls in Boston* (Boston: Published by the Society, 1919), 5.

51. Clarendon Street Baptist Church, *Brief History*, 16.

52. Watertown Female Charitable Sewing Society [First Baptist Church], "Report of the Watertown Female Charitable Sewing Society for the Year 1838," Andover-Newton Theological School, Special Collections, Newton Center, Mass. (hereafter cited as A-N).

53. Bethel Sewing Circle [Boston], Constitution and Minutes, 1846–1848, A-N.

54. Ibid.

55. Ladies Benevolent Society, Dudley Street Baptist Church, Roxbury, Constitution and Minutes, 1842–43, A-N.

56. Boston Female Society for Missionary Purposes, *Constitution*, 5.

57. Cheney, "Women of Boston," 348–49. Barbara Hobson, in "Sex in the Marketplace: Prostitution in an American City, Boston, 1820–1880" (Ph.D. diss., Boston University, 1982), 134–35, and Ginzberg, *Women and Benevolence*, also find that membership in different women's organizations in Boston was class based.

58. In *The Forging of an Aristocracy: Harvard and the Boston Upper Class, 1800–1870* (Middletown, Conn.: Wesleyan University Press, 1980), 35, Ronald Story notes that between 1800 and 1860 all but three members of Harvard's board were Unitarian.

59. Sewing Circle of the First Baptist Society, First Baptist Church, Boston, Constitution and Minutes, 1841–87, A-N.

60. *Friend of Virtue* 1 (July 1838): 109; 2 (15 July 1839): 200.

61. Quotes taken from *Friend of Virtue* 2 (1 July 1839): 182, 185, 190.

62. *Liberator*, 17 November 1832; *Friend of Virtue* 1 (November 1838): 175.

63. Josiah Quincy, *A Municipal History of the Town and City of Boston during Two Centuries . . .* (Boston: Charles C. Little and James Brown, 1852), 105.

4. Women in the Boston Female Anti-Slavery Society

1. Caroline Weston to Samuel J. May, 21 October 1871, BPL.

2. Anti-Slavery Convention of American Women, *Proceedings of the Anti-Slavery Convention of American Women, Held in the City of New York . . . 1837* (New York: William S. Dorr, 1837), 18.

3. Anti-Slavery Convention of American Women, *Proceedings of the Anti-Slavery Convention of American Women, Held in Philadelphia . . . 1838* (Philadelphia: Merrihew and Gunn, 1838), 9.

4. Sophia E. Thoreau to Maria Weston Chapman, 24 January [1839], BPL.

5. Women whose names appeared regularly on lists of petitioners, fair organizers and supporters, convention delegates, and meeting rolls were deemed active members.

6. Full-length biographies of Boston Female Anti-Slavery Society members include Helene Baer, *The Heart Is Like Heaven: The Life of Lydia Maria Child* (Philadelphia: University of Pennsylvania Press, 1964); William S. Osborne, *Lydia Maria Child* (Boston: Twayne, 1980); Milton Meltzer, *Tongue of Flame: The Life of Lydia Maria Child* (New York: Thomas Y. Crowell, 1965); and Sanford Salyer, *Marmee: The Mother*

of Little Women (Norman: University of Oklahoma Press, 1949). See also William Lloyd Garrison, *Helen Eliza Garrison: A Memorial* (Cambridge, Mass.: Riverside Press, 1876); Irving Bartlett, *Wendell and Ann Phillips: The Community of Reform, 1840–1880* (New York: W. W. Norton, 1979); [Frances J. Garrison], *Ann Phillips, Wife of Wendell Phillips: A Memorial Sketch* (Boston: Privately printed, 1886); *In Memoriam: Mary Ann W. Johnson, Wife of Oliver Johnson* (New York: Privately printed, 1872); and Nancy Prince, *Narrative of the Life and Travels of Mrs. Nancy Prince* (Boston: Published by the author, 1850). Articles about Boston's women abolitionists include Jane H. Pease and William H. Pease, "The Boston Bluestocking: Maria Weston Chapman," in *Bound with Them in Chains: A Biographical History of the Antislavery Movement* (Westport, Conn.: Greenwood Press, 1972), 28–59; Elizabeth Schlesinger, "Two Early Harvard Wives: Eliza Farrar and Eliza Follen," *New England Quarterly* 38 (June 1965): 147–67; Sheila Madden, "Mrs. Abba Alcott: Bulwark of a Famous Family," *New England Galaxy* 15 (2, 1973): 15–25; and Margaret Munsterberg's "The Weston Sisters and the 'Boston Controversy,'" *Boston Public Library Quarterly* 10 (January 1958): 38–50, and "The Weston Sisters and the Boston Mob," *Boston Public Library Quarterly* 9 (October 1958): 183–94. See also articles on Maria Weston Chapman, Eliza Follen, and Lydia Maria Child in the following biographical sources: *Dictionary of American Biography* (New York: Scribner, 1928–37); Edward James et al., *Notable American Women, 1607–1950* (Cambridge, Mass.: Belknap Press, 1971); and Alden Whitman, *American Reformers* (New York: H. W. Wilson, 1985), as well as the article on Martha V. Ball in Frances Willard and Mary Livermore, eds., *A Woman of the Century* (New York: Charles Wills Moulton, 1893).

7. More information is available concerning the husbands and fathers of Boston Female Anti-Slavery Society women. See, for example, J. Marcus Mitchell, "The Paul Family," *Old Time New England* 63 (Winter 1973): 73–77; Justin D. Fulton, *Memoir of Timothy Gilbert* (Boston: Lee and Shepard, 1866); J. C. Lovejoy, *Memoir of Rev. Charles T. Torrey, Who Died in the Penitentiary of Maryland* . . . (Boston: John P. Jewett, 1847); Ronald L. Numbers and Jonathan Butler, *The Disappointed: Millerism and Millenarianism in the Nineteenth Century* (Bloomington: Indiana University Press, 1987); Peter Burchard, *One Gallant Rush: Robert Gould Shaw and the Brave Black Regiment* (New York: St. Martin's Press, 1965); Gordon Milne, *George William Curtis: The Genteel Tradition* (Bloomington: University of Indiana Press, 1956); and Emma W. Sargent, *Epes Sargent of Gloucester and His Descendants* (Boston: Houghton Mifflin, 1923), as well as the better-known biographies of William Lloyd Garrison and Wendell Phillips. See also articles in the *Dictionary of American Biography* on Epes Sargent, Amasa Walker, Samuel Gilman, Charles Follen, Charles Tufts, Henry Highland Garnet, George William Russell, Francis G. Shaw, Thomas Clark, David Child, Ellis Gray Loring, and Henry G. Chapman, and those in *Appleton's Cyclopedia of American Biography* (New York: Appleton, 1894–1900) on Amos A. Phelps, Ellis Gray Loring, Rollin H. Neale, Nathaniel Colver, and William Collier. In addition to the more famous abolitionists, *Who Was Who in America* (Chicago: Marquis, 1942) has items on Joshua V. Himes, Alexander Young, and William S. Damrell.

8. William Lloyd Garrison to Helen Garrison, 30 December 1835, as quoted in Mary Caroline Crawford, *Romantic Days in Old Boston* . . . (Boston: Little, Brown,

1910), 129; Sarah Southwick, *Reminiscences of the Early Anti-Slavery Days* (1893; Macon, Ga.: Kingsley Press, 1971), 9.

9. Helen Garrison to Caroline Weston, 31 October 1835, BPL.

10. Josiah Brackett, quoted in *Liberator*, 7 June 1839.

11. Anne M. Boylan, in "Timid Girls, Venerable Widows, and Dignified Matrons: Life Cycle Patterns among Organized Women in New York and Boston, 1797–1840," *American Quarterly* 38 (Winter 1986): 779–97, has found that this diversity in age and marital status differentiates female reform groups from traditional benevolent societies and notes that single women reformers did not impose as many limits on their public activities as did women involved in traditional benevolent groups.

12. The occupational terms used in this chapter are based upon definitions provided in William Craigie, ed., *A Dictionary of American English on Historical Principles* (Chicago: University of Chicago Press, 1936–44). A *merchant* is one who engages in buying commodities (often foreign) and selling them at a profit, especially one who deals in large quantities or at wholesale. A *proprietor* is the owner of an established business or a shopkeeper. A *clerk* refers to one who either keeps accounts in a business or government office or is an assistant to a storekeeper and waits on customers. An *artisan* is one who is involved in a manual or skilled trade.

13. Economic data taken from the following sources: Lewis Bunker Rohrbach, *Boston Taxpayers in 1821* (Camden, Me.: Picton Press, 1988); Boston, *List of Persons, Copartnerships, and Corporations Who Were Taxed on Six Thousand Dollars and Upward in the Year 1850* (Boston: J. H. Eastburn, 1851), *List of Persons, Copartnerships, and Corporations Who Were Taxed in the City of Boston for the Year 1844* (Boston: J. H. Eastburn, 1845), *List of Persons, Copartnerships, and Corporations Who Were Taxed on Six Thousand Dollars and Upward in the Year 1855* (Boston: Moore and Crosby, 1856); Suffolk County, *Probate Records, 1636–1899*, microfilm (Salt Lake City: Genealogy Library, Church of Jesus Christ of Latter-day Saints, n.d.); and Abner Forbes and J. W. Greene, *The Rich Men of Massachusetts . . .* (Boston: W. V. Spencer, 1851).

14. See Barbara Hobson, "Sex in the Marketplace: Prostitution in an American City, Boston, 1820–1880" (Ph.D. diss., Boston University, 1982), 198.

15. Anne Warren Weston to Deborah Weston, 17 October 1837, BPL.

16. Annual donations to the Massachusetts Anti-Slavery Society are recorded in the *Annual Reports, 1833–1856*, 3 vols. (Westport, Conn.: Negro Universities Press, 1970).

17. Paul Johnson, in *A Shopkeeper's Millennium: Society and Revivals in Rochester, New York, 1815–1837* (New York: Hill and Wang, 1978), 137–38, provides a relevant discussion of how clerks and artisans were influenced by their employers (merchants and manufacturers) to take part in revivals.

18. Details regarding Boston's black activists can be found in James O. Horton and Lois E. Horton, *Black Bostonians: Family Life and Community Struggle in the Antebellum North* (New York: Holmes and Meier, 1979); Lois E. Horton, "Community Organization and Social Activism: Black Boston and the Antislavery Movement," *Sociological Inquiry* 55 (Spring 1985): 182–97; James O. Horton, "Generations of Protest: Black Families and Social Reform in Ante-bellum Boston," *New England*

Quarterly 49 (June 1976): 242–56; and George A. Levesque, "Black Boston: Negro Life in Garrison's Boston, 1800–1860" (Ph.D. diss., State University of New York, Binghamton, 1976). See also Julie Winch, *Philadelphia's Black Elite: Activism, Accommodation, and the Struggle for Autonomy, 1787–1848* (Philadelphia: Temple University Press, 1988).

19. *Home Guardian* 31 (July 1869): 195.

20. The identification of these working-class women—several of whom were named Jones—could not be corroborated in church histories or other local directories.

21. A high school for girls was established in Boston in 1825 under Ebenezer Bailey. The school was phenomenally popular and attracted so many students that Mayor Quincy closed it, claiming that the school was too expensive. Some have suggested that upper-class Bostonians feared that the education of poor females would render them unfit for domestic service. See Ednah Cheney, "The Women of Boston," in Justin Winsor, ed., *Memorial History of Boston . . .* (Boston: James R. Osgood, 1883), 4:343–44. Complained Isaac Homans in 1851: "It is rather a humiliating truth for a Bostonian to utter, when questioned as to our public aids to female culture, that we have no public institution to perfect young ladies in an advanced education"; *Sketches of Boston, Past and Present . . .* (Boston: Phillips, Sampson, 1851), 208.

22. Southwick, *Reminiscences of Anti-Slavery Days*, 37–38.

23. In a tribute to the young teacher and her father, Garrison wrote that when the elder Paul died "he had no money to leave his children." But, Garrison continued, "he left them what is better—a good character and a good education, by which means his daughter is enabled to instruct one of the primary schools for colored children in Boston and by her exertions and industry to assist in the support of her kind mother"; *Liberator*, 22 February 1834.

24. Prudence Crandall attempted to integrate her Canterbury, Connecticut, school in 1833, but public outcry, acts of vandalism, and finally legislative intervention forced her to close it.

25. Anne Warren Weston to Deborah Weston, 11 July 1839, BPL.

26. *Abolitionist*, 23 April 1840.

27. Abigail B. Ordway to Miss Foster [Salem Female Anti-Slavery Society], 21 May 1839, Essex Institute, Salem, Mass.

28. Emma Smith to Caroline Weston, 8 December 1839, BPL.

29. See announcement in *Liberator*, 30 November 1833.

30. Circumstances were described in Anne Warren Weston to Deborah Weston, 15 December 1839, BPL.

31. Carroll Smith-Rosenberg, "Beauty, the Beast, and the Militant Woman: A Case Study in Sex Roles and Social Stress in Jacksonian America," in *Disorderly Conduct: Visions of Gender in Victorian America* (New York: Oxford University Press, 1985), 123–24, discusses the New York Female Moral Reform Society's policy of hiring only women to perform society functions and comments on the feminist implications.

32. *Abolitionist*, 27 February 1840.

33. *Friend of Virtue* 27 (April 1864).

34. Mark Peel, "On the Margins: Lodgers and Boarders in Boston, 1860–1900," *Journal of American History* 72 (March 1986): 813–34.

35. Because the Quakers in the society were limited to one extended family of

comfortable income, generalizations as to patterns among Quakers would not be prudent. Elsewhere, Quakers were predominant in women's antislavery societies. For information on Quakers in the antislavery movement, see Thomas E. Drake, *Quakers and Slavery in America* (New Haven: Yale University Press, 1950); Jean R. Soderlund, *Quakers and Slavery: A Divided Spirit* (Princeton: Princeton University Press, 1985); and Carolyn Luverne Williams, "Religion, Race, and Gender in Antebellum American Radicalism: The Philadelphia Female Anti-Slavery Society, 1833–1870" (Ph.D. diss., University of California, Los Angeles, 1991).

36. Union Congregational Church, *Confession of Faith and Covenant, Also a Brief History of Union Church, Essex Street, Boston* (Boston: Crocker and Brewster, 1839), 5.

37. Clarendon Street Baptist Church, *A Brief History of the Clarendon Street Baptist Church . . .* (Boston: Gould and Lincoln, 1872), 14.

38. William G. McLoughlin, *New England Dissent, 1630–1883: The Baptists and the Separation of Church and State* (Cambridge, Mass.: Harvard University Press, 1971), 2:1271. See also Wendell P. Garrison and Frances Garrison, *William Lloyd Garrison, 1805–1879: The Story of His Life Told By His Children* (New York: Century, 1885–89), 1:68, 98.

39. As quoted in Aileen Kraditor, *Up from the Pedestal: Selected Writings in the History of American Feminism* (New York: Quadrangle, 1968), 51. In 1854 Adams penned *A South-Side View of Slavery*, in which he admonished abolitionists for their agitation and argued that left alone the South would voluntarily abolish slavery; *Dictionary of American Biography*, s.v. "Adams, Nehemiah."

40. Quoted in Boston Female Anti-Slavery Society, *Right and Wrong in Boston; Annual Report of the Boston Female Anti-Slavery Society . . . in 1837* (Boston: Isaac Knapp, 1837), 53.

41. *Dictionary of American Biography*, s.v. "Winslow, Hubbard."

42. Henry A. Cooke, comp., *Phineas Stowe and Bethel Work* (Boston: James H. Earle, 1874), 8.

43. Background on the Tremont Temple can be found in Fulton, *Memoir of Timothy Gilbert*, 49–66.

44. Ibid. The Tremont Temple burned to the ground the very day Colver preached his last sermon.

45. Quotes taken from Lydia Maria Child to Convers Francis, 22 December 1838, in *Lydia Maria Child: Selected Letters, 1817–1880*, ed. Milton Meltzer and Patricia Holland (Amherst: University of Massachusetts Press, 1982), 103. For a useful discussion of Boston's Unitarian abolitionists, including information on Boston Female Anti-Slavery Society members, see Douglas Stange, *Patterns of Antislavery among American Unitarians, 1831–1860* (Rutherford, N.J.: Fairleigh Dickinson University Press, 1977).

46. William Ellery Channing to Lydia Maria Child, 12 March 1842, Cornell University, Olin Library, Manuscript Division, Ithaca, N.Y. (hereafter cited as Cornell).

47. As quoted in Crawford, *Romantic Days in Old Boston*, 130–31. Some have suggested that Channing did not realize it was Garrison he was greeting.

48. Anne Warren Weston to Deborah Weston, 21 December 1836, BPL. For a good example of these transcendentalist connections, see Lydia Maria Child to Augusta G. King, 30 October 1844, in *Lydia Maria Child: Selected Letters*, 216–17. Child begins

this letter with "Emerson has sent me his new volume," and after discussing Emerson's *Essays*, she describes an engraving that Theodore Parker brought her from Italy.

49. Maria Weston Chapman to Mr. and Mrs. Garrison, 30 August 1838, BPL.

50. Lydia Maria Child to Convers Francis, 22 December 1838, in *Lydia Maria Child: Selected Letters*, 103.

51. Quotes taken from Deborah Weston, Diary, 18 October 1835, BPL.

52. Anne Warren Weston to Mary Weston, 27 October 1835, BPL.

53. Anne Warren Weston to Deborah Weston, 22 October 1836, BPL.

54. Ibid.

55. Alan Kraut, "The Forgotten Reformers: A Profile of Third Party Abolitionists in Antebellum New York," in Lewis Perry and Michael Fellman, eds., *Antislavery Reconsidered: New Perspectives on the Abolitionists* (Baton Rouge: Louisiana State University Press, 1979), 119–45; Edward Magdol, *The Antislavery Rank and File: A Social Profile of the Abolitionists' Constituency* (Westport, Conn.: Greenwood Press, 1986); and Gerald Sorin, *The New York Abolitionists: A Case Study of Political Radicalism* (Westport, Conn.: Greenwood Press, 1971). For an extremely useful synthesis of abolitionist social profiles, see Lawrence J. Friedman, "'Pious Fellowship' and Modernity: A Psychosocial Interpretation," in Alan M. Kraut, ed., *Crusaders and Compromisers: Essays on the Relationship of the Antislavery Struggle to the Antebellum Party System* (Westport, Conn.: Greenwood Press, 1983), 235–61. See also Edward Magdol, "Notes on Past Scholarship toward the Antislavery Profile," in *Antislavery Rank and File*, 143–55.

56. Kraut, "Forgotten Reformers," 129.

57. Friedman, "'Pious Fellowship' and Modernity."

58. David Donald, "Toward a Reconsideration of Abolitionists," in *Lincoln Reconsidered: Essays on the Civil War Era*, 2nd ed. (New York: Vintage Books, 1961), 19–36.

59. Leonard L. Richards, *"Gentlemen of Property and Standing": Anti-Abolition Mobs in Jacksonian America* (New York: Oxford University Press, 1970), 144.

60. Judith Wellman, "Women and Radical Reform in Antebellum Upstate New York: A Profile of Grassroots Female Abolitionists," in Mabel E. Deutrich and Virginia C. Purdy, eds., *Clio Was a Woman: Studies in the History of American Women* (Washington, D.C.: Howard University Press, 1980), 120.

61. Nancy Hewitt, "The Social Origins of Women's Antislavery Politics in Western New York," in Kraut, *Crusaders and Compromisers*, 208–9, and "On Their Own Terms: An Historiographical Essay," in Jean Fagan Yellin and John C. Van Horne, eds., *An Untrodden Path: Antislavery and Women's Political Culture* (Ithaca: Cornell University Press, forthcoming).

62. Amy Swerdlow, "Abolition's Conservative Sisters: The Ladies' New York City Anti-Slavery Societies, 1834–1840" (Paper presented at the Third Berkshire Conference on the History of Women, Bryn Mawr College, 9–11 June 1976), 2–3.

63. Williams, "Religion, Race, and Gender," 188.

64. Abel Bowen, *Bowen's Picture of Boston . . .*, 3rd ed. (Boston: Otis, Broaders, 1838), a standard city guidebook, did not include a single Presbyterian church among the sixty churches described. Also, Lemuel Shattuck, *Report to the Committee of the City Council Appointed to Obtain the Census of Boston for the Year 1845 . . .* (Boston:

John H. Eastburn, 1846), 122–26, does not include Presbyterians in tables covering the churches in the city at that time.

65. For a comprehensive discussion of African-American female abolitionists, see Shirley Yee, *Black Women Abolitionists: A Study in Activism, 1828–1860* (Knoxville: University of Tennessee Press, 1992).

66. As Jane Pease complained in her review of Gerald Sorin's *New York Abolitionists*, because his sample was primarily drawn from Liberty party voters his profile was "heavily weighted toward political antislavery people," which allowed for "little distinction among antislavery types"; *Journal of American History* 53 (September 1971): 459.

67. Edward Magdol, "A Window on the Abolitionist Constituency: Antislavery Petitions, 1836–1839," in Kraut, *Crusaders and Compromisers*, 48, 56–57. David Brion Davis's description of postrevolutionary abolitionism in the nation's two largest cities, Philadelphia and New York, also demonstrated that abolitionist leaders "represented an extremely narrow and affluent" group of merchants, bankers, lawyers, high government officials, and professionals; see David Brion Davis, *The Problem of Slavery in the Age of Revolution, 1770–1823* (Ithaca: Cornell University Press, 1975), 239.

68. Donald, "Toward a Reconsideration of Abolitionists," 26.

69. Blanche Glassman Hersh, *The Slavery of Sex: Feminist-Abolitionists in America* (Urbana: University of Illinois Press, 1978); Ellen Du Bois, "Women's Rights and Abolition: The Nature of the Connection," in Perry and Fellman, *Antislavery Reconsidered*, 238–51.

70. Kraut, "Forgotten Reformers"; and Sorin, *New York Abolitionists*.

71. Some excellent analyses of the differences among abolitionists include Nancy A. Hewitt, *Women's Activism and Social Change: Rochester, New York, 1822–1872* (Ithaca: Cornell University Press, 1984); Lawrence Friedman, *Gregarious Saints: Self and Community in American Abolitionism, 1830–1870* (New York: Cambridge University Press, 1982); and John R. McKivigan, *The War against Proslavery Religion: Abolitionism and the Northern Churches, 1830–1865* (Ithaca: Cornell University Press, 1984).

5. Divisions in the Boston Female Anti-Slavery Society

1. Anne Warren Weston to Deborah Weston, 11 July 1839, BPL.

2. Quotes from Anne Warren Weston to Mary Weston, 9 July 1838, BPL; Anne Warren Weston to Deborah Weston, 10 April 1838, BPL; *Massachusetts Abolitionist*, 14 May 1840.

3. Caroline Weston to Samuel J. May, 21 October 1871, BPL.

4. Quotes from Maria Weston Chapman to Elizabeth Pease, 20 April 1840, BPL; Lydia Maria Child to Caroline Weston, 7 March 1839, BPL; Lydia Maria Child to Lydia B. Child, 12 December 1839, in *Lydia Maria Child: Selected Letters, 1817–1880*, ed. Milton Meltzer and Patricia Holland (Amherst: University of Massachusetts Press, 1982), 125–26; *Liberator*, Extra [April 1840].

5. Martha V. Ball to Elizabeth Pease, 6 May 1840, BPL.

6. Quotes from *Liberator*, 15 November 1839, 22 November 1839, and Extra.

7. Quotes from Maria Weston Chapman to Elizur Wright [September 1837], BPL; Boston Female Anti-Slavery Society, "Meeting Minutes," 1837, BPL.

8. Caroline Weston to Deborah Weston, 3 March 1839, BPL; Martha V. Ball to Mrs. Chapman, 13 March 1839, BPL.

9. Anne Warren Weston to Deborah Weston, 10 April 1838, BPL; Maria Weston Chapman to Elizabeth Pease, 20 April 1840, BPL.

10. Maria Weston Chapman to Misses Ball, n.d., BPL; Lucy and Martha Ball to Mrs. Chapman, 29 September 1839, BPL.

11. Deborah Weston to Lucia Weston, 8 January 1839, BPL; Anne Warren Weston to Mary Weston, 27 February 1839, BPL.

12. As quoted in Jean Strouse, *Alice James: A Biography* (New York: Bantam Books, 1982), 80.

13. The Boston Public Library originally stood on the site of the Westons' school, the result of bequests from their London uncle, Joshua Bates. See Horace G. Wadlin, *The Public Library of the City of Boston: A History* (Boston: Boston Public Library, 1911), 42–46. Biographical information on the Weston family can be found in John Warner Barber, *Historical Collections . . . Relating to the History and Antiquities of Every Town in Massachusetts* (Worcester, Mass.: Dorr, Howland, 1839); William R. Cutter, *Genealogical and Personal Memoir Relating to the Families of the State of Massachusetts* (New York: Lewis Historical Publishing, 1910), vol. 3; Weymouth Historical Society, *History of Weymouth, Massachusetts* (Weymouth: Published by the Society, 1923); Edmund Soper Hunt, *Weymouth Ways and Weymouth People* (Boston: Privately printed, 1907); Maria Weston Chapman's obituary, *Woman's Journal*, 18 July 1885; John Jay Chapman, *Memories and Milestones* (New York: Moffat, Yard, 1915); and M. A. De Wolfe, *John Jay Chapman and His Letters* (Boston: Houghton Mifflin, 1937).

14. Quotes from Dorothy Bass, "The Best Hopes of the Sexes: The Woman Question in Garrisonian Abolitionism" (Ph.D. diss., Brown University, 1980), 131; Lee Chambers-Schiller, *Liberty, a Better Husband: Single Women in America, the Generations of 1780–1840* (New Haven: Yale University Press, 1984), 132.

15. Gordon Milne, *George William Curtis: The Genteel Tradition* (Bloomington: University of Indiana Press, 1956), 85; George Willis Cooke, ed., *Early Letters of George William Curtis and John S. Dwight: Brook Farm and Concord* (1898; Port Washington, N.Y.: Kennikat Press, 1971), 17; Emma W. Sargent, *Epes Sargent of Gloucester and His Descendants* (Boston: Houghton Mifflin, 1923), 13; *Dictionary of American Biography*, s.v. "Tufts, Charles"; [Frances J. Garrison] *Ann Phillips, Wife of Wendell Phillips: A Memorial Sketch* (Boston: Privately printed, 1886), 5; Carlos Martyn, *Wendell Phillips, the Agitator* (New York: Funk and Wagnalls, 1890), 86–87; Irving Bartlett, *Wendell and Ann Phillips: The Community of Reform, 1840–1880* (New York: W. W. Norton, 1979), 18–20.

16. Deborah Weston, Diary, 6–8 May 1835, BPL. Benjamin Silliman (1779–1864), professor of chemistry and natural history at Yale, was considered America's foremost scientist during the first half of the nineteenth century. His lectures at the Boston Society of Natural History in the spring of 1835 were said to have created "nothing less than a sensation"; *Dictionary of American Biography*, s.v. "Silliman, Benjamin." See also Margaret W. Rossiter, "Benjamin Silliman and the Lowell Institute: The Popularization of Science in Nineteenth-Century America," *New England Quarterly* 44 (December 1971): 602–26.

17. For information on the British–American abolitionist connection, see Frank Thistlethwaite, *America and the Atlantic Community: Anglo-American Aspects, 1790–1850* (New York: Harper and Row, 1959); Christine Bolt, *The Anti-Slavery Movement and Reconstruction: A Study of Anglo-American Cooperation, 1833–1877* (New York: Oxford University Press, 1969); Kathryn Kish Sklar, "Women Who Speak for an Entire Nation: American and British Women Compared at the World Anti-Slavery Convention, London, 1840," *Pacific Historical Review* 59 (November 1990): 453–99.

18. Anne Warren Weston to Aunt Mary, 13 January 1839, BPL. By "sky scraping," Weston probably refers to the social status of the Quincys and Sargents in Boston. Maria Mack moved to Brook Farm with her husband, David, in early 1842.

19. Anne Warren Weston to Deborah Weston, 21 December 1836, BPL.

20. Deborah Weston to Aunt Mary, 6 November 1836, BPL.

21. Anne Warren Weston to Deborah Weston, 8 April 1839, BPL.

22. Deborah Weston to Anne Warren Weston, 1 February 1837, BPL; Maria Weston Chapman, to *Evening Post*, letter frag. [May 1864?], BPL.

23. Deborah Weston to Anne Warren Weston, 1 February 1837, BPL.

24. Deborah Weston to Anne Warren Weston, 1 March 1840, BPL.

25. Quotes taken from Anne Warren Weston to Deborah Weston, 23 March 1839, BPL; Caroline Weston to Samuel Joseph May, 21 October 1871, BPL; *Liberator*, 1 January 1841.

26. William Lloyd Garrison to Helen Garrison, 4 November 1835, in William Lloyd Garrison, *Letters of William Lloyd Garrison*, ed. Walter Merrill (Cambridge, Mass.: Belknap Press, 1971), 1:546.

27. *Liberator*, Extra.

28. Lydia Maria Child to Caroline Weston, 7 March 1839, in *Lydia Maria Child: Selected Letters*, 109.

29. Quotes from *Liberator*, Extra; Maria Weston Chapman to Deborah Weston, 6 December 1839; BPL; *Liberator*, 26 April 1839.

30. Quotes from *Liberator*, Extra; Maria Weston Chapman, October 1835, BPL.

31. Quotes from *Liberator*, Extra; Boston Female Anti-Slavery Society, "Meeting Minutes," 1837, BPL; Maria Weston Chapman to Sarah and Angelina Grimké, 15 May 1839, as quoted in Jane H. Pease and William H. Pease, *Bound with Them in Chains: A Biographical History of the Antislavery Movement* (Westport, Conn.: Greenwood Press, 1972), 41.

32. Boston Female Anti-Slavery Society, "Meeting Minutes," 1837, BPL; Maria Weston Chapman to Salem Female Anti-Slavery Society, 16 October 1841, Essex Institute, Salem; *Liberator*, Extra.

33. Maria Weston Chapman, obituary, *Woman's Journal*, 18 July 1885.

34. A list of early officers in the Boston Female Asylum can be found in Boston Female Asylum, *Reminiscences of the Boston Female Asylum* (Boston: Eastburn's Press, 1844), 77–88.

35. *Liberator*, Extra.

36. Anne Warren Weston to Deborah Weston, 8 March 1839, BPL; Maria Weston Chapman to Deborah Weston, 6 December 1839, BPL; *Liberator*, 1 January 1841.

37. Quotes from Anne Warren Weston to Deborah Weston, 10 April 1838, BPL; William Lloyd Garrison to Mary Benson, 23 December 1838, in Garrison, *Letters*,

2:408. For more information on nonresistance, see Lewis Perry, *Radical Abolitionism, Anarchy, and the Government of God in Antislavery Thought* (Ithaca: Cornell University Press, 1973).

38. Quotes from Boston Female Anti-Slavery Society, "Meeting Minutes," 1837, BPL; Caroline Weston to Deborah Weston, 3 March 1839, BPL.

39. Maria Weston Chapman to Mary Estlin, 5 March 1858, as quoted in Pease and Pease, *Bound with Them in Chains*, 39–40; *Liberator*, 1 November 1839.

40. Quotes taken from Lydia Maria Child to Caroline Weston, 13 August 1838, in *Lydia Maria Child: Selected Letters*, 83, and Ethel K. Ware, "Lydia Maria Child and Anti-Slavery," *Boston Public Library Quarterly* 31 (October 1951): 261.

41. Boston Female Anti-Slavery Society, *Report of the Boston Female Anti-Slavery Society; with a Concise Statement of Events Previous and Subsequent to the Annual Meeting of 1835* (Boston: Published by the Society, 1836), 34–35.

42. Maria Weston Chapman, "Names Checked on Miss L. M. Ball's List Used at the Adjourned Meeting of the Boston Female A.S. Society" [1840], BPL.

43. Anne Warren Weston to Deborah Weston, 22 October 1836, BPL; Anne Warren Weston to Deborah Weston, 13 January 1839, BPL; Caroline Weston to Deborah Weston, letter frag., 1839, BPL.

44. Anne Warren Weston to Deborah Weston, 22 October 1836, BPL.

45. Information on the Parker sisters was gleaned from Albert Annett and Alice Lehtinen, *The History of Jaffrey (Middle Monadnock), New Hampshire . . .* (Jaffrey, N.H.: Published by the Town, 1937), 2:570–71; *The Town Register: Marlboro, Troy, Jaffrey, Swanzey* (Augusta, Me.: Mitchell-Cany, 1908), 70; Daniel B. Cutler, *History of the Town of Jaffrey, New Hampshire, 1749–1880* (n.p., 1881), 413–17; Charles Henry Chandler, *The History of New Ipswich, New Hampshire, 1735–1914* (Fitchburg, Mass.: Sentinel Printing, 1914), 546–47; *Jaffrey Town Reports, 1889–1901*, 24; *Invoices and Taxes of the Town of Jaffrey, New Hampshire, Taken April 1, 1875* (Peterboro, N.H.: Farnum and Scott, 1875), 13; Mary Parker, obituary, *Liberator*, 23 July 1841. Unfortunately, too little documentation remains to capture Parker's personality and opinions fully or to appreciate the rare qualities that earned her the presidency of the Boston Female Anti-Slavery Society.

46. Information on Lucy and Martha Ball taken from Frances Willard and Mary Livermore, eds., *A Woman of the Century* (New York: Charles Wills Moulton, 1893), 50; obituaries of Lucy Ball in *Home Guardian* 53 (June 1891): 279–81, and *Boston Evening Transcript*, 20 April 1891; Mount Auburn Cemetery Records, Lot no. 4428; Suffolk County, *Probate and Death Records*; and Martha V. Ball, Will, 8 January 1895.

47. African Baptists were divided in their allegiances with two supporting the board and two supporting the Chapmanites.

48. Anne Warren Weston to Aunt Mary, 6 May 1839, BPL. This comment was made in discussing the Reverend Amos Phelps's attitude toward radical women abolitionists.

49. Maria Weston Chapman to Abby Kelley, 14 March 1839, as quoted in Pease and Pease, *Bound with Them in Chains*, 43.

50. Quotes from Massachusetts Female Emancipation Society, "To the Public," 9 February 1841, Cornell; Lucy M. Ball to William Lloyd Garrison, 19 January 1836,

BPL; Boston Female Anti-Slavery Society, *Fifth Annual Report of the Boston Female Anti-Slavery Society* (Boston: Isaac Knapp, 1838), 26.

51. Quotes from *Home Guardian* 31 (October 1869): 305; Boston Female Anti-Slavery Society, *Fifth Annual Report*, 27; *Friend of Virtue* 2 (15 July 1839): 203.

52. Massachusetts Female Emancipation Society, "Address . . . to the Women of Massachusetts," 1 April 1840, BPL; Abigail B. Ordway to Salem Female Anti-Slavery Society, 25 August 1839, Essex Institute; *Friend of Virtue* 2 (1 February 1839): 32. Abigail Ordway was an interesting exception to the class-based divisions in the Boston Female Anti-Slavery Society. As a self-employed widow, Ordway earned an income as a milliner and by working in various capacities for women's organizations. After the Boston Female Anti-Slavery Society divided, she devoted herself to the Boston Female Moral Reform Society. Though dismissed by Anne Weston as vulgar and uneducated, Ordway sided with Weston's faction during the important votes in the abolition society.

53. Massachusetts Female Emancipation Society, "Address . . . to the Women of Massachusetts," 1 April 1840, BPL.

54. Quotes from *Home Guardian* 43 (July 1881): 371; *Friend of Virtue* 1 (January 1838): 14, 1 (August 1838): 126, 1 (September 1838): 143.

55. Quotes from *Friend of Virtue* 1 (February 1838): 17, 2 (15 July 1839): 190, 1 (November 1838): 172, 175.

56. Quotes from *Friend of Virtue* 1 (January 1838): 2, 2 (15 July 1839): 201, 2 (1 February 1839): 18, 2 (15 July 1839): 204; *Home Guardian* 1 (December 1868): 310. Mount Auburn Cemetery excited much acclaim during the nineteenth century. Contemporary discussions of its beauty, purpose, and meaning can be found in Isaac Smith Homans, *Sketches of Boston, Past and Present* . . . (Boston: Phillips, Sampson, 1851), 103–8; Frank Foxcroft, "Mount Auburn," *New England Magazine* 14 (June 1896): 419–38. For a good description of Mount Auburn and analysis of middle-class mourning practices, see Karen Halttunen, *Confidence Men and Painted Women: A Study of Middle-Class Culture in America, 1830–1870* (New Haven: Yale University Press, 1982), chap. 5.

57. Quotes from *Home Guardian* 53 (June 1891): 179, 1 (July 1868): 168; Boston Baptist Sewing and Social Circle, "Minute Book," January 1855, A-N; *Liberator*, 3 April 1840.

58. Anne Warren Weston to Deborah Weston, 5 December 1839, BPL; Harriet Martineau, *Retrospect of Western Travel* (1838; New York: Greenwood Press, Publishers, 1969), 3:155; Martha V. Ball to Elizabeth Pease, 6 May 1840, BPL.

59. *Liberator*, Extra; Boston Female Anti-Slavery Society, "Meeting Minutes," 1837, BPL.

60. Boston Female Anti-Slavery Society, "Meeting Minutes," 1837, BPL.

61. Boston Female Anti-Slavery Society husbands who associated with the "evangelical abolitionists" were Charles Fitch (Congregational minister), Willard Sears (housewright), Harvey Newcomb, Charles Briggs (bookseller/bookbinder), Abner Campbell (proprietor), Henry Blodgett (housewright), and William Damrell (printer/stationer). "Voting abolitionists" included Josiah Brackett (leather dealer), H. M. Chamberlain, Nathaniel Colver (Baptist minister), John E. Fuller (boardinghouse keeper), and Alanson St. Clair (Congregational minister).

62. *Liberator*, 14 June 1839.

63. Boston Female Anti-Slavery Society, *Fifth Annual Report*, 6.

64. Boston Baptist Sewing and Social Circle, "Minute Book," A-N. Melissa Neale died in January 1855. In 1861 the Baptist women's group elected Rollin Neale's new wife as president of their group. In the years prior to the Civil War, these Baptist women again gave voice to a lingering abolitionist sentiment. In January 1857 the society voted to contribute goods to Boston's Emigrant Aid Society, an organization formed to encourage the settlement of Kansas by New Englanders. "The ladies here are all on your side," the secretary wrote. "We will use all the influence we have with our husbands, our brothers, and lovers, all for peace and Kansas a Free State"; see "Minute Book," 15 January 1857, A-N.

65. *Friend of Virtue*, 1 (April 1838): 61.

66. Ibid., 1 (July 1838): 112. For more on the moral reform movement, see David J. Pivar, *Purity Crusade: Sexual Morality and Social Control, 1868–1900* (Westport, Conn.: Greenwood Press, 1973); Carroll Smith-Rosenberg, "Evangelicalism and the New City: A History of the City Mission Movement in New York, 1812 to 1870" (Ph.D. diss., Columbia University, 1968); and Howard H. Bell, "The American Moral Reform Society, 1836–1841," *Journal of Negro Education* 27 (Winter 1958): 34–40. Studies of the Boston Female Moral Reform Society, which later became the New England Female Moral Reform Society, include Barbara Hobson, "Sex in the Marketplace: Prostitution in an American City, Boston, 1820–1880" (Ph.D. diss., Boston University, 1982); Hobson's *Uneasy Virtue: The Politics of Prostitution and the American Reform Tradition* (New York: Basic Books, 1987); and Marlou Belyea, "The New England Female Moral Reform Society, 1835–1850: 'Put Down the Libertine, Reclaim the Wanderer, Restore the Outcast,'" typescript, 1976, Schlesinger Library, Radcliffe College.

67. Stephen Nissenbaum, *Sex, Diet, and Debility in Jacksonian America: Sylvester Graham and Health Reform* (Westport, Conn.: Greenwood Press, 1980), 144. Nissenbaum's analysis of the social composition of the American Physiological Society demonstrated that Boston Grahamites, like middle-class abolitionists, were largely skilled artisans and tradesmen. Members included six housewrights, five piano makers, four grocers, four merchants, three cabinetmakers, three bookbinders, three machinists, and assorted proprietors.

68. *Liberator*, 11 March 1837. The riot was also mentioned in Willard Sears's (owner of the meetinghouse) obituary in the *Boston Transcript*, 26 June 1890.

69. For an analysis of how moral reformers used the discussion of personal deportment and sexual activity to achieve some power and influence as well as to delineate class ideology, see Mary P. Ryan, "The Power of Women's Networks," in Judith L. Newton, Mary P. Ryan, and Judith R. Walkowitz, *Sex and Class in Women's History* (London: Routledge and Kegan Paul, 1983), 180–81. See also Lori D. Ginzberg, *Women and the Work of Benevolence: Morality, Politics, and Class in the Nineteenth-Century United States* (New Haven: Yale University Press, 1990), 24–25.

70. "Homeless," by Martha V. Ball, in *Home Guardian* 34 (May 1872): 202–3. For more on this, see Christine Stansell, "Women, Children, and the Uses of the Streets: Class and Gender Conflict in New York City, 1850–1860," *Feminist Studies* 8 (Summer 1982): 309–36; Hobson, *Uneasy Virtue*; and Linda Gordon, *Heroes of Their Own*

Lives: The Politics and History of Family Violence, Boston, 1880–1960 (New York: Penguin, 1988).

71. Friend of Virtue 1 (January 1838): 5.

72. For quotes, see Friend of Virtue 1 (January 1838): 2, 1 (October 1838): 153, 1 (September 1838): 141; Martha V. Ball to Elizabeth Pease, 1 April 1840, BPL.

73. Benjamin Frost letter printed in Liberator, 26 January 1838.

74. For more on the politicization of the Boston Female Anti-Slavery Society, see my article, "The Boston Female Anti-Slavery Society and the Limits of Gender Politics," in Jean Fagan Yellin and John C. Van Horne, eds., An Untrodden Path: Antislavery and Women's Political Culture (Ithaca: Cornell University Press, forthcoming).

75. Deborah Bingham Van Broekhoven, "'A Determination to Labor . . .': Female Antislavery Activity in Rhode Island," Rhode Island History 44 (1985): 42–44.

76. Amy Swerdlow, "Abolition's Conservative Sisters: The Ladies' New York City Anti-Slavery Societies, 1834–1840" (Paper presented at the Third Berkshire Conference on the History of Women, Bryn Mawr College, 9–11 June 1976), 16.

77. Judith Wellman, "Women and Radical Reform in Antebellum Upstate New York: A Profile of Grassroots Female Abolitionists," in Mabel E. Deutrich and Virginia C. Purdy, eds., Clio Was a Woman: Studies in the History of American Women (Washington, D.C.: Howard University Press, 1980), 124.

78. Carolyn Luverne Williams, "Religion, Race, and Gender in Antebellum American Radicalism: The Philadelphia Female Anti-Slavery Society, 1833–1870" (Ph.D. diss., University of California, Los Angeles, 1991).

79. Nancy Hewitt, "The Social Origins of Women's Antislavery Politics in Western New York," in Alan M. Kraut, ed., Crusaders and Compromisers: Essays on the Relationship of the Antislavery Struggle to the Antebellum Party System (Westport, Conn.: Greenwood Press, 1983), 205–6. See also Hewitt's "On Their Own Terms: An Historiographical Essay," in Yellin and Van Horne, An Untrodden Path.

80. For more of Hewitt's writing on the socioeconomic differences among women activists, see Women's Activism and Social Change: Rochester, New York, 1822–1872 (Ithaca: Cornell University Press, 1984), and "Feminist Friends: Agrarian Quakers and the Emergence of Women's Rights in America," Feminist Studies 12 (Spring 1986): 27–49.

81. Ginzberg, Women and Benevolence, 83, 85, 96.

82. Ibid., 8.

83. Nonresistance also was an elite institution through which its members engaged other elites in a dialog concerning the structure and process of politics and governments. As Ronald Formisano has described, elite Bostonians were suspicious of partisanship, particularly political parties, and nonresistance might be understood as part of this antipolitical orientation. In any event, the fact that upper-class abolitionist women participated in this dialog concerning the organization and conduct of the state is significant, I think, particularly when evangelical women rarely spoke to such issues—except to criticize their sisters for addressing them. See Ronald Formisano, The Transformation of Political Culture: Massachusetts Parties, 1790s–1840s (New York: Oxford University Press, 1983).

84. John R. McKivigan, The War against Proslavery Religion: Abolitionism and

the Northern Churches, 1830–1865 (Ithaca: Cornell University Press, 1984), chaps. 3 and 4.

85. Lawrence Friedman, *Gregarious Saints: Self and Community in American Abolitionism, 1830–1870* (New York: Cambridge University Press, 1982), 46, 70, 144.

86. Hewitt, "On Their Own Terms." The limited attention also derives from the fact that feminist-abolitionists were conscious record keepers whereas evangelical women were not. Thus few personal documents remain for the latter.

87. Blanche Glassman Hersh, *The Slavery of Sex: Feminist-Abolitionists in America* (Urbana: University of Illinois Press, 1978), 137.

88. Blanche Glassman Hersh, "'Am I Not a Woman and a Sister'? Abolitionist Beginnings of Nineteenth-Century Feminism," in Lewis Perry and Michael Fellman, eds., *Antislavery Reconsidered: New Perspectives on the Abolitionists* (Baton Rouge: Louisiana State University Press, 1979), 266.

89. Belyea, "New England Female Moral Reform Society."

90. Hobson, "Sex in the Marketplace," 136, 138–40. See also Hobson's book-length study, *Uneasy Virtue.*

91. Smith-Rosenberg, "Evangelicalism and the New City," 182.

92. See Carroll Smith-Rosenberg, "Beauty, the Beast, and the Militant Woman: A Case Study in Sex Roles and Social Stress in Jacksonian America," in *Disorderly Conduct: Visions of Gender in Victorian America* (New York: Oxford University Press, 1985), 126; elsewhere in this chapter (p. 122), she argues that the "New York Female Moral Reform Society could be considered a militant women's organization." Mary P. Ryan, in "The Power of Female Networks," makes a similar case.

93. Shirley Yee, *Black Women Abolitionists: A Study in Activism, 1828–1860* (Knoxville: University of Tennessee Press, 1992), 102.

94. Benjamin Quarles, *Black Abolitionists* (New York: Oxford University Press, 1969), makes this same observation.

6. The Boston Female Anti-Slavery Society Fair

1. Quotes from Anne Warren Weston to Deborah Weston, 8 April 1839, BPL; Deborah Weston to Anne Warren Weston, 13 April 1839, BPL.

2. Anne Warren Weston to Deborah Weston, 8 April 1839, BPL. For a sample letter describing the divisions among antislavery societies and urging financial support for the pro-Garrison faction, see Maria Weston Chapman to "Dear Friends," 1840, BPL.

3. *Liberator,* 12 April 1839. Women were admitted as full members to the Massachusetts Anti-Slavery Society in January 1839.

4. Ibid., 14 June 1839.

5. Ibid. For the different advertisements, see *Liberator,* 19 April 1839.

6. Quotes from *Liberator,* Extra, and 5 July 1839; and Caroline Weston to Samuel J. May, 21 October 1971, BPL.

7. See Jane H. Pease and William H. Pease, *Bound with Them in Chains: A Biographical History of the Antislavery Movement* (Westport, Conn.: Greenwood Press, 1972), 45–47.

8. James Russell Lowell's poem quoted in Chapman's obituary, *Woman's Journal,* 18 July 1885.

9. The Chapmans' Chauncy Place mansion boasted of conservatories and hothouses and valuable plants intended for the fair could be housed there; see *Liberator*, 13 December 1839.

10. Anne Warren Weston to Deborah Weston, 21 December 1836.

11. *Liberator*, 12 April 1839, 23 October 1840, 13 March 1840. For an informative discussion of the goals and uses of 1830s mechanics' fairs, see Sean Wilentz, "Artisan Republican Festivals and the Rise of Class Conflict in New York City, 1788–1837," in Michael Frisch and Daniel Walkowitz, eds., *Working-Class America: Essays on Labor, Community, and American Society* (Urbana: University of Illinois Press, 1983).

12. Henry G. Chapman to Caroline Weston [1841], Cornell.

13. *Liberator*, 1 January 1841.

14. See circular, "The Sixteenth National Anti-Slavery Bazaar," Boston, 21 December 1849, Columbia University, Butler Library, Department of Manuscripts, New York.

15. Boston Female Anti-Slavery Society, fair circular, 1839, BPL; *Liberator*, 1 January 1841; Anne Warren Weston, *Report of the Twenty-first National Anti-Slavery Bazaar* (Boston: J. B. Yerrinton and Son, 1855), 32.

16. Weston, *Report of Twenty-first Bazaar*, 32.

17. Margaret Fuller to Mother, 24 December 1841, in Margaret Fuller, *The Letters of Margaret Fuller*, ed. Robert N. Hudspeth (Ithaca: Cornell University Press, 1983), 2:261.

18. Caroline Weston to Samuel J. May, 21 October 1871, BPL; *Liberator*, 1 January 1841.

19. *Liberator*, 18 October 1839.

20. Ibid.

21. Deborah Weston to Anne Warren Weston, 7 December 1840, BPL.

22. *Liberator*, 2 January 1837; Anne Warren Weston to Deborah Weston, 21 December 1836, BPL.

23. Anne Warren Weston to Deborah and Caroline Weston, 10 February 1845, as quoted in Lee Chambers-Schiller, "'A Good Work among the People': The Political Culture of the Boston Antislavery Fair," in Jean Fagan Yellin and John Van Horne, eds., *An Untrodden Path: Antislavery and Women's Political Culture* (Ithaca: Cornell University Press, forthcoming). Charles Sumner also paid a visit to the radicals' sale, as he indicates in an 1841 letter to Lord Morpeth: "After quitting Prescott, I went to the Anti-slavery Fair, where I talked with Mrs. Loring and Mrs. Chapman about you"; Charles Sumner to Lord Morpeth, 28 December 1841, in *Memoir and Letters of Charles Sumner*, ed. Edward L. Pierce (Boston: Roberts Brothers, 1898), 2:189.

24. Caroline Weston to Samuel Joseph May, 21 October 1871, BPL.

25. Deborah Weston to Anne Warren Weston, 7 December 1840, BPL; Caroline Weston to "Dear Folk," 1–3 December 1840, as quoted in Chambers-Schiller, "Good Work among the People," n. 51.

26. *Liberator*, Extra.

27. Amos A. Phelps to James G. Birney, 13 November 1839, BPL.

28. Mary S. Parker to James G. Birney, 11 November 1839, BPL; Lucy M. Ball to Amos A. Phelps, 29 May 1843, BPL.

29. Women of the Massachusetts Anti-Slavery Society, fair circular [1839], BPL; Massachusetts Female Emancipation Society, *Third Annual Report* (Boston: James Loring, 1843), 7, 8.

30. *Liberator*, 14 June 1839.

31. Ibid.

32. *Liberator*, 22 May 1840.

33. *Liberator*, 21 August 1838.

34. Ibid., and 28 December 1838.

35. *Liberator*, 28 December 1838, 21 December 1838.

36. Henry A. Cooke, comp., *Phineas Stowe and Bethel Work* (Boston: James H. Earle, 1874), 94.

37. Charles Sumner to Maria Weston Chapman, 30 November 1842, in Charles Sumner, *The Selected Letters of Charles Sumner*, ed. Beverly Palmer (Boston: Northeastern University Press, 1990).

38. Ralph Thompson, "The *Liberty Bell* and Other Anti-Slavery Gift-Books," *New England Quarterly* 7 (March 1934): 161.

39. Massachusetts Female Emancipation Society, *Star of Emancipation* (Boston: Published by the Society, 1841), iii–iv.

40. Ibid., 85.

41. Ibid., 77–78.

42. Ibid., 14.

43. Ibid., 70.

44. Ibid., 75–76.

45. New England Female Moral Reform Society, *Twentieth Annual Report of the New England Female Moral Reform Society . . . 1858* (Boston: W. and E. Howe, 1858), 13.

46. *Liberator*, 1 January 1841; Abigail B. Ordway to Salem Female Anti-Slavery Society, 25 August 1839, Essex Institute.

47. Anne Warren Weston to Deborah Weston, 21 December 1836, BPL.

48. Benjamin Quarles, "Sources of Abolitionist Income," *Mississippi Valley Historical Review* 32 (June 1945): 74.

49. For a discussion of the symbolic meaning of the fairs, see Ronald Walters, *The Antislavery Appeal: American Abolitionism after 1830* (Baltimore: Johns Hopkins University Press, 1976).

50. *Liberator*, 1 January 1841.

51. For a thorough analysis of the organization, conduct, and long-term impact of the fairs, see Chambers-Schiller, "A Good Work among the People."

7. Models of Womanhood within the Boston Female Anti-Slavery Society

1. Lydia Maria Child to Charlotte Phelps, 2 January 1834, BPL.

2. Lydia Maria Child to Lucretia Mott, 5 March 1839, in *Lydia Maria Child: Selected Letters, 1817–1880*, ed. Milton Meltzer and Patricia Holland (Amherst: University of Massachusetts Press, 1982), 106; Boston Female Anti-Slavery Society, *Right and Wrong in Boston: Annual Report of the Boston Female Anti-Slavery Society . . . in 1837* (Boston: Isaac Knapp, 1837), 40.

3. Anne Warren Weston to Aunt Mary, 15–16 April 1836, BPL.

4. Boston Female Anti-Slavery Society, *Right and Wrong in Boston*, 1837, 26.

5. *Old Anti-Slavery Days: Proceedings of the Commemorative Meeting Held by the Danvers Historical Society . . . April 26, 1893* (Danvers, Mass.: Danvers Mirror Print, 1893), 137.

6. Anne Warren Weston to Deborah Weston, 19 January 1838, BPL.

7. Anne Warren Weston to Aunt Mary, 9 July 1838, BPL. Legend has it that it was Phelps who slipped into the back of a hall to hear the Grimkés speak, opening the doors to "promiscuous" meetings.

8. Anne Warren Weston to Aunt Mary, 6 May 1839, BPL.

9. *Abolitionist*, 9 July 1840; Boston Female Anti-Slavery Society, *Right and Wrong in Boston*, 1837, 74.

10. *Liberator*, Extra; Angelina Grimké to Theodore Weld, 12 August 1837, in Larry Ceplair, ed., *The Public Years of Sarah and Angelina Grimké: Selected Writings, 1835–1839* (New York: Columbia University Press, 1989), 277–78.

11. *Friend of Virtue* 1 (June 1838): 89.

12. *Friend of Virtue* 1 (January 1838): 3, 2 (1 August 1839): 209, 1 (October 1838): 149, 2 (1 August 1839): 211.

13. *Friend of Virtue* 1 (July 1838): 98, 1 (April 1838): 51.

14. *Friend of Virtue* 1 (November 1838): 161–62.

15. *Friend of Virtue* 1 (December 1838): 177, 1 (November 1838): 171, 2 (1 February 1839): 29.

16. Anne Warren Weston to Deborah Weston, 15 December 1839, BPL. The radical women involved in moral reform were Quaker and Congregationalist, not Unitarian, which perhaps explains their initial interest.

17. *Home Guardian* 33 (September 1871): 283.

18. *Friend of Virtue* 2 (1 August 1839): 209.

19. *Friend of Virtue* 1 (December 1838): 177, 1 (April 1838): 51, 1 (June 1838): 89, 1 (November 1838): 161.

20. *Friend of Virtue* 1 (February 1838): 24–25, 1 (July 1838): 111.

21. *Friend of Virtue* 1 (July 1838): 98–99.

22. *Friend of Virtue* 2 (1 February 1839): 29.

23. *Friend of Virtue* 1 (January 1838): 3; Massachusetts Female Emancipation Society, "To the Public," 9 February 1841, Cornell; *Friend of Virtue* 1 (March 1838): 39.

24. *Friend of Virtue* 1 (April 1838): 51; Boston Female Moral Reform Society, "Third Annual Meeting," in *Friend of Virtue* 1 (October 1838): 154, 157; Abigail B. Ordway to Salem Female Anti-Slavery Society, 25 August 1839, Essex Institute. For more on this sense of solidarity among women, see Carol Lasser, " 'Let Us Be Sisters Forever': The Sororal Model of Nineteenth-Century Female Friendship," *Signs* 14 (Autumn 1988): 158–81.

25. *Friend of Virtue* 1 (July 1838): 97.

26. Massachusetts Female Emancipation Society, "Address . . . to the Women of New England," in *Abolitionist*, 16 July 1840.

27. Ironically, there were fifteen evangelical and nine radical women from Boston who signed the rolls of the New England Anti-Slavery Society's 1838 annual meeting,

suggesting that evangelical women were not automatically opposed to certain forms of women's equality; see *Liberator*, 8 June 1838.

28. Lewis Tappan to Theodore Weld, 26 May 1840, in Weld–Grimké *Letters*, 836.

29. Maria Weston Chapman, *Right and Wrong in Massachusetts* . . . (1839; New York: Negro Universities Press, 1969), 44; *Liberator*, 1 November 1839.

30. Boston Female Anti-Slavery Society, *Seventh Annual Report* . . . *1840* (Boston: Published by the Society, 1840), 27; *Liberator*, 6 July 1838.

31. Anti-Slavery Convention of American Women, *Proceedings of the Anti-Slavery Convention of American Women, Held in the City of New York* . . . *1837* (New York: William S. Dorr, 1837), 9.

32. Boston Female Anti-Slavery Society, *Right and Wrong in Boston, 1837*, 75; *Liberator*, 6 September 1839.

33. *Friend of Virtue* 1 (March 1838): 36.

34. Boston Female Anti-Slavery Society, *Right and Wrong in Boston, 1837*, 42–43.

35. *Friend of Virtue* 1 (March 1838): 33.

36. Maria Weston Chapman, letter frag., 1840, BPL.

37. *Friend of Virtue* 1 (February 1838): 21.

38. Anne Warren Weston to Aunt Mary, 9 July 1838, BPL. The Westons found Miss Grey a position with Groton abolitionist physician Amos Farnsworth.

39. *Liberator*, Extra; Deborah Weston to Anne Warren Weston, 25 November 1839, as quoted in Lori Ginzberg, *Women and the Work of Benevolence: Morality, Politics, and Class in the Nineteenth-Century United States* (New Haven: Yale University Press, 1990), 57.

40. *Friend of Virtue* 1 (November 1838): 172. For more, see Christine Stansell, "Women, Children and the Uses of the Streets: Class and Gender Conflict in New York City, 1850–1860," *Feminist Studies* 8 (Summer 1982): 309–36.

41. Anne Warren Weston to Deborah Weston, 4 October 1836, BPL. During the mid 1830s, Anne showed marked interest in Richard Hildreth and John Greenleaf Whittier. The latter she quickly dropped, seeing no romantic future for herself with a Quaker. Lee Chambers-Schiller, in *Liberty, a Better Husband: Single Women in America, the Generations of 1780–1840* (New Haven: Yale University Press, 1984), 246, n. 21, surmises that Anne was also involved with George Thompson.

42. Anne Warren Weston to Deborah Weston, 21 December 1836, 15 December 1839, BPL.

43. As quoted in Alden Whitman, *American Reformers* (New York: H. W. Wilson, 1985), 164.

44. Sarah Southwick, *Reminiscences of Early Anti-Slavery Days* (1893; Macon, Ga.: Kingsley Press, 1971), 11. Phillis Salem was also a member of the Boston Female Anti-Slavery Society.

45. Deborah Weston, Diary, 7 January 1835, 4 March 1835, BPL.

46. Anne Warren Weston to Maria Weston Chapman, 5 November 1838, BPL; Caroline Weston to Deborah Weston, 24 June 1842, Cornell.

47. Maria Weston Chapman to Elizabeth Pease, 20 April 1840, BPL. Chapman preferred "Anti-Slavery Society of Boston Women."

48. In January 1838 a Boston Lyceum program was devoted to the issue of women's rights. Entrepreneur Amasa Walker, husband of Boston Female Anti-Slavery Society

member Hannah, spoke on behalf of the women. Women have always "been found on the side of humanity and religion," Walker maintained, "and the nearer they approximated to an equality of rights with the men, the better it would be for society." The *Liberator* report of this debate noted that the men present "almost unanimously decided against the women—of course," and went on to compare it to a meeting of slaveholders discussing whether slaves should be freed. Of course, women had not been allowed to vote. See *Liberator*, 12 January 1838.

49. Boston Female Anti-Slavery Society, *Fifth Annual Report of the Boston Female Anti-Slavery Society* (Boston: Isaac Knapp, 1838), 21, 27.

50. Lucy M. Ball to Amos A. Phelps, 29 May 1839, BPL; *Friend of Virtue* 1 (June 1838): 91.

51. Anne Warren Weston to the Boston Female Anti-Slavery Society, 21 August 1837, BPL.

52. Boston Female Anti-Slavery Society, *Seventh Annual Report*, 1840, 23.

53. Ibid., 29.

54. *Friend of Virtue* 1 (April 1838): 58; Boston Female Anti-Slavery Society, *Right and Wrong in Boston, 1837*, 82.

55. For an important discussion of the rise and significance of gender consciousness, see Nancy F. Cott's, *The Bonds of Womanhood: Woman's Sphere in New England, 1780–1835* (New Haven: Yale University Press, 1977).

56. Ginzberg, *Women and Benevolence*, 215.

57. Nancy A. Hewitt, "Feminist Friends: Agrarian Quakers and the Emergence of Woman's Rights in America," *Feminist Studies* 12 (Spring 1986): 29. Although Barbara Epstein, in *The Politics of Domesticity: Women, Evangelism, and Temperance in Nineteenth-Century America* (Middletown, Conn.: Wesleyan University Press, 1981), 6–9, notes the "protofeminist" implications of the middle-class model of womanhood (because it was "centered in women's experience and critical of society as it was"), she too concludes that it also represented an accommodation to the status quo.

58. Some good examples are Mary P. Ryan, *Cradle of the Middle Class: The Family in Oneida County, New York, 1790–1865* (New York: Cambridge University Press, 1981), and Suzanne Lebsock, *The Free Women of Petersburg: Status and Culture in a Southern Town, 1784–1860* (New York: W. W. Norton, 1984).

59. Carl N. Degler, *At Odds: Women and the Family in America from the Revolution to the Present* (New York: Oxford University Press, 1980); Daniel Scott Smith, "Family Limitation, Sexual Control, and Domestic Feminism in Victorian America," in Mary S. Hartman and Lois W. Banner, eds., *Clio's Consciousness Raised: New Perspectives on the History of Women* (New York: Harper and Row, 1974), 119–36.

60. See Ginzberg, *Women and Benevolence*, 215, for a similar assessment.

61. Thomas Carlyle, *On Heroes, Hero Worship and the Heroic in History* (1841). Unlike the Boston radicals, Carlyle advocated a strong governmental presence.

62. See, for example, Hewitt, "Feminist Friends." Ann Braude, in *Radical Spirits: Spiritualism and Women's Rights in Nineteenth-Century America* (Boston: Beacon Press, 1989), 56–81, finds that the feminist-abolitionists who became spiritualists also were predominantly lower-middle-class Quakers. However, the New England Garrisonians who she indicates experimented with spiritualism—Thomas Wentworth Higginson, Francis Jackson, Henry Wright, Ellis Gray Loring, Lydia Maria Child, and

Oliver Johnson—were actually Congregationalists and Unitarians, and many were of the upper class.

63. See, for example, Keith E. Melder, *Beginnings of Sisterhood: The American Woman's Rights Movement, 1800–1850* (New York: Schocken Books, 1977); Blanche Glassman Hersh, *The Slavery of Sex: Feminist-Abolitionists in America* (Urbana: University of Illinois Press, 1978). As Ellen Du Bois has observed, many women abolitionists were already conscious of the inequities experienced by their sex. The importance of the abolitionist movement in the development of feminism, she explains, was in teaching "women what to do with that perception, how to develop it into a social movement"; see "Women's Rights and Abolition: The Nature of the Connection," in Lewis Perry and Michael Fellman, eds., *Antislavery Reconsidered: New Perspectives on the Abolitionists* (Baton Rouge: Louisiana State University Press, 1979), 242.

8. Conclusion

1. Michael McGerr defines political style as "the different ways that people perceive, speak, and act politically"; see "Political Style and Women's Power, 1830–1930," *Journal of American History* 77 (December 1990): 865.

2. See Blanche Glassman Hersh, *The Slavery of Sex: Feminist-Abolitionists in America* (Urbana: University of Illinois Press, 1978); Ellen Carol Du Bois, *Feminism and Suffrage: The Emergence of an Independent Women's Movement in America, 1848–1869* (Ithaca: Cornell University Press, 1978); and Keith E. Melder, *Beginnings of Sisterhood: The American Woman's Rights Movement, 1800–1850* (New York: Schocken Books, 1977).

3. *Friend of Virtue* 1 (November 1838): 163.

4. By the mid 1850s, Massachusetts, as well as other states, was reforming legislation governing women's earnings and property. See Du Bois, *Feminism and Suffrage*, 41–42. Suzanne Lebsock, in *The Free Women of Petersburg: Status and Culture in a Southern Town, 1784–1860* (New York: W. W. Norton, 1984), 84–85, maintains that changes in married women's property laws resulted more from economic insecurity than from feminist demands.

5. That upper-class women identified more with individuals of their own socioeconomic background and standing than with women generally is evidenced in their intimate and long-term relationships with men of their own class. Maria Weston Chapman, for example, was perhaps closer to Edmund Quincy than to any woman, save her sisters. Lydia Maria Child had deep and abiding friendships with Ellis Gray Loring and Wendell Phillips. The subject of male–female friendship in the nineteenth century begs for study along the lines of Karen Lystra's *Searching the Heart: Women, Men, and Romantic Love in Nineteenth-Century America* (New York: Oxford University Press, 1989).

6. Karen Offen, "Defining Feminism: A Comparative Historical Approach," *Signs* 14 (Autumn 1988): 119–57. This ideology has also been labeled "liberal feminism." For an excellent overview of the origins and content of early-nineteenth-century liberal feminism, see Josephine Donovan, *Feminist Theory: The Intellectual Traditions of American Feminism* (New York: Frederick Ungar, 1985), 1–30.

7. Offen, in "Defining Feminism," 135–36, uses "relational feminists" to describe nineteenth-century cultural feminists. As Offen explains, relational feminists "emphasized women's rights *as women* (defined principally by their childbearing and/or nurturing capacities) in relation to men. It insisted on *women's* distinctive contributions in these roles to the broader society and made claims on the commonwealth on the basis of these contributions." Daniel Scott Smith coined another useful label for this type of activist, the "domestic feminist"; see "Family Limitation, Sexual Control, and Domestic Feminism in Victorian America," in Mary S. Hartman and Lois W. Banner, eds., *Clio's Consciousness Raised: New Perspectives on the History of Women* (New York: Harper and Row, 1974).

8. As Michael McGerr observed, they took "politics off the street, a male preserve, and put it in the home, a female preserve"; see "Political Style and Women's Power," 870.

9. Lori D. Ginzberg has made this same observation about moral reformers, many of whom were middle-class abolitionists; see *Women and the Work of Benevolence: Morality, Politics, and Class in the Nineteenth-Century United States* (New Haven: Yale University Press, 1990), 19.

10. Lisa Tuttle, *Encyclopedia of Feminism* (New York: Facts on File, 1986), 73. For a good discussion of the nineteenth-century origins of cultural feminism, see Donovan, *Feminist Theory*, 31–63.

11. Alcoff states further: "For cultural feminists, the enemy of women is not merely a social system or economic institution or set of backward beliefs but masculinity itself and in some cases male biology. Cultural feminist politics revolve around creating and maintaining a healthy environment—free of masculinist values and all their offshoots such as pornography—for the female principle." See Linda Alcoff, "Cultural Feminism versus Poststructuralism: The Identity Crisis in Feminist Theory," *Signs* 13 (Spring 1988): 408.

12. Karen Blair, *The Clubwoman as Feminist: True Womanhood Redefined, 1868–1914* (New York: Holmes and Meier, 1980), 118.

13. Hester Eisenstein, *Contemporary Feminist Thought* (Boston: G. K. Hall, 1983), xvi–xvii. See also Alice Echols, "The New Feminism of Yin and Yang," in Ann Snitow, Christine Stansell, and Sharon Thompson, eds., *Powers of Desire: The Politics of Sexuality* (New York: Monthly Review Press, 1983), 439–59.

14. In "Cultural Feminism versus Poststructuralism," 414, Alcoff makes a similar critique of cultural feminists, noting that, although they "valorize" positive feminine attributes "developed under pressure," in so doing they promote the "restrictive conditions that gave rise to those attributes."

15. For more on this important topic, see Joan W. Scott, "Deconstructing Equality-versus-Difference; or, The Uses of Poststructuralist Theory for Feminism," *Feminist Studies* 14 (Spring 1988): 33–50. Lori Ginzberg, in *Women and Benevolence*, 214–20, provides an outstanding discussion of the origins and significance of this debate.

16. See, for instance, the exchange between Joan W. Scott and Linda Gordon in "Book Reviews," *Signs* 15 (Summer 1990): 848–60. Particularly instructive is the controversy surrounding the *EEOC* v. *Sears, Roebuck & Co.* gender-discrimination suit in which two feminist historians, Rosalind Rosenberg and Alice Kessler-Harris, testified

for the defendant and the plaintiff, respectively, and the uproar that this created in the profession. For a good overview, see Ruth Milkman, "Women's History and the Sears Case," *Feminist Studies* 12 (Summer 1986): 375–400; Jacquelyn Dowd Hall, "Women's History Goes to Trial: *EEOC v. Sears, Roebuck and Company*," *Signs* 11 (Summer 1986): 751–56; and Scott, "Deconstructing Equality-versus-Difference."

Bibliography

Manuscript Collections

American Antiquarian Society, Worcester, Mass.
Abby Kelley Foster Papers
Local History Collection

Andover-Newton Theological School, Special Collections, Newton Center, Mass.
Bethel Sewing Circle, Boston. Constitution and Minutes, 1846–1848
Dudley Street Baptist Church, Roxbury. Ladies' Benevolent Society, Constitution and
    Minutes, 1842–1843
First Baptist Church, Boston. Women's Sewing Circle, Constitution and Minutebook,
    1841–1887
First Baptist Church, Watertown. Female Charitable Sewing Society, Constitution and
    Minutebook, 1829–1906
First Baptist Church, Watertown. Female Foreign Mission Society, Minutebook,
    1845–1910

Boston Public Library, Department of Rare Books and Manuscripts, Boston, Mass.
Antislavery Collection
Lydia Maria Child Papers
William Lloyd Garrison Papers
Weston Family Papers

Brown University, John Hay Library, Providence, R.I.
Phillip Ammidon Papers

Columbia University, Butler Library, Department of Manuscripts, New York, N.Y.
Lydia Maria Child Papers
Sydney Howard Gay Papers

Cornell University, Olin Library, Manuscript Division, Ithaca, N.Y.
Henry G. Chapman Papers
Lydia Maria Child Papers
Samuel J. May Papers

Essex Institute, Salem, Mass.
Salem Female Anti-Slavery Society Papers

Massachusetts Historical Society, Boston, Mass.
Boston Female Anti-Slavery Society Papers

Smith College, Sophia Smith Collection, Northampton, Mass.
Antislavery Papers
Garrison Family Papers
U.S. Organizations Collection

Memoirs and Published Correspondence

Birney, James G. *Letters of James G. Birney, 1831–1857.* Edited by Dwight L. Dumond. 2 vols. 1938. Gloucester, Mass.: Peter Smith, 1966.

Child, Lydia Maria. *Letters of Lydia Maria Child . . .* Edited by John G. Whittier and Wendell Phillips. Boston: Houghton Mifflin, 1883.

———. *Lydia Maria Child: Selected Letters, 1817–1880.* Edited by Milton Meltzer and Patricia Holland. Amherst: University of Massachusetts Press, 1982.

Cushing, Thomas. "Reminiscences of Schools and Teachers in Dorchester and Boston." *American Journal of Education* 34 (1884): 177–92.

Fuller, Margaret. *The Letters of Margaret Fuller.* Edited by Robert N. Hudspeth. 5 vols. Ithaca: Cornell University Press, 1983.

Fulton, Justin D. *Memoir of Timothy Gilbert.* Boston: Lee and Shepard, 1866.

[Garrison, Frances J.]. *Ann Phillips, Wife of Wendell Phillips: A Memorial Sketch.* Boston: Privately printed, 1886.

Garrison, William Lloyd. *Helen Eliza Garrison: A Memorial.* Cambridge, Mass.: Riverside Press, 1876.

———. *Letters of William Lloyd Garrison.* Edited by Walter Merrill et al. 6 vols. Cambridge, Mass.: Belknap Press, 1971–81.

Grew, Mary. "Annals of Women's Anti-Slavery Societies." In *Proceedings of the American Anti-Slavery Society at Its Third Decade.* 1864. New York: Arno Press, 1969.

Grimké, Angelina, and Sarah Grimké. *The Letters of Theodore Weld, Angelina Grimké Weld, and Sarah Grimké, 1822–1844.* Edited by Gilbert H. Barnes and Dwight L. Dumond. 2 vols. 1934. Gloucester: Peter Smith, 1965.

In Memoriam: Mary Ann W. Johnson, Wife of Oliver Johnson. New York: Privately printed, 1872.

Johnson, Oliver. *William Lloyd Garrison and His Times.* Boston: B. B. Russell, 1880.

Lovejoy, J. C. *Memoir of Rev. Charles T. Torrey, Who Died in the Penitentiary of Maryland* . . . Boston: John P. Jewett, 1847.

Martineau, Harriet. *Harriet Martineau's Autobiography.* Edited by Maria Weston Chapman. 2 vols. London: Smith, Elder, 1877.

May, Samuel J. *Some Recollections of Our Anti-Slavery Conflict.* 1869. New York: Arno Press, 1968.

A Memorial of Wendell Phillips from the City of Boston. Boston: City Council, 1884.

Quincy, Josiah Phillips. "Memoir of Edmund Quincy." *Proceedings of the Massachusetts Historical Society* 18 (October 1904): 401–16.

Smith, Rev. Justin A. *Memoir of Nathaniel Colver.* Boston: Durkee and Foxcroft, 1873.

Southwick, Sarah. *Reminiscences of the Early Anti-Slavery Days.* 1893. Macon, Ga.: Kingsley Press, 1971.

Sumner, Charles. *The Selected Letters of Charles Sumner.* Edited by Beverly Palmer. 2 vols. Boston: Northeastern University Press, 1990.

Tiffany, Nina M. *Samuel E. Sewell: A Memoir.* Boston: Houghton Mifflin, 1898.

Walker, James. *Memoir of Josiah Quincy.* Cambridge, Mass.: John Wilson and Son, 1867.

Wyman, Lillie B. Chace. "Reminiscences of Wendell Phillips." *New England Magazine* 27 (February 1903): 725–40.

Contemporary Newspapers and Magazines

Abolitionist
Boston Transcript
Friend of Virtue
Gleason's Drawing Room Companion
Home Guardian
Liberator
New England Magazine

Printed Primary Sources

[Abbott, Jacob]. *New England and Her Institutions: By One of Her Sons.* Hartford: S. Andrus, 1847.

Alcott, William A. *The Moral Reformer and Teacher on the Human Constitution.* Boston: Light and Horton, 1835.

Anti-Slavery Convention of American Women. *Proceedings of the Anti-Slavery Convention of American Women, Held in the City of New York . . . 1837.* New York: William S. Dorr, 1837.

———. *Proceedings of the Anti-Slavery Convention of American Women, Held in Philadelphia . . . 1838.* Philadelphia: Merrihew and Gunn, 1838.

———. *Proceedings of the Anti-Slavery Convention of American Women, Held in Philadelphia . . . 1839.* Philadelphia: Merrihew and Thompson, 1839.

"Asylum for the Blind." *North American Review* 31 (July 1830): 66–85.

Barber, John Warner. *Historical Collections . . . Relating to the History and Antiquities of Every Town in Massachusetts.* Worcester, Mass.: Dorr, Howland, 1839.

Berkeley Street Church. *Articles of Faith and Covenant of the Berkeley Street Congregational Church* . . . Boston: Isaac W. May, 1868.

Bethesda Society. *Annual Report, November 15, 1854.* Boston: John Wilson and Son, 1854.

Boston. *List of Persons, Copartnerships, and Corporations Who Were Taxed in the City of Boston for the Year 1844.* Boston: J. H. Eastburn, 1845.

—————. *List of Persons, Copartnerships, and Corporations Who Were Taxed on Six Thousand Dollars and Upward in the Year 1850.* Boston: J. H. Eastburn, 1851.

—————. *List of Persons, Copartnerships, and Corporations Who Were Taxed on Six Thousand Dollars and Upward in the Year 1855.* Boston: Moore and Crosby, 1856.

Boston Children's Aid Society. *First Report of the Executive Committee of the Boston Children's Aid Society* . . . Boston: John Wilson and Son, 1865.

Boston Directory . . . *1835.* Boston: Charles Stimpson, 1835.

Boston Directory . . . *1837.* Boston: Charles Stimpson, 1837.

Boston Directory . . . *1840.* Boston: Charles Stimpson, 1841.

Boston Directory . . . *1849.* Boston: George Adams, 1849.

Boston Female Anti-Slavery Society. *Annual Reports, 1834–1844.* [Publisher varies.]

Boston Female Asylum. *Reminiscences of the Boston Female Asylum.* Boston: Eastburn's Press, 1844.

Boston Female Moral Reform Society. *Second Annual Report of the Boston Female Moral Reform Society, 1837.* Boston: Isaac Knapp, 1837.

—————. *Third Annual Report of the Boston Female Moral Reform Society, 1838.* Boston: George P. Oakes, 1838.

Boston Female Society for Missionary Purposes. *Constitution.* Boston: Nathaniel Willis, 1816.

The Boston Mob of "Gentlemen of Property and Standing." Proceedings of the Anti-Slavery Meeting . . . *on the Twentieth Anniversary of the Mob of October 21, 1835.* Boston: R. F. Wallcut, 1855.

Boston Provident Association. *Annual Report.* Boston: General Office, 1852.

—————. *Manual of the Boston Provident Association, Adopted October 1853.* Boston: General Office, 1859.

Boston Seaman's Friend Society. *Twenty-Sixth Annual Report of the Boston Seaman's Friend Society.* Boston: T. R. Marvin, 1854.

Bowdoin Street Congregational Church. *The Articles of Faith and Covenant of the Bowdoin Street Church, Boston* . . . Boston: Perkins and Marvin, 1837.

Bowen, Abel. *Bowen's Picture of Boston* . . . 3rd ed. Boston: Otis, Broaders, 1838.

Bradford, Alden. *Biographical Notices of Distinguished Men in New England.* Boston: S. G. Simpkins, 1842.

Caldwell, Charles. "Thoughts on the Moral and Other Indirect Influences of Rail-Roads," *New England Magazine* 2 (April 1832): 288–300.

Chapman, John Jay. *Memories and Milestones.* New York: Moffat, Yard, 1915.

Chapman, Maria Weston. *Right and Wrong in Massachusetts.* 1839. New York: Negro Universities Press, 1969.

—————, ed. *Liberty Bell.* 15 vols. 1839–1858. [Publisher varies.]

Child, Lydia Maria. *An Appeal in Favor of That Class of Americans Called Africans.* 1836. New York: Arno Press, 1868.

————. "William Lloyd Garrison." *Atlantic Monthly* 44 (August 1879): 234–38.

Clarendon Street Baptist Church. *A Brief History of the Clarendon Street Baptist Church . . .* Boston: Gould and Lincoln, 1872.

Collins, John A. *Right and Wrong among Abolitionists in the U.S.* Glasgow: G. Gallie, 1841.

Cooke, Henry A., comp. *Phineas Stowe and Bethel Work.* Boston: James H. Earle, 1874.

Damrell, William, et al. *The Boston Almanac for the Year 1857.* Boston: Jewett, 1857.

Dearborn, Nathaniel. *Dearborn's Reminiscences of Boston and Guide through the City and Environs.* Boston, 1851.

Derby, E. H. *Boston: A Commercial Metropolis in 1850.* Boston: Redding, 1850.

Dickinson, S. N. *The Boston Almanac for the Year 1840.* Boston: Thomas Groom, 1840.

————. *The Boston Almanac for the Year 1849.* Boston: B. B. Mussey, 1849.

Dix, J. R. *Local Loiterings and Visits in the Vicinity of Boston.* Boston: Redding, 1845.

Edwards, Justin. *Joy in Heaven over the Penitent: A Sermon Delivered in Park Street Church before the Penitent Females Refuge Society, and Annual Report for 1825.* Boston: T. R. Marvin, 1826.

Eliot, Samuel Atkins. *An Article on Public and Private Charities in Boston.* Cambridge, Mass.: Metcalf, 1845.

Evangelical Baptist Benevolent and Missionary Society. *Constitution of the Evangelical Baptist Benevolent and Missionary Society, with a History of the Tremont Temple Enterprise.* Boston: J. M. Hewes, 1876.

Federal Street Baptist Church, Maternal Society. *Constitution.* Boston: J. Ford, 1833.

"Female Education." *New England Magazine* 3 (October 1832): 278–84.

First Free Congregational Church. *Brief History of the First Free Congregational Church . . .* Boston: Dow and Jackson, 1840.

Forbes, Abner, and J. W. Greene. *The Rich Men of Massachusetts . . .* Boston: W. V. Spencer, 1851.

Franklin Street Congregational Church. *Origin and Formation of the Franklin Street Church in Boston . . .* Boston: Light and Stearns, 1836.

Garrison, William Lloyd, Jr. "Boston Anti-Slavery Days." *Bostonian Society Publications* 2 (1905): 81–104.

George, Elijah. *Index to the Probate Records of the County of Suffolk, Massachusetts, from the Year 1836 to and including the Year 1893.* 2 vols. Boston: Rockwell and Churchill, 1895.

Grimké, Sarah M. *Letters on the Equality of the Sexes and Other Essays.* 1838. New Haven: Yale University Press, 1988.

Hancock, J. *The Merchant's and Trader's Guide and Stranger's Memorandum Book for the Year of Our Lord, 1836 . . .* Boston: J. Hancock, 1836.

Homans, Isaac Smith. *History of Boston from 1630–1856 . . .* Boston: F. C. Moore, 1856.

————. *Sketches of Boston, Past and Present . . .* Boston: Phillips, Sampson, 1851.

Index to Boston Births, 1800–1849. Microfilm. Salt Lake City: Genealogy Library, Church of Jesus Christ of Latter-day Saints.

Index to [Boston] Deaths, 1882–1891. Microfilm. Salt Lake City: Genealogy Library, Church of Jesus Christ of Latter-day Saints.

Invoices and Taxes of the Town of Jaffrey, New Hampshire, Taken April 1, 1875. Peterboro, N.H.: Farnum and Scott, 1875.

Jaffrey Town Reports, 1889–1901.

Ladies' American Home Education Society. *Annals and Family Manual.* Boston: Published by the Society, 1852.

Ladies' American Home Education Society and Temperance Union. *Annals.* Boston: Emery N. Moore, 1859.

Ladies' Association, Auxiliary to the American Colonization Society. *First Annual Report of the Ladies' Association, Auxiliary to the American Colonization Society, Presented May 7, 1833.* Philadelphia: Lydia R. Bailey, 1833.

Lyman, Theodore, III. *Papers Relating to the Garrison Mob.* Cambridge, Mass.: Welch, Bigelow, 1870.

McGlennon, Edward W., comp. *Boston Marriages from 1700 to 1809.* 2 vols. Baltimore: Genealogical Publishing, 1977.

Martineau, Harriet. *The Martyr Age of the United States.* 1839. New York: Arno Press, 1969.

———. *Retrospect of Western Travel.* 3 vols. 1838. New York: Greenwood Press, 1969.

———. *Society in America.* 1837. Garden City, N.Y.: Anchor Books, 1962.

Massachusetts Abolition Society. *The Second Annual Report of the Massachusetts Abolition Society, Together with the Proceedings of the 2d Annual Meeting, May 20, 1841.* Boston: David Ela, 1841.

———. *The True History of the Late Division in the Anti-Slavery Societies . . .* Boston: David Ela, 1841.

Massachusetts Anti-Slavery Society, *Annual Reports, 1833–1856.* Westport, Conn.: Negro Universities Press, 1970.

Massachusetts Female Emancipation Society. *Star of Emancipation.* Boston: Published by the Society, 1841.

———. *Third Annual Report.* Boston: James Loring, 1843.

"Mobs." *New England Magazine* 7 (December 1834): 471–77.

Moore, Martin. *Boston Revival, 1842: A Brief History of the Evangelical Churches of Boston.* Boston: John Putnam, 1842.

Neale, Rollin H. *The Pastor and Preacher: A Memorial of the Late Baron Stow, D.D.* Boston: Gould and Lincoln, 1870.

New England Female Moral Reform Society. *Twentieth Annual Report of the New England Female Moral Reform Society . . . 1858.* Boston: W. and E. Howe, 1858.

Old Anti-Slavery Days: Proceedings of the Commemorative Meeting Held by the Danvers Historical Society . . . April 26, 1893. Danvers, Mass.: Danvers Mirror Print, 1893.

Old South Church. *List of the Pastors, Officers, and Members of Old South Church in Boston . . .* Boston: J. Frank Farmer, 1870.

Old South Society. *Act of Incorporation and By-laws of the Old South Society in Boston*. Boston: M. Stevens, 1870.

Old Boston Town, Early in This Century, by an 1801er. New York: George F. Nesbitt, 1880.

Penitent Females Refuge. *Annual Report, January 1830*. Boston: T. R. Marvin, 1830.

———. *Appeal to the Public in Behalf of the Penitent Females Refuge in the City of Boston*. Boston: Perkins and Marvin, 1839.

———. *Brief History of the Rise and Progress of the Penitent Females Refuge, Instituted Jan. 12, 1825*. Boston: William D. Ticknor, 1849.

———. *Eleventh Annual Report of the Auxiliary Penitent Females Refuge Society for the Year Ending December 1835*. Boston: Published by the Society, 1837.

———. *The Penitent Females Refuge and Bethesda Societies in the City of Boston . . .* Boston: T. R. Marvin and Son, 1859.

———. *A Short Account of the Penitent Females Refuge in the City of Boston*. Boston: Perkins, Marvin, 1834.

Pennsylvania Hall Association. *The History of Pennsylvania Hall, Which Was Destroyed by a Mob on the 17th of May 1838*. 1838. New York: Negro Universities Press, 1969.

"Philanthropy of the Present Age." *New England Magazine* 6 (January 1834): 55–59.

Pike, James, ed. *History of the Churches of Boston . . .* Boston: Ecclesia Publishing, 1883.

Quincy, Josiah. *A Municipal History of the Town and City of Boston during Two Centuries . . .* Boston: Charles C. Little and James Brown, 1852.

"Reminiscences of a Walker Round Boston." *United States Magazine and Democratic Review* 3 (September 1838): 79–87.

Report of a Delegate to the Anti-Slavery Convention of American Women. Boston: Isaac Knapp, 1838.

Report of the Committee of Delegates from the Benevolent Societies of Boston. Boston: Tuttle and Weeks, 1834.

Sargent, Aaron. "Recollections of Boston Merchants in the Eighteen-Forties." *Proceedings of the Bostonian Society*, 1904, 25–37.

Shattuck, Lemuel. *Bills of Mortality, 1810–1849, City of Boston*. Boston: Registry Department, 1893.

———. *Report to the Committee of the City Council Appointed to Obtain the Census of Boston for the Year 1845 . . .* Boston: John H. Eastburn, 1846.

Snow, C. H. *A Geography of Boston, County of Suffolk, and the Adjacent Towns, with Historical Notes*. Boston: Carter and Hendee, 1830.

The Stranger's Guide; or, Information about Boston and Vicinity. Boston: J. B. Hall, 1844.

Stranger's Guide While in the City of Boston. Boston: Andrews, 1848.

Suffolk County [Massachusetts]. *Probate Records, 1636–1899*. Microfilm. Salt Lake City: Genealogy Library, Church of Jesus Christ of Latter-day Saints.

Union Congregational Church. *Confession of Faith and Covenant, Also a Brief History of Union Church, Essex Street, Boston*. Boston: Crocker and Brewster, 1839.

United States, Bureau of the Census. *Historical Statistics of the United States: Colo-*

nial Times to 1970. 2 vols. Washington, D.C.: Government Printing Office, 1975.

United States, Department of State. *Aggregate Amount of Each Description of Persons within the United States and Their Territories, According to the Census of 1840.* Washington, D.C.: Blair and Rives, 1841.

———. *Enumeration of the Inhabitants of the United States: 1830.* Washington, D.C.: Duff Green, 1832.

Weston, Anne Warren. *Report of the Twenty-first National Anti-Slavery Bazaar.* Boston: J. B. Yerrinton, 1855.

Wilson, T. L. V. *The Aristocracy of Boston.* Boston: Privately printed, 1848.

Wines, E. C. A *Trip to Boston, in a Series of Letters to the Editor of the "United States Gazette."* Boston: Charles C. Little and James Brown, 1838.

Secondary Sources

Abbott, Richard H. *Cotton and Capital: Boston Businessmen and Antislavery Reform, 1854–1868.* Amherst: University of Massachusetts Press, 1991.

Alcoff, Linda. "Cultural Feminism versus Poststructuralism: The Identity Crisis in Feminist Theory." *Signs* 13 (Spring 1988): 405–36.

Annett, Albert, and Alice Lehtinen. *The History of Jaffrey (Middle Monadnock), New Hampshire . . .* 2 vols. Jaffrey, N.H.: Published by the Town, 1937.

Bacon, Edwin M. *Rambles around Old Boston.* Boston: Little, Brown, 1921.

———. *Washington Street, Old and New.* Boston: Macullar Parker, 1913.

Baer, Helene. *The Heart Is Like Heaven: The Life of Lydia Maria Child.* Philadelphia: University of Pennsylvania Press, 1964.

Baker, Paula. "The Domestication of Politics: Women and American Political Society, 1780–1920." *American Historical Review* 89 (June 1984): 620–47.

Banner, Lois. "Women's History: Culture and Feminization." *Reviews in American History* 6 (June 1978): 155–62.

Barnes, Gilbert H. *The Antislavery Impulse, 1830–1844.* 1933. New York: Peter Smith, 1973.

Bartlett, Irving. *Wendell and Ann Phillips: The Community of Reform, 1840–1880.* New York: W. W. Norton, 1979.

———. *Wendell Phillips, Brahmin Radical.* Boston: Beacon Press, 1961.

Bass, Dorothy. "The Best Hopes of the Sexes: The Woman Question in Garrisonian Abolitionism." Ph.D. diss., Brown University, 1980.

Bedell, Madelon. *The Alcotts: Biography of a Family.* New York: Clarkson Potter, 1980.

Bell, Howard H. "The American Moral Reform Society, 1836–1841." *Journal of Negro Education* 27 (Winter 1958): 34–40.

Belyea, Marlou. "The New England Female Moral Reform Society, 1835–1850: 'Put Down the Libertine, Reclaim the Wanderer, Restore the Outcast.'" Typescript. 1976. Schlesinger Library, Radcliffe College.

Bernard, Richard M., and Maris A. Vinovskis. "The Female School Teacher in Antebellum Massachusetts." *Journal of Social History* 10 (March 1977): 332–45.

Bisson, Wilfred Joseph. "Some Conditions for Collective Violence: The Charlestown Convent Riot of 1834." Ph.D. diss., Michigan State University, 1974.

Bibliography

Blair, Karen. *The Clubwoman as Feminist: True Womanhood Redefined, 1868–1914.* New York: Holmes and Meier, 1980.

Bolt, Christine. *The Anti-Slavery Movement and Reconstruction: A Study of Anglo-American Cooperation, 1833–1877.* New York: Oxford University Press, 1969.

Bond, Henry F. "Old Summer Street, Boston." *New England Magazine* 19 (November 1898): 333–56.

Boston Children's Friend Society. *One Hundred Years of Service to the Children of Boston.* Boston: Published by the Society, 1933.

Boston Society for the Care of Girls. *One Hundred Years of Work with Girls in Boston.* Boston: Published by the Society, 1919.

Boylan, Anne M. "Timid Girls, Venerable Widows, and Dignified Matrons: Life Cycle Patterns among Organized Women in New York and Boston, 1797–1840." *American Quarterly* 38 (Winter 1986): 779–97.

———. "Women in Groups: An Analysis of Women's Benevolent Organizations in New York and Boston, 1797–1840." *Journal of American History* 71 (December 1984): 497–523.

———. "Women's History: Some Axioms in Need of Revision." *Reviews in American History* 6 (September 1978): 340–47.

Braude, Ann. *Radical Spirits: Spiritualism and Women's Rights in Nineteenth-Century America.* Boston: Beacon Press, 1989.

Brown, Ira V. "Cradle of Feminism: The Philadelphia Female Anti-Slavery Society, 1833–1840." *Pennsylvania Magazine of History and Biography* 102 (April 1978): 143–66.

———. "Racism and Sexism: The Case of Pennsylvania Hall." *Phylon* 37 (June 1976): 126–36.

Burchard, Peter. *One Gallant Rush: Robert Gould Shaw and the Brave Black Regiment.* New York: St. Martin's Press, 1965.

Ceplair, Larry, ed. *The Public Years of Sarah and Angelina Grimké: Selected Writings, 1835–1839.* New York: Columbia University Press, 1989.

Chafe, William. *Women and Equality: Changing Patterns in American Culture.* New York: Oxford University Press, 1977.

Chamberlin, Joseph Edgar. "Winter on Boston Common." *New England Magazine* 11 (December 1894): 425–37.

Chambers-Schiller, Lee. *Liberty, a Better Husband: Single Women in America, the Generations of 1780–1840.* New Haven: Yale University Press, 1984.

———. "The Single Woman Reformer: Conflicts between Family and Vocation, 1830–1860." *Frontiers* 3 (3,1978): 41–48.

Chandler, Charles Henry. *The History of New Ipswich, New Hampshire, 1735–1914.* Fitchburg, Mass.: Sentinel Printing, 1914.

Colver, Frederic. *Colver–Culver Genealogy.* Boston: Privately printed, 1910.

Conzen, Michael P., and George K. Lewis. *Boston: A Geographical Portrait.* Cambridge, Mass.: Ballinger, 1976.

Cott, Nancy F. *The Bonds of Womanhood: Woman's Sphere in New England, 1780–1835.* New Haven: Yale University Press, 1977.

———. *The Grounding of Modern Feminism.* New Haven: Yale University Press, 1987.

Crawford, Mary Caroline. *Famous Families of Massachusetts.* 2 vols. Boston: Little, Brown, 1930.

―――. *Romantic Days in Old Boston: The Story of the City and of Its People during the Nineteenth Century.* Boston: Little, Brown, 1910.

Crocker, George Glover. *From the Stage Coach to the Railroad Train and the Street Car: . . . Public Conveyances in and around Boston in the Nineteenth Century.* Boston: W. B. Clarke, 1900.

Curti, Merle. "Non-Resistance in New England." *New England Quarterly* 2 (January 1929): 34–57.

Cushing, John D. "Notes on Disestablishment in Massachusetts, 1780–1833." *William and Mary Quarterly,* 3rd ser. 26 (April 1969): 169–90.

Cutler, Daniel B. *History of the Town of Jaffrey, New Hampshire, 1749–1880.* N.p., 1881.

Cutter, William R. *Genealogical and Personal Memoir Relating to the Families of the State of Massachusetts.* 3 vols. New York: Lewis Historical Publishing, 1910.

Davis, Lance E., and Peter L. Payne. "From Benevolence to Business: The Story of Two Savings Banks." *Business History Review* 32 (1958): 386–406.

Deems, Mervin M. *A Home away from Home: The Boston Seaman's Friend Society, Inc., 1827–1975.* Bangor, Me.: Furbush-Roberts, 1975.

Degler, Carl N. *At Odds: Women and the Family in America from the Revolution to the Present.* New York: Oxford University Press, 1980.

Dodd, Jill S. "The Working Classes and the Temperance Movement in Ante-bellum Boston." *Labor History* 19 (Fall 1978): 510–31.

Donald, David. "Toward a Reconsideration of Abolitionists." In *Lincoln Reconsidered: Essays on the Civil War Era.* 2nd ed. New York: Vintage Books, 1961.

Donovan, Josephine. *Feminist Theory: The Intellectual Traditions of American Feminism.* New York: Frederick Ungar, 1985.

Douglas, Ann. *The Feminization of American Culture.* New York: Alfred A. Knopf, 1978.

Drake, Thomas E. *Quakers and Slavery in America.* New Haven: Yale University Press, 1950.

Duberman, Martin, ed. *The Antislavery Vanguard: New Essays on the Abolitionists.* Princeton: Princeton University Press, 1965.

Dublin, Thomas. "Rural Migrants in Industrial New England: The Case of Lynn, Massachusetts, in the Mid-Nineteenth Century." *Journal of American History* 73 (December 1986): 623–44.

―――. *Women at Work: The Transformation of Work and Community in Lowell, Massachusetts, 1826–1860.* New York: Columbia University Press, 1979.

―――. "Women Workers and the Study of Social Mobility." *Journal of Interdisciplinary History* 9 (Spring 1979): 647–65.

Du Bois, Ellen Carol. *Feminism and Suffrage: The Emergence of an Independent Women's Movement in America, 1848–1869.* Ithaca: Cornell University Press, 1978.

―――. "Politics and Culture in Women's History: A Symposium." *Feminist Studies* 6 (Spring 1980): 26–64.

————. "Struggling into Existence: The Feminism of Sarah and Angelina Grimké." *Women's Journal of Liberation* 11 (September 1970): 4–11.

Dunston, J. Leslie. *A Light to the City: 150 Years of the City Missionary Society of Boston, 1816–1966*. Boston: Beacon Press, 1966.

Easton, Barbara. "Industrialization and Femininity: A Case Study of Nineteenth-Century New England." *Social Problems* 23 (April 1976): 389–401.

Edel, Matthew, et al. *Shaky Palaces: Homeownership and Social Mobility in Boston's Suburbanization*. New York: Columbia University Press, 1984.

Eisenstein, Hester. *Contemporary Feminist Thought*. Boston: G. K. Hall, 1983.

Elbert, Sarah. *A Hunger for Home: Louisa May Alcott's Place in American Culture*. New Brunswick, N.J.: Rutgers University Press, 1987.

Emerson, George B. "Schools as They Should Be: Reminiscences of an Old Teacher." *American Journal of Education* 28 (1878): 257–74.

Epstein, Barbara. *The Politics of Domesticity: Women, Evangelism, and Temperance in Nineteenth-Century America*. Middletown, Conn.: Wesleyan University Press, 1981.

Evans, Sara. *Personal Politics: The Roots of Women's Liberation in the Civil Rights Movement and the New Left*. New York: Alfred A. Knopf, 1979.

Farber, Bernard. *Guardians of Virtue: Salem Families in 1800*. New York: Basic Books, 1972.

Filler, Louis. *Crusade against Slavery, 1830–1860*. New York: Harper and Row, 1960.

Firor Scott, Anne. "Most Invisible of All: Black Women's Voluntary Associations." *Journal of Southern History* 56 (February 1990): 3–22.

Formisano, Ronald. *The Transformation of Political Culture: Massachusetts Parties, 1790s–1840s*. New York: Oxford University Press, 1983.

Formisano, Ronald, and Constance Burns. *Boston, 1700–1980: The Evolution of Urban Politics*. Westport, Conn.: Greenwood Press, 1984.

Foxcroft, Frank. "Mount Auburn." *New England Magazine* 14 (June 1896): 419–38.

Friedman, Lawrence. "Garrisonian Abolitionism and the Boston Clique: A Psychosocial Inquiry." *Psychohistory Review* 7 (Fall 1978): 6–19.

————. *Gregarious Saints: Self and Community in American Abolitionism, 1830–1870*. New York: Cambridge University Press, 1982.

Frisch, Michael. "American Urban History as an Example of Recent Historiography." *History and Theory* 18 (3, 1979): 350–77.

Frisch, Michael, and Daniel Walkowitz. *Working-Class America: Essays on Labor, Community, and American Society*. Urbana: University of Illinois Press, 1983.

Garrison, Wendell P., and Frances Garrison. *William Lloyd Garrison, 1805–1879: The Story of His Life Told by His Children*. 4 vols. New York: Century, 1885–89.

Gilmore, James R. "Recollections of a New England School Mistress." *New England Magazine* 28 (July 1898): 566–76.

Ginzberg, Lori D. "Moral Suasion Is Moral Balderdash: Women, Politics, and Social Activism in the 1850s." *Journal of American History* 73 (December 1986): 601–22.

————. *Women and the Work of Benevolence: Morality, Politics, and Class in the Nineteenth-Century United States*. New Haven: Yale University Press, 1990.

Gold, Ellen Reid. "The Grimké Sisters and the Emergence of the Woman's Rights Movement." *Southern Speech Communication Journal* 46 (Summer 1981): 341–60.

Goldin, Claudia. "The Changing Economic Role of Women: A Quantitative Approach." *Journal of Interdisciplinary History* 13 (Spring 1983): 707–33.

———. "The Economic Status of Women in the Early Republic: Quantitative Evidence." *Journal of Interdisciplinary History* 16 (Winter 1986): 375–404.

Goodman, Paul. "Ethics and Enterprise: The Values of a Boston Elite, 1800–1860." *American Quarterly* 18 (Fall 1966): 437–51.

Gordon, Linda. *Heroes of Their Own Lives: The Politics and History of Family Violence, Boston, 1880–1960.* New York: Penguin, 1988.

Grimké, Archibald H. "Anti-Slavery Boston." *New England Magazine,* n.s. 3 (December 1890): 441–59.

Hall, Peter Dobkin. "Family Structure and Class Consolidation among the Boston Brahmins." Ph.D. diss., State University of New York, Stony Brook, 1973.

———. "Marital Selection and Business in Massachusetts Merchant Families, 1700–1900." In *The American Family in Social-Historical Perspective.* Edited by Michael Gordon. 2nd ed. New York: St. Martin's Press, 1978.

———. "The Model of Boston Charity: A Theory of Charitable Benevolence and Class Development." *Science and Society* 38 (Winter 1974/75): 464–77.

Halttunen, Karen. *Confidence Men and Painted Women: A Study of Middle-Class Culture in America, 1830–1870.* New Haven: Yale University Press, 1982.

Hammett, Theodore M. "Two Mobs of Jacksonian Boston: Ideology and Interest." *Journal of American History* 62 (March 1976): 845–68.

Handlin, Oscar. *Boston's Immigrants, 1790–1880: A Study in Acculturation.* Cambridge, Mass.: Harvard University Press, 1941.

Hansen, Karen. "Feminist Conceptions of Public and Private: A Critical Analysis." *Berkeley Journal of Sociology* 32 (1987): 105–28.

Hastings, John K. "Anti-Slavery Landmarks in Boston." *Boston Transcript,* 1 September 1897.

Henretta, James A. "Economic Development and Social Structure in Colonial Boston." *William and Mary Quarterly* 22 (January 1965): 75–92.

———. *The Evolution of American Society, 1700–1815: An Interdisciplinary Analysis.* Lexington, Mass.: D. C. Heath, 1973.

———. "The Morphology of New England Society in the Colonial Period." *Journal of Interdisciplinary History* 2 (Autumn 1971): 379–98.

Hersh, Blanche Glassman. *The Slavery of Sex: Feminist-Abolitionists in America.* Urbana: University of Illinois Press, 1978.

Hewitt, Nancy A. "Feminist Friends: Agrarian Quakers and the Emergence of Women's Rights in America." *Feminist Studies* 12 (Spring 1986): 27–50.

———. *Women's Activism and Social Change: Rochester, New York, 1822–1872.* Ithaca: Cornell University Press, 1984.

Hobson, Barbara. "Sex in the Marketplace: Prostitution in an American City, Boston, 1820–1880." Ph.D. diss., Boston University, 1982.

———. *Uneasy Virtue: The Politics of Prostitution and the American Reform Tradition.* New York: Basic Books, 1987.

Hogeland, Ronald W. "The Female Appendage: Feminine Life-Styles in America, 1820–1860." *Civil War History* 17 (June 1971): 101–14.

Horton, James O. "Freedom's Yoke: Gender Conventions among Antebellum Free Blacks." *Feminist Studies* 12 (Spring 1986): 51–76.

———. "Generations of Protest: Black Families and Social Reform in Ante-bellum Boston." *New England Quarterly* 49 (June 1976): 242–56.

Horton, James O., and Lois E. Horton. *Black Bostonians: Family Life and Community Struggle in the Antebellum North.* New York: Holmes and Meier, 1979.

Horton, Lois E. "Community Organization and Social Activism: Black Boston and the Antislavery Movement." *Sociological Inquiry* 55 (Spring 1985): 182–99.

Howe, Daniel Walker. *The Unitarian Conscience: Harvard Moral Philosophy, 1805–1861.* Cambridge, Mass.: Harvard University Press, 1970.

Howe, M. A. De Wolfe. *Boston: The Place and the People.* New York: Macmillan, 1903.

Hunt, Edmund Soper. *Weymouth Ways and Weymouth People.* Boston: Privately printed, 1907.

Huse, Charles P. *The Financial History of Boston, from May 1, 1822, to January 31, 1909.* Cambridge, Mass.: Harvard University Press, 1916.

Jaher, Frederic Cople. "Nineteenth-Century Elites in Boston and New York." *Journal of Social History* 6 (Fall 1972): 32–77.

Jeffrey, Kirk. "Marriage and Feminine Ideology in Nineteenth-Century America: Reconstructing the Marital Experience of Lydia Maria Child, 1821–1874." *Feminist Studies* 2 (Spring/Summer 1975): 113–30.

Johnson, Paul. *A Shopkeeper's Millennium: Society and Revivals in Rochester, New York, 1815–1837.* New York: Hill and Wang, 1978.

Jones, Jacqueline. *Labor of Love, Labor of Sorrow: Black Women, Work, and the Family from Slavery to the Present.* New York: Vintage Books, 1985.

Kantrowitz, Nathan. "Racial and Ethnic Residential Segregation in Boston, 1830–1970." *Annals of the American Academy of Political and Social Science* 441 (January 1979): 41–54.

Kay, Jane Holtz. *Lost Boston.* Boston: Houghton Mifflin, 1980.

Kerber, Linda. "Separate Spheres, Female Worlds, Woman's Place: The Rhetoric of Women's History." *Journal of American History* 75 (June 1988): 9–39.

———. *Women of the Republic: Intellect and Ideology in Revolutionary America.* Chapel Hill: University of North Carolina Press, 1980.

Kessler-Harris, Alice. *Out to Work: A History of America's Wage-Earning Women.* New York: Oxford University Press, 1982.

Knights, Peter R. *The Plain People of Boston, 1830–1860: A Study in City Growth.* New York: Oxford University Press, 1971.

Knights, Peter R., and Leo F. Schnore. "Residence and Social Structure: Boston in the Antebellum Period." In *Nineteenth-Century Cities: Essays in the New Urban History.* Edited by Stephan Thernstrom and Richard Sennett. New Haven: Yale University Press, 1969.

Kraut, Alan M. *Crusaders and Compromisers: Essays on the Relationship of the Antislavery Struggle to the Antebellum Party System.* Westport, Conn.: Greenwood Press, 1983.

Kulikoff, Allan. "The Progress of Inequity in Revolutionary Boston." *William and Mary Quarterly* 28 (July 1971): 375–412.

Lader, Lawrence. *The Bold Brahmins: New England's War against Slavery, 1831–1863.* New York: Dutton, 1961.

Lane, Roger. *Policing the City: Boston, 1822–1885.* Cambridge, Mass.: Harvard University Press, 1967.

Lasser, Carol S. "The Domestic Balance of Power: Relations between Mistress and Maid in Nineteenth-Century New England." *Labor History* 28 (Winter 1987): 5–22.

————. "A 'Pleasingly Oppressive Burden': The Transformation of Domestic Service and Female Charity in Salem, 1800–1840." *Essex Institute Historical Collections* 116 (April 1980): 156–75.

Laurie, Bruce. *Artisans into Workers: Labor in Nineteenth-Century America.* New York: Hill and Wang, 1989.

Lawrence, Robert. *Old Park Street and Its Vicinity.* Boston: Houghton Mifflin, 1922.

Lebsock, Suzanne. *The Free Women of Petersburg: Status and Culture in a Southern Town, 1784–1860.* New York: W. W. Norton, 1984.

Lerner, Gerda. *The Grimké Sisters from South Carolina: Rebels against Slavery.* Boston: Houghton Mifflin, 1967.

————. "New Approaches to the Study of Women in American History." *Journal of Social History* 3 (1969–70): 53–62.

————. "Placing Women in History: Definitions and Challenges." *Feminist Studies* 3 (Fall 1975): 5–14.

————. "The Political Activities of Antislavery Women." In *The Majority Finds Its Past: Placing Women in History.* New York: Oxford University Press, 1979.

Levesque, George A. "Black Boston: Negro Life in Garrison's Boston, 1800–1860." Ph.D. diss., State University of New York, Binghamton, 1976.

Levy, Leonard. "The 'Abolition Riot': Boston's First Slave Rescue." *New England Quarterly* 25 (March 1952): 85–92.

Linden-Ward, Blanche. *Putting the Past in Place: The Making of Mount Auburn Cemetery.* Cambridge, Mass.: Cambridge Historical Society, 1985.

Lubow, Lisa Beth. "Artisans in Transition: Early Capitalist Development and the Carpenters of Boston, 1787–1837." Ph.D. diss., University of California, Los Angeles, 1987.

Lutz, Alma. *Crusade for Freedom: Women of the Antislavery Movement.* Boston: Beacon Press, 1968.

McCaughey, Robert A. "From Town to City: Boston in the 1820s." *Political Science Quarterly* 88 (June 1973): 191–213.

McGerr, Michael. "Political Style and Women's Power, 1830–1930." *Journal of American History* 77 (December 1990): 864–85.

McKivigan, John R. *The War against Proslavery Religion: Abolitionism and the Northern Churches, 1830–1865.* Ithaca: Cornell University Press, 1984.

McLoughlin, William G. *New England Dissent, 1630–1833: The Baptists and the Separation of Church and State.* Cambridge, Mass.: Harvard University Press, 1971.

Magdol, Edward. *The Antislavery Rank and File: A Social Profile of the Abolitionists' Constituency.* Westport, Conn.: Greenwood Press, 1986.

Marsden, George M. *Religion and American Culture.* San Diego: Harcourt Brace Jovanovich, 1990.

Martyn, Carlos. *Wendell Phillips, the Agitator.* New York: Funk and Wagnalls, 1890.

Meckel, Richard A. "Immigration, Mortality, and Population Growth in Boston, 1840–1880." *Journal of Interdisciplinary History* 15 (Winter 1985): 393–417.

Melder, Keith E. *Beginnings of Sisterhood: The American Woman's Rights Movement, 1800–1850.* New York: Schocken Books, 1977.

————. "The Beginnings of the Women's Rights Movement in the United States, 1800–1840." Ph.D. diss., Yale University, 1964.

————. "Forerunners of Freedom: The Grimké Sisters in Massachusetts, 1837–1838." *Essex Institute Historical Collections* 103 (3, 1967): 223–49.

————. "Ladies Bountiful: Organized Woman's Benevolence in Early Nineteenth-Century America." *New York History* 48 (Spring 1967): 231–52.

————. "Woman's High Calling: The Teaching Profession in America, 1830–1860." *American Studies* 13 (2, 1972): 19–32.

Meltzer, Milton. *Tongue of Flame: The Life of Lydia Maria Child.* New York: Thomas Y. Crowell, 1965.

Milne, Gordon. *George William Curtis: The Genteel Tradition.* Bloomington: University of Indiana Press, 1956.

Mitchell, J. Marcus. "The Paul Family." *Old Time New England* 63 (Winter 1973): 73–77.

Munsterberg, Margaret. "The Weston Sisters and the 'Boston Controversy.'" *Boston Public Library Quarterly* 10 (January 1958): 38–50.

————. "The Weston Sisters and the Boston Mob." *Boston Public Library Quarterly* 9 (October 1958): 183–94.

Nash, Gary. "The Failure of Female Factory Labor in Colonial Boston." In *Race, Class, and Politics: Essays on American Colonial and Revolutionary Society.* Urbana: University of Illinois Press, 1986.

————. *The Urban Crucible: Social Change, Political Consciousness, and the Origins of the American Revolution.* Cambridge, Mass.: Harvard University Press, 1979.

Nash, Gilbert, comp. *Historical Sketch of the Town of Weymouth, Massachusetts, from 1622 to 1884.* Boston: A. Mudge and Son, 1885.

Newton, Judith L., Mary P. Ryan, and Judith R. Walkowitz. *Sex and Class in Women's History.* London: Routledge and Kegan Paul, 1983.

Nissenbaum, Stephen. *Sex, Diet, and Debility in Jacksonian America: Sylvester Graham and Health Reform.* Westport, Conn.: Greenwood Press, 1980.

Norton, Mary Beth. "The Evolution of White Women's Experience in Early America." *American Historical Review* 89 (June 1984): 593–619.

————. *Liberty's Daughters: The Revolutionary Experience of American Women, 1750–1800.* Boston: Little, Brown, 1980.

Numbers, Ronald L., and Jonathan Butler. *The Disappointed: Millerism and Millenarianism in the Nineteenth Century.* Bloomington: Indiana University Press, 1987.

Nye, Russell B. *William Lloyd Garrison and the Humanitarian Reformers*. Boston: Little, Brown, 1955.

O'Connor, Thomas H. *Bibles, Brahmins, and Bosses: A Short History of Boston*. 2nd ed. Boston: Boston Public Library, 1984.

Offen, Karen. "Defining Feminism: A Comparative Historical Approach." *Signs* 14 (Autumn 1988): 119–57. [Ellen Carol Du Bois and Nancy Cott], "Comment and Reply," *Signs* 15 (Autumn 1989): 195–209.

O'Neill, William L. *Everyone Was Brave: A History of Feminism in America*. New York: Quadrangle/New York Times, 1969.

Osborne, William S. *Lydia Maria Child*. Boston: Twayne, 1980.

Palmieri, Patricia A. "'This Single Life': Respectable Spinsterhood, 1780–1840." *American Quarterly* 37 (Fall 1985): 599–606.

Pease, Jane H., and William H. Pease. *Bound with Them in Chains: A Biographical History of the Antislavery Movement*. Westport, Conn.: Greenwood Press, 1972.

―――. *Ladies, Women, and Wenches: Choice and Constraint in Antebellum Charleston and Boston*. Chapel Hill: University of North Carolina Press, 1990.

Pease, William H., and Jane H. Pease. "Paternal Dilemmas: Education, Property, and Patrician Persistence in Jacksonian Boston." *New England Quarterly* 53 (June 1980): 147–67.

―――. *The Web of Progress: Private Values and Public Styles in Boston and Charleston, 1828–1843*. New York: Oxford University Press, 1985.

Peel, Mark. "On the Margins: Lodgers and Boarders in Boston, 1860–1900." *Journal of American History* 72 (March 1986): 813–34.

Perry, Lewis. *Radical Abolitionism, Anarchy, and the Government of God in Antislavery Thought*. Ithaca: Cornell University Press, 1973.

Perry, Lewis, and Michael Fellman, eds. *Antislavery Reconsidered: New Perspectives on the Abolitionists*. Baton Rouge: Louisiana State University Press, 1979.

Pessen, Edward. "Did Fortunes Rise and Fall Mercurially in Antebellum America? The Tale of Two Cities: Boston and New York." *Journal of Social History* 4 (Spring 1971): 339–57.

Pivar, David J. *Purity Crusade: Sexual Morality and Social Control, 1868–1900*. Westport, Conn.: Greenwood Press, 1973.

Powell, E. P. "Harriet Martineau in New England." *New England Magazine* 15 (November 1896): 282–89.

Quarles, Benjamin. *Black Abolitionists*. New York: Oxford University Press, 1969.

―――. "Sources of Abolitionist Income." *Mississippi Valley Historical Review* 32 (June 1945): 63–76.

Radford, John P. "Blacks in Boston." *Journal of Interdisciplinary History* 12 (Spring 1982): 677–84.

"The Reading Room and Marine Diary in the Exchange Coffee House, 1810." *Bostonian Society Publications* 8 (1911): 123–31.

Rice, C. Duncan. "The Anti-Slavery Mission of George Thompson to the United States, 1834–1835." *Journal of American Studies* 2 (April 1968): 13–31.

Rich, Robert. "'A Wilderness of Whigs': The Wealthy Men of Boston." *Journal of Social History* 4 (Spring 1971): 263–76.

Richards, Leonard L. *"Gentlemen of Property and Standing": Anti-Abolition Mobs in Jacksonian America.* New York: Oxford University Press, 1970.

Rose, Anne C. "Social Sources of Denominationalism Reconsidered: Post-Revolutionary Boston as a Case Study." *American Quarterly* 38 (Summer 1986): 243–64.

————. *Transcendentalism as a Social Movement, 1830–1850.* New Haven: Yale University Press, 1981.

Rosenberger, Jesse Leonard. *Through Three Centuries: Colver and Rosenberger Lives and Times, 1620–1922.* Chicago: University of Chicago Press, 1922.

Rossiter, Margaret W. "Benjamin Silliman and the Lowell Institute: The Popularization of Science in Nineteenth-Century America." *New England Quarterly* 44 (December 1971): 602–26.

Rossiter, William S., ed. *Days and Ways in Old Boston.* Boston: R. H. Stearns, 1915.

Rostenberg, Leona. "Number Thirteen West Street." *Book Collector's Packet,* September 1945, 7–9.

Rotundo, Barbara. "Mount Auburn Cemetery: A Proper Boston Institution." *Harvard Library Bulletin* 22 (July 1974): 268–79.

Ruchames, Louis. "Race, Marriage, and Abolition in Massachusetts." *Journal of Negro History* 40 (July 1955): 250–73.

Rush, N. Owin. "Lucretia Mott and the Philadelphia Anti-Slavery Fairs." *Bulletin of the Friends Historical Society,* Autumn 1946, 23–40.

Ryan, Mary P. *Cradle of the Middle Class: The Family in Oneida County, New York, 1790–1865.* New York: Cambridge University Press, 1981.

————. *The Empire of the Mother: American Writing about Domesticity, 1830 to 1860.* New York: Institute for Research in History and Haworth Press, 1982.

————. *Womanhood in America: From Colonial Times to the Present.* 3rd ed. New York: Franklin Watts, 1983.

Salyer, Sandford. *Marmee: The Mother of Little Women.* Norman: University of Oklahoma Press, 1949.

Sargent, Emma W. *Epes Sargent of Gloucester and His Descendants.* Boston: Houghton Mifflin, 1923.

Schlesinger, Elizabeth. "Two Early Harvard Wives: Eliza Farrar and Eliza Follen." *New England Quarterly* 38 (June 1965): 147–67.

Schneider, Eric C. "In the Web of Class: Youth, Class, and Culture in Boston, 1840–1940." Ph.D. diss., Boston University, 1980.

Scott, Joan W. "Deconstructing Equality-versus-Difference; or, The Uses of Poststructuralist Theory for Feminism." *Feminist Studies* 14 (Spring 1988): 33–50.

————. "Women in History: The Modern Period." *Past and Present,* November 1983, 141–57.

Sklar, Kathryn Kish. *Catharine Beecher: A Study in American Domesticity.* New York: W. W. Norton, 1976.

————. "Women Who Speak for an Entire Nation: American and British Women Compared at the World Anti-Slavery Convention, London, 1840." *Pacific Historical Review* 59 (November 1990): 453–99.

Smith, Daniel Scott. "Family Limitation, Sexual Control, and Domestic Feminism in Victorian America." In *Clio's Consciousness Raised.* Edited by Mary S. Hartman and Lois W. Banner. New York: Harper and Row, 1974.

Smith-Rosenberg, Carroll. *Disorderly Conduct: Visions of Gender in Victorian America*. New York: Oxford University Press, 1985.

————. "Evangelicalism and the New City: A History of the City Mission Movement in New York, 1812 to 1870." Ph.D. diss., Columbia University, 1968.

————. "The New Women and the New History." *Feminist Studies* 3 (Fall 1975): 185–98.

Soderlund, Jean R. *Quakers and Slavery: A Divided Spirit*. Princeton: Princeton University Press, 1985.

Sorin, Gerald. *The New York Abolitionists: A Case Study of Political Radicalism*. Westport, Conn.: Greenwood Press, 1971.

Srole, Carol. "'A Position that God Has Not Particularly Assigned to Men': The Feminization of Clerical Work, Boston, 1860–1915." Ph.D. diss., University of California, Los Angeles, 1984.

Stange, Douglas. *Patterns of Antislavery among American Unitarians, 1831–1860*. Rutherford, N.J.: Fairleigh Dickinson University Press, 1977.

Stansell, Christine. *City of Women: Sex and Class in New York, 1789–1860*. New York: Alfred A. Knopf, 1986.

————. "Women, Children, and the Uses of the Streets: Class and Gender Conflict in New York City, 1850–1860." *Feminist Studies* 8 (Summer 1982): 309–36.

State Street Trust Company. *Old Shipping Days in Boston*. Boston: State Street Trust, 1918.

————. *Some Merchants and Sea Captains of Old Boston*. Boston: State Street Trust, 1918.

Sterling, Dorothy, ed. *We Are Your Sisters: Black Women in the Nineteenth Century*. New York: W. W. Norton. 1984.

Stewart, James Brewer. *Holy Warriors: The Abolitionists and American Slavery*. New York: Hill and Wang, 1976.

Story, Ronald. "Class and Culture in Boston: The Athenaeum, 1807–1860." *American Quarterly* 27 (May 1975): 178–99.

————. *The Forging of an Aristocracy: Harvard and the Boston Upper Class, 1800–1870*. Middletown, Conn.: Wesleyan University Press, 1980.

Stromberg, Roland N. "Boston in the 1820s and 1830s." *History Today* 11 (September 1961): 591–98.

Strouse, Jean. *Alice James: A Biography*. New York: Bantam Books, 1982.

Sweet, Leonard. *The Minister's Wife: Her Role in Nineteenth-Century American Evangelism*. Philadelphia: Temple University Press, 1983.

Swerdlow, Amy. "Abolition's Conservative Sisters: The Ladies' New York City Anti-Slavery Societies, 1834–1840." Paper presented at the Third Berkshire Conference on the History of Women, Bryn Mawr College, 9–11 June 1976.

Thistlethwaite, Frank. *America and the Atlantic Community: Anglo-American Aspects, 1790–1850*. New York: Harper and Row, 1959.

Thompson, E. P. "The Moral Economy of the English Crowd in the Eighteenth Century." *Past and Present* 50 (February 1971): 76–136.

Thompson, Ralph. "The *Liberty Bell* and Other Anti-Slavery Gift-Books." *New England Quarterly* 7 (March 1934): 154–68.

The Town Register: Marlboro, Troy, Jaffrey, Swanzey. Augusta, Me.: Mitchell-Cany, 1908.

Van Broekhoven, Deborah Bingham. "'A Determination to Labor . . .': Female Antislavery Activity in Rhode Island." *Rhode Island History* 44 (1985): 35–44.

Vinovskis, Maris. "Mortality Rates and Trends in Massachusetts before 1860." *Journal of Economic History* 32 (March 1972): 184–213.

Wadlin, Horace G. *The Public Library of the City of Boston: A History.* Boston: Boston Public Library, 1911.

Walters, Ronald. *American Reformers, 1815–1860.* New York: Hill and Wang, 1978.

————. *The Antislavery Appeal: American Abolitionism after 1830.* Baltimore: Johns Hopkins University Press, 1976.

Ward, David. "The Industrial Revolution and the Emergence of Boston's Central Business District." *Economic Geography* 42 (April 1966): 152–71.

Ware, Ethel K. "Lydia Maria Child and Anti-Slavery." *Boston Public Library Quarterly* 31 (October 1951): 251–75.

Wellman, Judith. "Women and Radical Reform in Antebellum Upstate New York: A Profile of Grassroots Female Abolitionists." In *Clio Was a Woman: Studies in the History of American Women.* Edited by Mabel E. Deutrich and Virginia C. Purdy. Washington, D.C.: Howard University Press, 1980.

Welter, Barbara. "The Cult of True Womanhood, 1820–1860." *American Quarterly* 18 (Summer 1966): 151–74.

Weymouth Historical Society. *History of Weymouth, Massachusetts.* 4 vols. Weymouth: Published by the Society, 1923.

Whitehill, Walter Muir. *Boston: A Topographical History.* 2nd ed. Cambridge, Mass.: Belknap Press, 1968.

Williams, Carolyn Luverne. "Religion, Race, and Gender in Antebellum American Radicalism: The Philadelphia Female Anti-Slavery Society, 1833–1870." Ph.D. diss., University of California, Los Angeles, 1991.

Winsor, Justin, ed. *The Memorial History of Boston . . .* 4 vols. Boston: James R. Osgood, 1883.

Wood, Nathan E. *The History of the First Baptist Church of Boston (1665–1899).* Philadelphia: American Baptist Publication Society, 1899.

Wyatt-Brown, Bertram. *Lewis Tappan and the Evangelical War Against Slavery.* Cleveland: Press of Case Western Reserve University, 1969.

Wyman, Lillie B. Chace. "Black and White." *New England Magazine* 5 (December 1891): 476–81.

Yee, Shirley. *Black Women Abolitionists: A Study in Activism, 1828–1860.* Knoxville: University of Tennessee Press, 1992.

Yellin, Jean Fagan. *Women and Sisters: The Antislavery Feminists in American Culture.* New Haven: Yale University Press, 1989.

Yellin, Jean Fagan, and John C. Van Horne. *An Untrodden Path: Antislavery and Women's Political Culture.* Ithaca: Cornell University Press, forthcoming.

Zorn, Roman. "The New England Anti-Slavery Society: Pioneer Abolitionist Organization." *Journal of Negro History* 43 (July 1957): 157–76.

Index

221

114, 121; founding of, 79; abolitionists in, 79, 80, 114, 121; women employed by, 79–80, 108; women's residences of, 80; and antislavery divisions, 114, 121, 144; conservatism of, 114–15, 144; fundraising by, 137. *See also* New England Female Moral Reform Society
Boston Female Society for Missionary Purposes, 60–61
Boston Harbor, 29–30, 32
Bowdoin Street Congregational Church, 35, 56, 81, 82, 83–84, 145
Bowring, John, 135
Boylan, Anne, 9
Brackett, Josiah, 69, 73
Brackett, Mrs., 68
Bremer, Fredrika, 135
Briggs, Charles, 73
Brook Farm, 86, 104
Browning, Elizabeth Barrett, 135
Building trades, 36, 72
Bulfinch, Charles, 30, 34
Burleigh, Charles, 102
Businesswomen. *See* Proprietors
Byron, Lady, 135

Cabot, Samuel, 6, 70
Cabot, Samuel, Jr., 70
Cabot, Susan, 67, 97, 99
Cambell, David, 115
Carlyle, Thomas, 154, 156
Carpenter, M. B., 73
Carpenter, Orin, 73
Chamberlain, H. M., 68–69
Chamberlain, Mrs., 68
Chambers-Schiller, Lee, 50
Channing, William Ellery, 16, 44, 85–86, 103
Chapman, Ann G., 68, 69, 75
Chapman, Henry G., 68, 69, 98, 100, 106, 127, 128
Chapman, Henry, Sr., 6, 69, 127
Chapman, Maria Weston: and Garrison Mob, 4, 106; description, 4–5, 98, 104, 126–27; and religion, 16, 24,

85, 86–87, 88, 95, 103, 109, 147, 148; on women's rights, 21, 22, 24, 25, 141, 142, 148, 149, 154; and Ball sisters, 24, 96–97, 102; and antislavery divisions, 24–28, 94, 95, 105, 124–26, 147; fair work, 26–27, 124–30, 134–36, 138; family background, 66–67, 69–70, 98; teaching and editing, 76, 78, 98, 134–35, 136; supporters, 97–98, 107, 122; elitism of, 101, 105, 107; and racial integration, 101–2; social activities, 101–2, 106; political philosophy, 103–5; reform interests, 104, 105, 119; criticisms of, 117, 126. See also *Right and Wrong in Boston*
Chapman, Mary, 17, 68, 69, 75, 104
Chapman, Sarah, 100, 127
Chapman family, 66, 69–70, 72
Charitable organizations. *See* Women's organizations
Charles Street Baptist Church, 109
Cheney, Ednah, 43, 57
Child, David L., 68, 134, 140
Child, Laura Dwight, 106
Child, Lydia Maria, 64, 68; on racism, 14; antislavery activities, 14, 15, 17, 19–20, 106, 126; and women's rights, 21, 22, 24, 103, 140, 148, 149; and antislavery divisions, 25, 94; family background, 65–66, 98, 74; teaching and writing, 76, 78, 134, 140; religious beliefs, 85, 86, 87, 102, 149; political philosophy, 103; reform interests, 85, 105
Choate, Mrs. Rufus, 21
Choate, Rufus, 17
Clark, Caroline, 74
Clark, Thomas, 74
Clergy. *See* Ministers
Clerical Appeal, 23, 93–94, 95, 121
Clerks, 34–35, 73
Clough, Ebenezer, 73
Clough, Mary Ann, 73, 75–76
Codman, John, 61
Collier, Mary Ann, 69, 75, 84, 114